Working
with
Groups

edited by Lily Becker

OXFORD
UNIVERSITY PRESS

OXFORD
UNIVERSITY PRESS

Great Clarendon Street, Oxford OX2 6DP

Oxford University Press is a department of the University of Oxford.
It furthers the University's objective of excellence in research, scholarship,
and education by publishing worldwide in

Oxford New York

Auckland Cape Town Dar es Salaam Hong Kong Karachi
Kuala Lumpur Madrid Melbourne Mexico City Nairobi
New Delhi Shanghai Taipei Toronto

with offices in
Argentina Austria Brazil Chile Czech Republic France Greece
Guatemala Hungary Italy Japan Poland Portugal Singapore
South Korea Switzerland Thailand Turkey Ukraine Vietnam

Oxford is a registered trade mark of Oxford University Press
in the UK and in certain other countries

Published in South Africa
by Oxford University Press Southern Africa, Cape Town

Working with Groups
ISBN 0 19 578140 6 (10-digit, current)
ISBN 9 78 0 19 578140 3 (13-digit, from 2007)

© Oxford University Press Southern Africa 2005

Commissioning Editor: Arthur Attwell/Zarina Adhikari
Editor: Marisa Montemarano
Proofreader: Inge du Plessis
Designer: Sharna Sammy
Cover design: Sharna Sammy
Indexer: Jeanne Cope

Published by Oxford University Press Southern Africa
PO Box 12119, N1 City, 7463, Cape Town, South Africa

Set in 10 pt on 12 pt Palatino by Global Graphics
Cover photo: Gallo Images/Getty
Reproduction by Castle Graphics
Cover reproduction by The Image Bureau
Printed and bound by ABC Press, Cape Town

The authors and publishers gratefully acknowledge permission to reproduce material
in this book. Every effort has been made to trace copyright holders, but where this
has proved impossible, the publishers would be grateful for information that
would enable them to amend any omissions in future editions.

Contents

List of contributors

Lily Becker, M.Soc.Sc (ClinSW) is a Senior Lecturer in the Department of Social Development, University of Cape Town, the Principal Lecturer in Groupwork and in Clinical Practice in Social Work, and Coordinator of the postgraduate programmes in Clinical Practice.

Willem de Jager, MA (ClinPsych) is a Senior Clinical Psychologist at the Child and Family Unit, Red Cross Children's Hospital, Cape Town, and a Lecturer in the Department of Psychiatry and Mental Health, Faculty of Health Sciences at the University of Cape Town.

Prof. Sandra J Drower, Ph.D. is Professor and Head of Social Work in the School of Human and Community Development at the University of the Witwatersrand, Johannesburg.

Madeleine Duncan, M.ScOT, D.Phil. (Psych) candidate is an occupational therapist, and a Senior Lecturer in the Division of Occupational Therapy, School of Health and Rehabilitation Sciences, Faculty of Health Sciences at the University of Cape Town.

Dr Assie Gildenhuys, D.Phil. is a Senior Lecturer in the Department of Psychology at the University of Pretoria and Programme Director of the Ph.D. (Psychotherapy) course.

Nelleke Keet, MA (MedSW) is a Lecturer in the Department of Social Development at the University of Cape Town, and an executive member of the South African Association for Psychosocial Rehabilitation (SAAPSR).

Pat Mayers, M.Sc.Med (Psych) is a mental health nurse, and a Senior Lecturer in the Division of Nursing and Midwifery, School of Health and Rehabilitation Sciences at the University of Cape Town and Convenor of the Masters in Nursing programmes.

Dr Connie O'Brien, Ph.D. is a Lecturer in the Department of Social Development at the University of Cape Town, Coordinator of the post-graduate research programme, and is an active member of various NGO boards.

Peter Powis, MA (ClinPsych) is a Clinical Psychologist, and Director of Psychological Services and Co-founder of Stepping Stones Addiction Centre, Kommetjie, Cape Town.

Assoc. Prof. André de V Smit, M.Pub.Ad is an Associate Professor and Head of the Department of Social Development at the University of Cape Town.

Dr Monica Spiro, Ph.D. is a Clinical Psychologist in private practice, working with individuals, couples, and groups, with a special focus on long-term groups for single mothers, university students, and refugees.

Shona Sturgeon, M.Soc.Sc (ClinSW) is a Senior Lecturer in the Department of Social Development at the University of Cape Town, and is President of the South African Federation for Mental Health and President Elect of the World Federation for Mental Health.

Ben Truter, MA (ClinPsych) is a Community Clinical Psychologist in the Department of Health, Provincial Government of the Western Cape.

Foreword

I am honoured to be asked to contribute a foreword to this important book. A few years ago, I attended the first Psychoanalytic Congress in South Africa – an occasion when I was suddenly asked to organize and conduct a large group to explore the rising tensions in the conference and give the participants an opportunity to voice their concerns. I gained the impression that the scope and practice of groupwork in South Africa was limited. That was prior to reading this book – how wrong I was!

I have learned, and the reader will learn, that the contributors have established strong 'beach heads', entry points into the vast psychosocial problems facing this young nation. I have an interest in fostering group analysis, which is well presented here in Chapter Five, though its influence is evident throughout the book.

The aims are well set out by the editor Lily Becker in her Introduction: groupwork emphasising empowerment, the intertwining of democratising goals within the framework of the group, the importance of leader behaviour in facilitating the process and the galvanising of mutuality in groups.

Although the authors work in diverse areas: psychotherapy, organizations, feminist issues, peacemaking, support groups for professionals, HIV/AIDS, mental disability, there is a striking commonality. They all march to this common tune: clear writing, comprehensive cover of relevant literature, and recognition of the complex nature of their work areas. They look both outwards and inwards, using psychodynamic insights balanced by their understanding of the great social forces that have arisen from the troubled history of South Africa.

I applaud the editor's work in ensuring high standards from all the authors. I have learned much from their chapters. The range of references is comprehensive and I particularly enjoyed the creative use of articles and books in my own sphere of group analysis.

When I finished reading I knew that I had been on a long, difficult journey with the authors and felt inspired and empowered by their achievements.

Working with Groups should be widely read, not only in South Africa but in developing and developed countries. Through it we can see what has to be done and how it should be done.

Malcolm Pines

FRCP, FRCPsych, DPM, M.Inst.Group Analysis
Former Consultant Psychotherapist Tavistock Clinic, Maudsley St Georges and Cassel Hospitals
Past President International Association Group Psychotherapy
Founder Member Institute of Group Analysis London
Past President Group Analytic Society London

Preface

This book has evolved from a three-fold objective: to capture in hard copy some of the essence of groupwork that is happening in South Africa today, to further promote groupwork as a valuable commodity in pursuing therapeutic and community goals, and to bring home to local practice some depth insights of groups and groupwork practice to inform practitioners and students in training. A further overarching plan was to demonstrate how the values embedded in key issues of groups, groupwork practice, and leadership contribute to the development of a just, democratic, and cohesive society.

During many years as a teacher and supervisor of groupwork I have long felt the need for a book which would address areas appropriate to contemporary needs in a developing country, and also be an advanced text available to students and practitioners in South Africa. I hope that this book will help to fill that gap. The chapters addressing different client concerns are written by a range of local experts. Learning objectives in each chapter, contextualisation and theoretical frameworks provide a basis, while case examples/vignettes illuminate theory.

I would like to express appreciation for the many opportunities afforded me in my professional development, such as the privilege of facilitating weekly staff groups for many years at Groote Schuur and Red Cross Hospitals. I have learnt much from my teachers, students and clients. In compiling this volume, I wish to thank all the contributors for sharing their knowledge so willingly. I want to especially thank group colleagues Willem de Jager, Madie Duncan and Monica Spiro whose reading of the manuscript and suggestions helped to stimulate inquiry and improvements. I am very appreciative of the support and encouragement of my colleagues in the Department of Social Development at the University of Cape Town and at other universities and organizations. The meticulous ability of Marisa Montemarano, academic editor at Oxford University Press, in tuning the finished product is particularly appreciated.

In a more personal sense, I am deeply grateful to my family, my husband Ronnie, my children Joanne Videtzky, Cathy Katz and Debbie Becker, my grandchildren and families for love, support and a secure base while I happily pursued this challenge.

Lily Becker

Introduction

Lily Becker

… a stone in the pond produces a ripple effect in the long term.
(Becker, 1988: 122)

Working in groups has far-reaching effects, which resonate beyond the boundaries of particular groups. This book evolved from a need to proclaim the value of groups in South Africa today, to reflect the groupwork that was already happening, and to highlight the potential contributions of groups to our rapidly changing context. Changes are happening in South Africa in many domains: from the consolidation of the country as a democratic state, to developing and empowering community and society, to attempts to find compatibility between the great needs of the population and the provision of structures to meet those needs. The many challenges facing this country range from economic need to transformation, with change as a constant theme. Blackwell (1998) reminds us that in times of rapid change and uncertainty, there is a potential for both chaos and creativity. Much depends on the way that the anxiety generated by such instability is managed, and working in groups can counteract regressive tendencies by promoting communication and dialogue.

This book explores the groupwork method of practice in different human service settings in South Africa. Groups, the 'space' where people can meet, interact, connect to others, be empowered and healed are becoming more utilised in various diverse communities and populations in South Africa. The communication network that is set up in groups, whether conflict resolution groups, or therapeutic groups, or support groups, becomes a vital conduit through which the work of the group is done, but is also the base on which connectedness is entrenched. An important facet of groupwork practice is how it is able to interface between individuals, families, communities and the broader society. Working with groups has also helped to provide a deeper understanding of collective and individual intersecting dimensions such as cultural issues, trauma, and community conflicts, as well as being a tool for transformational work.

Groupwork carries a number of hats: it operates at the therapeutic level as a model offering a variety of therapeutic strategies to different client groups. At the same time, it operates at the cultural level, where it has an important role to play in empowerment, as it functions in an anti-oppressive framework, engaging with issues of difference and power. Implicit in the approach of groupwork in any client population, is the ideal of fostering a democratic approach in the group, where each member's contribution to the whole is valued and encouraged. The ideal leader/facilitator of a group is a democratic one, fostering the strengths in the group as a whole to benefit both the group as an entity, and the members within the group as entities within their own right. The experience and training that occurs in a group helps members to think about others, and to see the 'other' as a visible entity, deserving of due care and respect, an important foundation for social justice and human dignity.

There is compatibility in the training and practice of groupworkers in the helping professions in social work, psychology and health care professional training programmes and practice. Internship training, and professional practice often take place in the same units in multidisciplinary teams, and co-leadership of a mix of disciplines is common in settings where groupwork is practised. As we in the different professions dialogue, we identify commonalities in our work, but also differences, which are enriching. The interdisciplinary nature of this book draws on commonalities in groupwork and bypasses the isolationism still experienced in different professions. What has been so exciting in this book is to gather together 'like-minded' individuals, who enjoy groups and working in groups, and who have found positive change emerging from utilising a group approach. They all have a profound respect for the circular space of the group – that inner, interpersonal, and transpersonal matrix created when individuals meet, are influenced by and together influence the contemplative sacred inner/outer space of the group.

My own learning about groups was given impetus by my involvement in a small group of practitioners and academics drawn from the helping professions, who met on a regular monthly basis for many years. The task of this group was to learn about groups, think about groups, to offer peer supervision within the group, and to further our interest in groups through readings and discussions. This group task has excitingly led us into many diverse areas in the group arena. Of the original small group, which started eight years ago, four members remain, although this core group has since expanded into a larger reading group. This core group was germane in our immersion into 'thinking group', as we thoughtfully joined in a buoyant spirit of enquiry into the richness of groups. Each member of this small core group has individually contributed a chapter in this volume, and together as a small group, we have contributed the conclusion chapter. There has been ongoing input into my own group learning, discoveries as we unpack a concept or link with a group experience, and ever present humour. Warmth, trust and open communication have characterised the small group, qualities which have permeated also into the now larger group. My own learning, faith and trust in groups has been enriched through this eight-year-long experience with our original group members, Willem de Jager, Madie Duncan, and Monica Spiro, who with me, formed the core group.

In the chapters that follow we will see a range of authors, drawn from different professions and a variety of contexts, contribute their experiences of groups and groupwork practice. In the process of compiling this volume, I have asked each contributor to explore an understanding of groupwork in his/her own way. The total field across practice contexts emerging in the book identifies connections and common threads that bind the practice of groupwork at this time in South Africa. The commonalities are seen in the sheer diversity of groups which mirrors the diverse nature of the society, the emphasis on empowerment, the intertwining of democratising goals with the work of the group, the importance of leader behaviour in facilitating the process, and the galvanising of mutuality in groups. Some of the contributors think psychoanalytically, some are involved in organizational work, transformation, feminist psychotherapy, peacemaking, and support groups with professionals. Some are active in groups in the fields of substance dependency, HIV/AIDS, and the empowerment of persons with mental disability. Many of the contributors combine academic teaching and supervision of groups with practice. It is hoped that the rich variability of the different models of groupwork as seen in this volume will continue to develop exponentially.

In Chapter One, Becker introduces the reader to an overview of groups and groupwork practice, with the aim of exploring how groups have relevance in South Africa, as treatment and task modalities. She highlights the richness and variability of groups in different frameworks, that groups have healing potential and encourages a stance of 'thinking group' in a broader perspective. She emphasises that the value system of groups is entirely compatible with that of democratic societies, and given the current situation in South Africa, one decade after the new dispensation, she advances the view that groups can be used more actively to contribute to social healing and the development of a cohesive society.

In Chapter Two, Becker and Duncan reappraise the 'nuts and bolts' of groupwork in context. They offer a framework of some essential dimensions of groupwork theory and its interface with practice. They outline the principles of setting up and running a group and key domains in the planning process. The characteristics of groups such as levels, processes, dynamics, and development are explored and the reader is offered a systematic framework for appreciating group functioning. The role, functions, qualities, skills and techniques of group leadership are explained, and the ethics of practice elaborated in order to promote a critical, reflective stance to groupwork in South Africa.

In Chapter Three, O'Brien presents community groups as a way of peace-building in South Africa, which she describes as a 'post-settlement context' referring to its transition to democratic governance through a peace settlement. However, such contexts are characterised by various transitional issues that need to be addressed through peacebuilding initiatives. She contextualises community groups within its civil society context and argues that a critical perspective is needed when working with community groups that address community development and conflict resolution issues. She highlights a variety of strategies that contribute to peacebuilding in South Africa, noting that the stability of South Africa's democracy is centrally linked to the social and economic development of its people.

In Chapter Four, Smit demonstrates how groups are organizational building blocks. He identifies various types and functions of organization groups (or teams), and discusses how they are intrinsically connected to the attainment of organizational goals. Given the vast resources allocated annually to social service delivery in South Africa, the importance of effective and efficient management of these is important. He emphasises that leadership and management functions are requisite ingredients of any successful organizational enterprise, and that harnessing the power of groups in the organization contributes to goal attainment.

In Chapter Five, Gildenhuys offers an introduction to the theory and practice of group analysis. He argues that group analysis is positioned centrally in the social context as it addresses the complex process of psychosocial development. He discusses the psychological significance of the social context, and outlines group analysis as a model of practice. He emphasises that group analysis can assist in developing a 'community-based restorative paradigm' as it focuses on the total situation, and allows the socio-cultural, political and economic domains to be part of the developmental programme. He would like to see more creative applications of group analytic practice in the South African context, not only as a remedial instrument, but also to understand issues of social transformation, alienation and change.

In Chapter Six, Drower discusses how groupwork is well suited to address the wide range of issues arising from the HIV/AIDS challenge facing South Africa today. HIV/AIDS is a major threat to the country's social, economic and political stability. Groupwork, as an approach to helping people solve their own and their community problems and as means to develop their own and their community's strengths can be used in response to this challenge. Intervention strategies, skills and techniques relevant to the use of groupwork are outlined. A case study is presented as an example of how groupwork may be utilised to facilitate empowerment in the context of HIV/AIDS, and raises pertinent issues which the group facilitator working in this area, needs to consider.

In Chapter Seven, De Jager and Truter take a revisionist position and draw our attention to some of the adaptations of approach and technique therapists need to consider when doing psychodynamic groupwork with adolescents. They argue for an active management of the latent and manifest anxieties that are particular to the state of young adolescence and amplified when gathered in a group. Their case example illustrates the acting-out behaviour when this matter is not attended to and for which groupwork with adolescents is known (and feared!).

In Chapter Eight, Spiro examines how group therapy can provide a transformative experience for women who face the challenge of being single parents. She notes that South African statistics indicated that 42% of children in this country are living with single mothers and that locally and internationally, female headed households are identified as economically disadvantaged. She presents group therapy as a modality that can enhance women's growth and development from a relational/cultural perspective, and considers the value of groupwork for self-empowerment. A case example of a slow, open group intervention provided for single mothers demonstrates the therapeutic aspects of the group experience, in which members can reintegrate relationally.

In Chapter Nine, Sturgeon and Keet advocate for and describe the use of groupwork as a tool in improving the quality of life of people with mental illness and disability. Mental health problems represent five of the ten leading causes of disability worldwide, and the task of assisting the integration of people with mental disability into the community must be assumed by a wide range of professionals and other appropriate people from the community. They suggest that groupwork is particularly suited as a medium for equipping people with mental disability with knowledge, attitudes and skills needed for community living, and they outline techniques and skills particularly useful in working in the mental health field.

In Chapter Ten, Powis presents the reader with a basic understanding of substance dependency as well as a comprehensive treatment programme, within which groupwork assumes primary importance as a method of intervention in in-patient or specialist outpatient centres. He identifies substance dependence as one of the most common and invasive problems affecting all communities in South Africa and discusses the nature of this condition. He presents two types of group processes, which together constitute essential ingredients for a comprehensive group treatment programme, and illustrates facilitation skills required to work effectively with substance dependence.

In Chapter Eleven, Duncan proposes a model of using groups to transform attitudes in health professional education. The need to change the perspective and attitudes of health professionals became evident in the Truth and Reconciliation Commission (TRC) special hearings on the health sector. She describes how groups are used to promote sensitisation to issues of diversity, difference, power and interdependence in a teaching programme in a curriculum for health practitioners. She explains the use of median groups to effect attitudinal change as they pertain to the process of developing social responsiveness in a multi-cultural society.

In Chapter Twelve, Mayers proposes that groups be used to support health professionals in meeting the challenges faced in the Primary Health System in South Africa. She outlines how fundamental changes in the system of health care delivery have occurred since the new political dispensation in 1994. Comprehensive primary health care, an integral component of overall social and economic development and restructuring of the health care system is occurring, and has also been associated with an increased demand on the primary level services. She discusses some of the challenges encountered by health professionals, and suggests a support system for primary care health professionals. She demonstrates the usefulness of this approach in an example of such a support group for health professionals in the primary health system.

In the Conclusion, Becker, De Jager, Duncan and Spiro reaffirm the merits of groups, which have value as therapeutic as well as transformative tools in South Africa currently. They integrate and present a thematic analysis of the central principles and values of groupwork as emerging from the text, and make recommendations about the way forward.

We will see in the following chapters how groups have a substantive role to play in South Africa. I hope to give a flavour of particular areas in which groups are being used in South Africa as therapeutic and task groups, which includes the task of transformation. At another level, knowledge about groups and group behaviour can also illuminate aspects of large group and societal functioning, and if heeded, can be valuable cues to thinking about change and stability. In relation to applying group thinking on a broader level Cohen (2000) has drawn attention to the need to train political leaders. He asks: 'Will the body of knowledge concerning group dynamics, as accumulated in the 20th century, continue to expand beyond psychotherapy so as to provide useful approaches to the general problems of group life in the 21st' (Cohen, 2000: 101).

Pines (1998) eloquently reminds us that: 'The face of the other teaches justice and peace. As opposed to Hegel's master–slave philosophy, Levinas teaches that the relationship between the self and the other is that of master-disciple. It is by entering into language, through listening, that we are bound to the other' (86–87).

In the process of building a democratic and socially cohesive society in South Africa, it is imperative that we communicate through working together in groups and enter into a relationship with the other. As we in South Africa move beyond the restrictions of the past, we work together to create equilibrium and harmony. The variety of groupwork practice contexts as portrayed in this book reflects the complexity of the reality confronting us today.

1 An overview of groups and groupwork

Lily Becker

Learning objectives

By the end of this chapter you should be able to:

- Provide an overview of groups and groupwork practice, including the historical development of groupwork, as well as its current application to problems in today's society.
- Discuss the theoretical basis of groupwork, including the concepts of interpersonal connectedness and the value of groups.
- Outline the impact of clinical thinking on groups and group thinking on societies.
- Discuss the place of groups in nation-building, social development, and social healing in South Africa.

Introduction

Significance of groupwork   Groupwork has a great deal to offer in South Africa today. When we work together in small, large or medium-sized (median) groups, we can enhance the quality of life of a nation in a number of ways: groupwork can be used as a treatment modality to support and treat individuals in a group; and, in a broader context, as a task modality, it can be an instrument for community action. Groups can be used to create a more efficient and effective working environment in an organization. In groups we can transform prejudice and intolerance of difference. Groups can be used to problem solve and to resolve conflicts interpersonally, on an inter-group, inter-societal, and on the broader international level.

Groups can also be sources of conflict as the world has witnessed in the major group and inter-group conflicts currently and in the past. Interestingly, the same issues that we struggle with in the wider world, such as power, prejudice, an intolerance of difference, totalitarianism, democracy, conflict and hostility are also found in the microcosm of groups. In the early roots of groupwork groupworkers heard about the strength of groups as well as the 'story of the disastrous power of group associations and of the skilled misuse that could be made of them …'.[1] Groupwork as practised by helping professionals, however, focuses on the positive power of group associations, while trying to obviate negative or destructive potentials which may exist in the groups they work with. It is imperative that we learn about the potential for healing that exists in groups, and the interpersonal connectedness that can be promoted through groupwork. Within groups people can be supported, empowered, and can learn to be more humane and democratic. Ultimately, groups can be used to enhance, to repair, to transform, and to promote a culture of healing and collective learning. Importantly, as groups possess both positive and negative potentials, it is essential that we are able to promote the healing, transformative potential of groups, rather than collude with the negative, destructive aspects, which can perpetuate group problems.

Promoting healing and change in the 21st century   Today, in these early years of the 21st century, the relevance of group becomes even clearer. Seen against the background of the persistent themes of the 20th century – war, prejudice, migration, the break-up of the family and social groups, displacement, and the search for a new belonging (Nitsun, 2000), groupwork could be part of a route to foster understanding, constructive change, and interconnectedness. As a way of trying to increase communication and connectedness it conveys an important message about the value of belonging, sharing, and empowerment. The time of greater group awareness has dawned.

As helping professionals, we can use groups not only to improve individuals' lives; an understanding of groups and working with small groups also opens up a way of understanding and working with other groups – the community and society – in a 'discourse of both small and large groups, which can create and maintain dialogue across national, political and cultural divides' (Blackwell, 2000). Many theorists have responded to the challenge to study groups: their potentials, problems, and applications, resulting in a splendid diversity of theories from different strands of enquiry, as well as many questions. These questions revolve around the need for answers to group problems in both the microcosm and the macrocosm.

This chapter discusses groups and groupwork practice with the aim of exploring how groups have relevance in South Africa, not only as treatment and task modalities, but also to encourage the value of 'thinking group' in a broader perspective. Treatment and task groups used as a social healing medium can work towards nation-building, redress, social responsiveness, and capacity enhancement. This chapter contextualises groupwork methodology by outlining the early origins of groupwork as a discipline, before going on to explain how and why groupwork as practice has become so significant in the South African context, thereby extending the boundaries of practice into a continuum suited to the realities of a developing nation. Finally, this chapter upholds a firm commitment to groupwork as an important method in professional practice, and to its valuable role in promoting a democratic society.

History of groupwork

Although groupwork practice dates back to the 20th century, the formation of groups coincides with the earliest history of human beings. People have always gathered together in groups, often under the guidance of a leader, whether chief, medicine woman or shaman – to find meanings behind or beyond their everyday experiences.[2] Individuals have formed family groups or hunting groups, and these in turn formed communities in order most effectively to meet common human needs and to effect changes in their surroundings.

The origins of groupwork practice started at a time of progressive reform at the turn of the 20th century[3] in the self-help and recreational organizations, such as the settlement houses, YMCAs, Jewish centres and youth serving agencies of the time. These organizations were concerned with building character, socialising immigrants and young people, and establishing needed services, such as kindergartens and adult education, and promoting social exchange and social justice. Early groupwork encouraged social participation, democratic processes, and personal growth and learning. The major work of the agencies was with 'normal' individuals, whereas a far smaller use of groupwork emerged with those individuals who were physically or mentally ill.[4] Accordingly, democratic values are part of groupwork's early origins, with citizenship participation an important principle for bringing about social change. Collectivism and democracy were the underpinning ideologies bringing people together in these early contexts.

In Europe, the philosophical underpinning of groupwork was strengthened by the influence of immigrants who had fled Nazi persecution. Their experiences at the hands of totalitarianism inculcated them with strong humanistic beliefs in the rights of group members and a passion for democratic participation. Andrews (2001) writes of her interview with Konopka in 1998, when she told of her escape from Germany in the late 1930s and the contribution of her life experiences to her strong belief in the humanisation of social services. Similarly, in the realm of group analysis, Blackwell (2000) notes that Foulkes, a survivor of the collective destructiveness that prevailed in Germany and the Second World War, and Bion, a survivor of the collective destructiveness of the First World War, both turned their efforts to pioneering work in their study of group behaviour.

By 1940 groupwork as an active method of intervention took even greater hold, especially after the Depression when settlement houses, labour movements and community centres were providing support for immigrants, and for citizens trying to adjust to their current situation. In the area of groupwork and psychoanalysis, the 1940s, which unfolded against the background of World War Two and the period of post-war reconstruction, was described as the 'group decade' (Trist, 2000). Trist, in a drawing on Bion's 1948 Presidential Address on 'Psychiatry in a time of crisis', writes: 'Psychoanalysis and related disciplines, including work with groups, had brought a new type of knowledge to humankind. If used, it could be the means through which Western societies could learn how to surmount their manifold crises and develop to a further stage' (Trist, 2000: 26). At the International Congress on

Mental Health in 1948, held in London, for the first time at an international gathering, group methods were explored in a public arena.

Interestingly, the history of groupwork alerts us to the unpopularity of groupwork with conservative elements in American history. For example, Andrews (2001) writes that groupwork with its focus on humanity, equality, democracy, and social action was particularly affected by McCarthyism, and along with the witchhunts of that time in 1950–1954, thousands of citizens, including many groupworkers lost their jobs. In South Africa, the liberation movements in the apartheid era were nurtured within groups, which mirrored and articulated the aspirations of the oppressed population.

The first social work course in groupwork was developed by Grace Coyle in 1946 at the Case Western Reserve University in the United States.[5] Similar developments in the groupwork method in other professional courses, for example, in psychology, occupational therapy and nursing, developed in the post-World-War-Two period. As group theory developed, groups were viewed as having therapeutic or social action goals, depending on their purpose, forming part of both community and clinical work. This tension between the two emphases – drawing on the strengths of community members to improve their social environments and working with the ill to improve their health/mental health status – still persists today. What is clear, however, is that from its early beginnings, while rooted in social reform, the work done in groups considered both the individual and the group as a whole, as well as the wider community, a trend still evident in current practice. In South Africa, early groupwork methods, writes Helm (1962), included direct or material services, counselling methods, educative methods and information methods.

An important debate in the history of groupwork was the merger of groupwork with generic practice courses and there was particular concern about the consequences for the groupwork method. Groupwork receded in the 1960s and early 1970s and little groupwork content was offered in training schools, with generic practice courses including only minimal groupwork content. At the same time, reminds Andrews (2001), theory building continued, especially by Papell and Rothman, who in 1966 distinguished groups by articulating three models: social goals, reciprocal and remedial. [Refer to section on Typology of groups for more detail.]

An important event to herald the re-assertion of groupwork for example, was the launch of the journal, *Social Work with Groups: A Journal of Community and Clinical Practice* in 1978. This culmination of the come-back mode coincided with the start of regular conferences and symposia which underscored the re-discovery of groupwork practice. Despite this, today not enough education in groupwork is given in training schools internationally and nationally, with schools of professional training offering little more than foundation courses in groupwork, while a few are increasing their training to more advanced levels. However, Andrews (2001: 62) reassures and reminds us that 'groupwork ideology has stood up well over time because it is rooted in a clear understanding of the realities of human lives and the human condition, and that concepts of citizenship, participation, community, mutual aid and democracy are still powerful'.

Why groupwork?

Meeting the challenges   South Africa faces enormous challenges in managing the many factors that impact on the well-being of its citizens. Such factors include lack of resources (personal, material, educational, social), natural disasters (droughts, floods), events (illness, accidents), macro-system changes (economy, politics), social stratification (class issues), roles (performance, inadequacy) and life transitions (loss, change) (Potgieter, 1998). Against this background, groupwork as a method of practice is utilised by helping professionals and social development workers to promote individual and social change. Social workers, psychologists, health professionals, youth workers, and development/community workers, among others, have found the group method to be a particularly versatile method to use in a wide variety of contexts. The focus is the improvement of social functioning of people, and to this end, remedial, rehabilitative or preventive services are rendered, all with the overarching aim of advancing transformative human systems and enhancing the quality of life of the people of South Africa. Each helping profession in turn acquires specific knowledge and skills to do the job intrinsic to its professional mandate.

Inner strengths of groups   The nature of groupwork and the scope of projects can be seen to lie on a continuum, ranging from therapeutic groups working with a range of problem situations, to community groups dealing with social issues in communities. The group provides a context for communicating, sharing and mutual aid. Groups can focus on strengths, helping to search for and use human potential. The group can become a self-help instrument enabling people to take action to improve their life situations. The leader and group members can become transference objects (whereby early relationships are transferred onto the leader and other group members and worked through). This process can assist in therapeutic change in the group members individually and collectively; and the group collective strength can push for transformation in the broader societal context. In essence, the group itself in a mutually beneficial manner, through mutual aid, can become the source for healing and promoting desired change. The 'magic' of groupwork is the group's intangible collective strength that can be channelled in constructive ways.

The strengths perspective (Saleeby, 1996) assumes that group members possess inner resources, have the capacity for resilience and competence, and are participants in the helping process. This collaborative approach enriches the group experience and facilitates growth. A reliance on the capacity of the group also implies that the group has the ability to find solutions. However, a key determinant of whether a strengths perspective will become manifest, is the quality of the leader or facilitator, whose facilitation strategies and leadership can encourage the inherent strengths of the group to emerge, and be utilised for the benefit of the members.

Promoting interpersonal connectedness   We have all been in a number of groups in our everyday life beginning with the first group, the family, in which our basic relatedness to others was formed. Since those early formative years, and continuing throughout our lives, we have been in groups of various kinds and sizes. The peer group, the school group, the college and work environment group, have in simple and complex ways, connected us to others.

We are connected but also dependent on a wide context, the family, the community and the society. Foulkes[6] emphasised the inextricability and interrelated nature of the individual and society, maintaining that the individual cannot be separated from the social context. Thus in the beginning, each person is part of the group, and 'each individual ... is centrally and basically determined, inevitably, by the world in which he lives, by the community, the group of which he forms a part'.[7] The individual's identification with the groups of which he is a part, such as family, nation, culture, religion, tribe, is a feature of human existence.

The relevance of individuals' intrinsic connection to and dependence on groups is that individuals need to be considered within their social contexts, i.e. within the context of the interconnection of individuals, groups and communities, the relationships among these, and the convergent trends from different aspects of life.

Group approach and indigenous practice models   A group approach appears to be similar to the customarily used models of help in Africa, for it is often within the context of a family, kinship or the village group that solutions are found for problems of individuals. The need for indigenous models of practice is currently debated in the literature, with emphasis placed on the need to build on already existing strengths, and solutions that people have found works for them (Gray and Allegritti, 2003, and Ose-Hwedie, 2002).

Perhaps in the realm of the group and its collective approach we can start to find a meeting point in this challenge to develop indigenous practice. Groupwork coheres well with an overarching social developmental approach, the recommended model of change and development for South Africa.

Theoretical basis of groupwork

There are a number of theories which explain what groups are and how to work with them. Theory is useful to practitioners as it offers explanatory concepts, which help to order events. Lonergan (1994) writes that theories are tools which are useful to group leaders in three ways: they help to organize data, they generate new ideas for group interventions, and having a theory increases confidence as group leaders know what they are doing; group members pick up on this and this increases their engagement in the group process.

Sometimes it is hard to see whether theory or practice comes first, according to Whitaker (2001). Theory may come first for those groupworkers who have been schooled in a particular theory and then apply it in practice, or practice may come first for those who develop a characteristic way of working with groups, without recourse to an established theory. Explanations for events that are observed are usually looked for in theory. It is likely that groupworkers move back and forth between theory and practice and that theory and practice influence one another. Theories give rise to models, which are created to apply aspects of theory to fit situations in practice.

Definition of a group There are many ways of defining a group, just as we use numerous terms to describe a group, such as team, collective, meeting, congregation, association, forum, orchestra, jury, which attest to the many groupings that are present in everyday life.

According to Barnes, Ernst and Hyde (1999: 2):

> *A group is more than people who happen to be doing the same thing at the same time in the same place; to be a group, the people must have some connection, some way in which they come together (either literally or in their minds) with a common aim, purpose, or function. This defines the boundary of the group, separating it from the surrounding environment of which nevertheless it is a part.*

Definition of groupwork Brown (1992: 8) defines groupwork as follows:

> *Groupwork provides a context in which individuals help each other; it is a method of helping groups as well as helping individuals; it can enable individuals and groups to influence and change personal, group, organizational, and community problems.*

Theoretical positions

Drawing on the plethora of theories which explain group functioning, many texts including Toseland and Rivas (2001) and Corey (1990) offer overviews of the most influential theories. For example, Toseland and Rivas (2001) locate and debate the following five theories: **systems theory**, **psychodynamic theory**, **learning theory**, **field theory** and **social exchange theory**, as being most influential, with the emphasis that a thorough knowledge of systems theory is basic to all groupwork practice. There is however, no easy way of classifying the wide range of theories available, and there are 'difficulties inherent in the task of describing and categorising theories',[8] which resemble one another in some ways, and diverge in others. Rather than defining the above five theories, this chapter refers to specific vantage points (positions that allow an overall view of theories) from which to read theories and their usefulness for practice.

In offering a range of theories that contemporary groupwork practitioners draw on, McDermott (2002) views them from five vantage points. These are not mutually exclusive however, and practitioners happily mix and borrow among available theories, in an eclectic approach. The five vantage points from which group theories are surveyed are as follows:

The group as a power base Originating in Marxist political thought, theories that see the group as a power base begin from the premise that problems which individuals have are social and structural, rather than personal. Self-help groups, advocacy, and social action groups emerge from this perspective, with the focus on collective action, not on individual change. 'The group then becomes the site where perspectives, actions and outcomes are shared and the dialectical process which ensues has the potential to emancipate and empower' (McDermott, 2002: 38). Criticisms of this approach cite the absence of focus on individuals in the group. This criticism echoes an earlier criticism of the **social goals model**, one of the three models of groupwork as crystallised by Papell and Rothman (1966). [Refer to section on Group practice format.] An example of a theory which addresses the 'group-as-a-power-base' approach is Vinik's and Levin's (1991) social action group approach.

The group as a system Most groupworkers include the central elements of **systems theory** in conceptualising their practice, notes McDermott (2002). Systems theory focuses on the group as an entity, a system of interacting elements. Barnes, Ernst and Hyde (1999: 100) offer a fluid rendition of a system at work as follows: 'as people, their energy, presence and emotions move across the boundary of the group, the members resonate in their personal ways to the issues which arise'. Toseland and Rivas (2001) discuss the details and the implications of a systems theoretical approach, while Shulman (1992) derives his **mutual aid approach** from this theory. [Refer to section on Group practice format – also referred to as interactional approach or model.] In essence, the group, like all living organisms, is a system interacting with its environment, and in a healthy system, there is input and output. Healthy systems have semipermeable boundaries, are able to integrate new information, but also able to close their boundaries if necessary. As new energy enters the system, there is a disturbance to the equilibrium, and the system now has to seek harmony and a new balance. Therefore we need to ask questions about the impact of a particular event on the group or, rather than seeing a problem in isolation, we should see it as interconnected with other events. Blackwell (2000) and McDermott (2002) comment on some of the current critiques of systems theory, which address inter alia, the applicability of natural and physical sciences to the social world and the limitations in addressing conflict and change.

The group as a container of individuals As a contrast to the systems theory, this view focuses on the individual members who comprise the group. Two key examples of theories derived from individual psychology and applied to the group are **psychoanalytic theory** and **learning theory** (McDermott, 2002). These theories derive from psychological theories of personality, human development and psychopathology, and are adapted to explain collective group processes. The group is seen as a family, issues of transference and countertransference are worked with, and the group is used to gain insight into problems and dynamics, as well as to strengthen interpersonal skills.[9] A later section in this chapter, on clinical work and groups, will further examine this area. Another theoretical view that focuses on individuals in the group emanates from learning theories, with an emphasis on behavioural and rational emotive strategies, on self-management, and the role of cognition in behavioural change (Corey, 1990).

The group as a container of properties   This view holds that common properties of groups such as communication, interaction, cohesion, group culture, norms and roles can all be identified, studied and analysed in their own right. Further, they can also help to suggest factors, which enhance or inhibit group functioning.[10] As groups change in character at various times in the life of the group, the development of the group through various phases or stages has received attention. Most models of group development propose that groups move through similar stages, broadly seen as beginning, middle, and end stages, although different writers have different ideas about the number of stages, and the quality of the events that occur. For example, Garland, Jones and Kolodny (1976) describe the middle stage of development as being around issues of intimacy and differentiation, while Northen (1988) focuses on exploring, testing and problem solving. Both progressive and cyclical processes exist, so a group may move through the stages sequentially, but then come back, in a cyclical manner, to re-address an earlier concern. Critics of the group developmental view, writes McDermott (2002), refer to the uniqueness of any given group, arguing that this detracts from the creativity and uniqueness of particular types of groups.

The group as a site of meaning construction   This view recognises that the 'inter-subjective context of the group can be a site for the construction and reconstruction of meaning' (McDermott, 2002: 51). This post-modern view proposes that in the process of talking and communicating, people come to understand their experiences, and also reframe and control them. Members are seen to be agents who are re-authoring their own lives. There are changes in meaning as members tell their stories, interact and exchange. Within the group the stories and reflections shared by members and facilitators include social, personal factors, and the discovery of meaning about these. The importance of language, narrative and discourse as implicit in making meaning is reflected upon and these factors are seen as having the potential to initiate change (McDermott, 2002). Critics of this view are concerned about the fluidity inherent in this approach.

In practice however, groupworkers will draw from a mix of theories, in an eclectic approach. This can be as a response to the diverse needs of people, and the requirements of the service context. Fortunately, part of the richness of groupwork is that it is able to incorporate diverse theories and techniques according to the requirements of the situation, and the expertise of the facilitator.

Group practice format

Describing the format of group practice takes into consideration the area of practice into which it falls, the levels of operation involved, purpose and tasks involved, group size and time determinant.

Groupwork as a method of professional practice fits comfortably in the middle between the micro and the macro areas of practice, as it deals with personal and interpersonal change, as well as social change.[11]

Groupwork also takes place in a range of different formats depending on its purpose and tasks. The format continuum ranges from community, to self-help, to support groups, to psycho-educational groups, to process groups (such as training, or human relations or organizational training groups studying evolving dynamics) to psychotherapeutic groups (Ettin, 1999). The level of expertise ranges from leaderless groups, such as in self-help groups, to discussion groups with an untrained facilitator, to professionally run groups.

Groupwork occurs in groups of different sizes, from the small treatment group, to median groups, to large groups, with each of these having different characteristics and outcomes. There are also different intervention strategies, which aim to serve the various mandates specific to the type of group, the members in the group, and the treatment outcomes required for the group.

The size of a group often depends on the purpose, and membership demographics such as age, for example children's groups may be smaller. Groups range from 2–4 (very small, similar to individual therapy), to small (5–9 usual size for psychotherapy groups), mid-size (10–15 workshops or training groups), median groups (16–30, used in milieu settings), large groups (30–60 human relations conferences), and very large groups (100 or more, such as conferences) (Ettin, 1999).

The time determinant of groups range from single session, to crisis intervention (1–5 sessions), short-term contracted groups (6–20 sessions), medium-length contracts (20–52 sessions), and long-term groups (over one year's duration) (Ettin, 1999), or closed groups with no membership change, or open groups, which allows for membership change for the duration of the group contract.

Typology of groups Groups can be organized according to purpose, aims, and task requirements. Various intervention strategies differ according to the purpose, selection of members, type of leadership, focus of attention, and the inherent ideology underlying collective efforts.[12] Papell and Rothman (1966) outlined three historically significant models of groupwork which emphasise the relationship of the group to the social context, and which reflect different emphases characterising different eras in social work practice (McDermott, 2002). The social goals model emphasises empowerment and social change, through democratic principles of participation and collective action. The remedial model has a treatment focus, emphasising restoration and rehabilitation of individuals in the group, and the reciprocal model, also called the interactional model or mutual aid group, essentially sees the group as a system, seeing reciprocal connections between individuals, groups and the wider social environment.

Toseland and Rivas (2001) classify groups into formed and natural groups, and treatment and task groups.

- **Formed groups** are those that come together through some outside influence, and are convened for a particular purpose. Some examples are therapy groups, and social action groups.
- **Natural groups** occur spontaneously on interpersonal attraction or needs of members. Some examples of these are family groups and peer groups.

Formed groups (which are focused on in this book) are classified according to **treatment** and **task** groups.

- In **treatment groups**, the major purpose is to meet members' socio-emotional needs. The five primary purposes for treatment groups are: support, education, growth, therapy and socialisation.
- In contrast, in a **task group** the major purpose is to accomplish a goal that will affect the broader constituency, not only the members of the group. They have three primary purposes: meeting client needs, meeting organizational needs and meeting community needs (Toseland & Rivas, 2001).

A useful comparison between these two types of groups may be made,[13] whereby differences in terms of specific characteristics are defined according to bond, roles, communication patterns, procedures, composition, self-disclosure, confidentiality and evaluation.

Defining groups according to typology is helpful, as it outlines the importance of different purposes, and consequences, and the variety of groups offered in practice settings. Toseland and Rivas (2001) emphasise however, that often in direct service, both treatment and task groups are interchangeable, as attention is paid to meeting members' socio-emotional needs as well as accomplishing tasks.

In South Africa, both task and treatment groups can be used in social healing, focusing on social development, redress, capacity enhancement, empowerment, and reciprocity. These can reflect collaborative endeavours: task groups enhancing development, and therapeutic groups enhancing interpersonal restoration.

Value of groupwork

Benefits   Amongst other goals, the helping professions attempt to bridge the gap between the individual and society. Groupwork uses the power of the collective to assist the individual. The benefits of groups and groupwork are documented, and include:[14]

- the experience of commonality, where similar interests and goals can be shared in the group;
- the problem-solving potential of groups, where there can be an exchange of ideas, and the development of new approaches to a problem or issue;
- small-group forces which are potent and can be utilised for achieving social and individual change; and
- the convenience, efficiency and cost-effectiveness of groups.

Curative factors   The value of groupwork can also be delineated through curative (therapeutic) factors, as defined by Yalom (1985). These are: group cohesiveness, catharsis, socialisation, installation of hope, interpersonal learning, corrective emotional experience, reality testing, modelling, vicarious learning, the corrective recapitulation of the family group and universality. Scheidlinger (1997) cites Karasu (1986) and Kaul and Bednar (1986) who have demonstrated group therapy's effectiveness as being on a par with that of other therapies. It is therefore, useful to understand these unique curative (therapeutic) factors as rendered by Yalom (1985) as also by Bloch and Crouch (1985), the latter reflecting slightly nuanced changes, specific to the authors' theoretical orientations (Scheidlinger, 1997).

Healing effect Brown (1998) reminds us that Foulkes formulated what is called the Basic Law of Group Dynamics and used it to describe the healing effect of groups in these words: 'The deepest reason why [these] patients ... can reinforce each other's normal reactions and wear down and correct each other's neurotic reactions is that collectively they constitute the very norm from which individually they deviate'.[15] What this means is that each individual is to a large extent part of the group he belongs to, and the collective aspect permeates him to the core. Therefore, groups provide 'an opportunity to engage in reciprocal relationships of mutual empathy and understanding . . . simultaneously to recognise ourselves and others as feeling and autonomous subjects' (Brown, 1998: 393).

Connectedness On a broad level, groupwork gives us an opportunity to 'influence the pattern of connectedness, not only in the therapy group itself, but in the world of groups outside ...' (Nitsun, 2000: 117). Nitsun reminds us that at the start of the new millennium human beings have learned relatively little about communicating with one another. He comments that the 'tendency to entropy and fragmentation that could continue in society, the loss of human connectedness, the atomisation of the self, may give group psychotherapy added momentum as medium of social healing' (Nitsun, 2000: 117).

Ethics Ethical relationships are fostered by engagement in group life, writes Brown (1998). While this is an important part of the effectiveness of groupwork at the small-group level, it has wider social implications. By developing respect for and tolerance of difference in religious, class or racial affiliation, members acclimatise to a group norm that emphasises inclusion and justice. In addition to dealing with difference, there can be a focus on fostering interpersonal relatedness and mutuality, resolving conflict, and transforming attitudes of prejudice. In fostering a theme of communication, sharing and togetherness, a beginning can be made in the direction of broader healing of communities, and societies.

Social transformation Brown (1998) maintains that, given enough free speech and dialogue, groups have a wisdom and power that can lead to the fall of totalitarian regimes. By converting the group into the agent of change, Ormont (2000) suggests that we are coming full circle to Cody Marsh's prediction of eighty years ago: 'By the crowd they have been broken; by the crowd they shall be healed (1933: 406, in Ormont, 2000: 186).

Groups and clinical work

Group therapy

The group as a treatment modality is the vehicle through which a variety of group therapeutic models can be offered. Group therapy, akin to individual therapy, is used to promote healing and the restoration of group members. The therapy group is a vehicle for understanding the members' interpersonal world, experiencing the interaction of members within the group and reflecting upon that interaction. Bernard and Mackenzie (1994) point out that therapy is provided through the group, not through interaction with individual members, and that the entire group is conceptualised as a system, therefore a paradigm shift is required, akin to the paradigm shift required to do family therapy.

The therapeutic aspect of groupwork was part of groupwork's early roots. From the early focus on the mentally ill, it has evolved into a sophisticated therapeutic modality. The 'group decade' (Trist, 2000: 1) of the 1940s, particularly in Britain, brought with it exciting developments in group theory and clinical intervention, and has had a profound influence on group clinical theory and practice today. Group theory, starting with Freud's early insights about the 'primal horde' has continued to progress, and carries the imprints of influential original theoreticians, in particular, Foulkes (1948, 1964) and Bion (1961, 1962). Today, there are a number of group therapy approaches, which vary according to the underlying theoretical models. Some examples of group therapy offered in South Africa, are addressed in later chapters in this volume.

Models of group therapy

The different models of group therapy aim to offer members a secure context to promote change through a variety of therapeutic strategies. While 'every school of personality theory, such as Freudian, Sullivanian, Horneyan, etc, is represented in group practice',[16] models of group therapy range from Yalom's 'here and now' interactional approach (Yalom, 1985), the group analytic approach of Foulkes (1964), Bion's basic assumptions theory (Brown, 2000), group focal conflict theory (Whitaker & Lieberman, 1964), and cognitive and behavioural approaches (Lonergan, 1994). More recently, object relations (Alonso & Rutan, 1984) and self psychology approaches (Harwood & Pines, 1998) have been applied to group therapy, highlighting depth dimensions about group experience.

Contributions of clinical theory

Clinical theory as a whole has made significant contributions in group theory and group therapeutic interventions, as well as to the application of groups beyond the clinical domain.

Psychoanalytic perspective   The unconscious aspect of group behaviour has been the domain of the **psychoanalytic perspective**, starting with Freud. Freud, as did Le Bon, questioned why and how people, when part of a mob, could get out of control, and Freud's suggestion that 'a group mind' was at play[17] has continued to intrigue. In the group, the individual was said to regress to a primitive state. According to Freud: 'the feelings of a group are always very simple and very exaggerated. So that a group knows no doubt nor uncertainty … . In groups the most contradictory ideas can exist side by side … without any conflict arising from the logical contradiction'.[18] The instincts are said to run rampant, and while groups might be moral at times, it is not out of any natural tendency, only 'under the influence of suggestion'.[19]

Group analytic theory   Since then, group analytic theoretical contributions have continued to deepen understanding of group collective behaviour. Foulkes questioned the very basis of the division between individual and group (Pines, 1983), and this questioning forms the basis of his **group analytic theory**. Foulkes places the group, not the individual, at the centre of theory, helping to form a new view of groups. He believed that 'so-called inner processes in the individual are internalisation of the forces operating in the group to which he belongs'.[20] Foulkes emphasised the social nature of human beings.

The group context, the collective ground of the group was the focus of Foulkes' enquiry. What he defined as the 'group matrix' was 'the hypothetical web of communication and relationship in a group. It is the common shared ground which ultimately determines the meaning and significance of all events upon which all communication and interpretation, verbal and non-verbal, rest' (Foulkes, 1984: 118, in Brown, 2000).

Ego and object relations   The importance of the **holding environment** of the group and the relationships within the group is highlighted particularly in the works of Foulkes (1964). The group's ability to contain the group members is instrumental for its therapeutic potential. This is seen as akin to the holding, attunement and mirroring of the mother–infant dyad.[21] These insights and others from the **ego and object relations** clinical theorists have resonated with groupworkers, who now understand more fully the need to create a trusting, healing environment within the group to enable groupwork to proceed optimally.

Self psychology   The clinical perspective from **self psychology** has helped group therapists understand the intersubjective experiences of individuals within the group. Pines (1998) writes that the self-object, the other, is always integrally part of the self's development. As the individual's need for affiliation to others is nurtured, so development progresses optimally. This converges well with what we understand about the intrinsic value of groups for individuals. Self psychology has also helped groupworkers to understand the needs of some of the more vulnerable group patients, as well as the importance of empathic validation within a group. The similarity of Kohut's 'group as a self' and Foulkes' concept of the 'group matrix' has been commented on by Pines (1996a, in Karterud, 1998). The need for 'self-object' experiences through life, which support and enhance the self, is extended to the need for engagement with groups, be this as a member of family, religion, work, or political or social group.

Clinical theory and selection criteria   A clinical perspective assists group-workers in the selection and composition of the members of the group, as **assessment and selection criteria** draw mainly from clinical theory. The suitability and capacity of individual members is assessed, with reference to personality strengths and the ability of members to participate in a group experience (Piper & McCallum, 1994). The concept of 'group ego' or the 'group self' informs us about the group-as-a-whole group field (Pines, 2000; Harwood, 1998), and this can also be gauged for its collective strength.

Group-as-a-whole knowledge   This has deepened due to the influential theoretical advances of Bion (1961). Bion's theory on **basic assumptions** holds that a group behaves as a 'work' group at times and as a 'basic assumption' group at other times, when emotional states take over the group. Bion described these basic assumptions as primitive states of mind, which are generated automatically when people are in a group. Bion named three basic assumptions: dependency (expecting solutions to be bestowed by the leader/facilitator); fight/flight (fleeing from or fighting with adversaries, particularly outside the group; the group is united against vaguely perceived external enemies) and pairing (hoping for a coupling of individuals which would bring a new person or idea which would provide salvation) (Schermer, 2000; Brown, 2000). Melanie Klein's ideas about primitive mental mechanisms influenced Bion's formulations about group basic assumption behaviour (Klein, 1946).

Positive and negative group forces   The identification of **positive and negative forces** in groups has been enriched by a number of group analytic writers (Foulkes, 1964; Bion, 1961; Nitsun, 1996) among others. Nitsun's concept of the **anti-group** (Nitsun, 1996, 2000) suggests that there are destructive or potentially destructive attitudes towards groups. These may manifest before the group starts, or during the group, or be found outside of the group in the organization in which it is run, or indeed, in the group facilitator himself (Nitsun, 2000). Importantly, the anti-group processes needs recognition, as this provides a key to the creative development of the group. 'In parallel with Winnicott's theory of the "use of the object" (Winnicott, 1968), the survival of the group in the face of attack is itself growth promoting. It reinforces belief in the strength and durability of the group and it enhances trust in the group' (Nitsun, 2000: 120).

Influence of leadership   Clinical theory has amplified insights into the leader/facilitator role, and his manifest and latent influence on the group (Freud, 1922; Bion, 1961; Foulkes, 1964; Lipgar & Pines, 2003). Leadership behaviour, especially in relation to the power of a charismatic group leader, interests clinicians. Kohut (1971, 1977) for example, was concerned about destructive group dynamics, and how a messianic group leader was able to lead Germany into self-destruction, while systematically destroying millions of other human beings (Harwood, 1998). Harwood (2003) distinguishes between the facilitating and self-serving group leader and the importance of being aware of how self-serving charismatic leaders can utilise group pressure to their own ends.

Group- vs. individual-centred models The **clinical perspective** has, in the past and currently, debated **group-centred models** of group psychotherapy versus **individual-centred models** of group psychotherapy, with the focus alternatively on group-as-a-whole, or on individual members. Currently, the inseparability of individual and group-as-a-whole dynamics is more recognised, with group therapists attending both to the individual in the group, as well as addressing group-as-a-whole dynamics or themes.

In sum, the clinical perspective on the whole has furthered our understanding of group processes and dynamics and the therapeutic potential in a group. In addition to understanding individuals in groups and group-as-a-whole behaviour, group analytic theorists have also made major contributions to understanding societal behaviour.

Groups and culture

Culture and groups are intertwined (Weinberg, 2003). The concept of ' "culture" … is a collective term used to denote the symbolic and learned, nonbiological aspects of human society, including language, custom, and convention by which human social groups are distinguishable from one another. Each social group in society develops its own culture. A culture shares certain common features: language, religion, dress codes, customs and belief' (Mackintosh, 1998: 119). Different cultures vary in their norms, values, ethics, codes of conduct and common history (Weinberg, 2003), so we can assume that these variations will be seen in the groups from different cultures.

The formative effects of the social milieu (the family), and systems (societies, cultures and political climates), are felt in the group setting (Ettin, 1997). Thus, different ethnic origins in the group members, with different languages, religions, social attitude, non-verbal communication and customs (Weinberg, 2003), play out in the group. A group setting can re-create the effect of social forces, which affect the different individuals. As such, in some respects, a group meeting can be thought of as a cultural event, as individuals come from different milieus, cultural settings, family backgrounds and individual histories. This translates into the different ways different members from different cultures behave, communicate, express feelings, allow closeness and relate to authority. Similarly, gender differences can also manifest differences in group communication and the culture of a group.

There are challenges in groups given that different cultures can constitute groups. Nitsun (2000) reminds us that a love of one's own (cultural) group is professed often at the expense of the other's group, which is feared and hated. An awareness of the ambivalence about the 'other' is important, as is the opportunity to create common understanding and communication across cultural divides. Small groups mirror the social groupings in wider society. The leap (and the link) from the small group context to the larger social context (Nitsun, 2000) is crucial to recognise. If we can see the continuity, and how the small group is relevant to the broader societal realm in the area of culture, groups can become a valuable transformational tool to better society.

Cultural groups in South Africa   In South Africa, there are diverse cultural groups, which have different cultural values. These are reflected in groups, which often comprise membership of multiple cultures. Competent group practice must always rest on a respectful, sensitive attitude to others, whether culturally or personally, and must aim to create harmony and understanding, racially, ethnically and culturally. The necessity for cultural sensitivity in the culturally diverse South African society is explored by Mackintosh (1998) who suggests appropriate ways in which professional practice can respond to diversity, in keeping with values and ethics inherent to professional practice.

Different phenomena characteristic of the diverse cultures will be reflected in the group context; the 'social unconscious' (Hopper, 2001) of a culture, which is internalised by members, is often re-evoked in a group. In South Africa, groups are run in different settings and are usually multi-cultural, and differences in cultural background, family background and historical experiences, can become manifest during the course of the group. Cultural codes often play a role in defining how the members relate in a group and anxiety may be created where members appear to transgress a culture-specific code, for example, by expressing greater individuality where this is not the norm in a specific cultural group. This is similar to findings in Japanese society as found by Hofstede (in Weinberg, 2003) where Japanese cultural norms become reflected in the group behaviour. It presents a challenge to members and the leadership of groups, to be tolerant of the different cultures, social attitudes and norms. There is, in addition, a particular culture that is developed in a group. We are reminded that members are all both carriers of culture as well as creators of culture in a group (Weinberg, 2003). The group evolves its own culture, and its norms and values, as group members communicate, interact, talk, listen, and develop an 'impersonal fellowship' (Maxwell, 2000: 40), and a new 'culture of meaning' (40).

Groups and building society

Klein (1953: xv, in Papell, 1997) expresses well the way groupwork is relevant to its societal mission in an alienated world:

> *Society is seeking a way in which people can live together peacefully and productively. We must learn to use our tools and methods to help all of*

us to learn to live together ... it is in such face-to-face groups that people can be helped to develop mature personalities, learn constructive values and be educated to their roles as citizens.

How does our knowledge about groups and group dynamics assist us in better understanding societies and societal behaviour? How can groups be useful in building a better society?

Building blocks for society   Firstly, the small group is a base and a building block for the development of a democratic society, as it provides a venue where ideals of mutuality, sharing, giving, and citizenship can be developed. Differences of culture, religion, class, can be talked, worked and understood, and conflicts can be thought about, worked with and ultimately resolved. Within the work of the group, there are critical issues, which are characteristic of democratic-egalitarian systems (Ettin, 2000). In groups there is a struggle between balancing of personal needs and rights against the collective requirement of the group to which they belong; the will of the majority against the protection of the rights of the minority; the need to allow healthy competition, and the need to protect individual needs, as well as group needs. De Maré (1975, 1998, 2000), a pioneer of the large group has said that, while the function of the small group is to socialise the individual, the function of the large group is to humanise society. De Maré emphasised the importance of the group setting, particularly the median and large group, in bridging a gap between the individual and the socio-cultural environment. We have to learn to talk to each other, develop dialogue, and restore 'mindfulness' in society, rather than the mindlessness, which often prevails in society. De Maré believes that groups have the capacity to 'humanise' society. 'If we turn to present day industrial society, we can ask how it can be that intelligent individuals perpetuate cultures that are destructive. I believe that the answer lies in the clash between the individual mind and the group mind, and as I have already suggested, group mind is what the term 'culture' implies. Without dialogue, minds are cut off from one another and produce groups that are pathological' (De Maré, 2000: 206.)

De Maré sees large groups as an extension of small groups, and that societies, beyond the small, median and large groups, can be said to share a similar structure to large groups. Dalal (1998) has added that the small group too can humanise society. In this respect, 'koinoinia' (De Maré, 2000: 209), described as 'impersonal fellowship', can be seen to resonate with the African ethic of 'ubuntu', both emphasising collective mentality and fellowship.

Working with socio-political issues   Secondly, knowledge about group phenomena can help us to understand and to work with issues such as power, authority conflicts, the adherence to a 'powerful' leader figure, dependence and interdependence. Thus, leadership and conformity to the leader in large groups, communities and societies can become more transparent. Nitzgen cites Freud who defined the role of the leader as the collective ego-ideal and as an 'institutionalised love object' (Nitzgen, 2001: 335). Group members are left in a state of 'unconsciously chosen dependency on him or her, comparable to hypnotic suggestion.'[22] Group leadership should enhance and educate group members to a democratic way of thinking (Nitzgen, 2001). Foulkes (1964) has maintained that groups show a tendency to compliance and conformity towards their leaders, and that the goal of groupwork was to enhance cooperation rather than submission of the members to the leader.

Understanding trauma and large-group identity Thirdly, large-group identity, defined by Volkan (2002) as ethnic, religious, or national identity, tends to assume greater importance in times of stress. 'Under extreme conditions, members will rally round a leader who will help them to protect their large-group identity, no matter what means he or she might use' (Volkan, 2001: 84). He further explains that one aspect of clinical observation that is especially relevant to understanding certain components of large-group identity is the transgenerational transmission of trauma. There are processes at the group level that are similar to those of individuals who experience trauma. This is concerned with shared traumatic events, mental representations of which are 'deposited' into the next generation. Over generations such events become 'woven into the canvas of the ethnic or large-group tent' (Volkan, 2001: 88), and can become a 'chosen trauma' that forms part of the large group's collective identity, but which may lie dormant. It can be reactivated especially when there is a crisis. When such a trauma is fully reactivated within a large group by a stressful event, a 'time collapse' occurs whereby the past trauma and contemporary threat are felt as one. 'Thus an ancient enemy will be perceived in a new enemy and a sense of entitlement to regain what was lost, or to seek revenge against the contemporary enemy, becomes exaggerated' (Volkan, 2001: 89). While Volkan does not mean to reduce political events only to this phenomenon, he explains how it can become an important 'ethnic marker' in reactivation.

Hopper (2001) echoes the concept of a reactivation. He too refers to society as a large group, which can re-enact experiences of social trauma which have occurred at another time, or another place, and can be conscious or unconscious. In the recreation of old situations into new situations, aspects of social trauma, which have occurred at another time, or another place, can become re-enacted. He refers to this recreation of an old situation into a new one as 'equivalence' (Hopper, 2001: 13). This re-enactment is as a result of 'attempts to communicate non-verbal and ineffable experience, all of which may be considered as elements of repetition compulsion' (Hopper, 2001: 13). He suggests that this re-enactment is most likely to occur in large groups, such as organizations, or societies. Traumatised social systems are like groups, explains Hopper (1997) and the role of unconscious factors in the life of social systems is especially important in traumatised societies. Thus, for example when a society goes through a massive trauma, such as the holocaust, it is engraved in the memory of the population for generations. Therefore, Israel, established as a state as a result of the holocaust, is very sensitive to threats on its security, and unconsciously sees them as threats of annihilation. In South Africa, the apartheid legacy has left deep imprints and sensitivity to race and difference.

Understanding progression and regression Fourthly, larger groups such as societies behave in a similar way to smaller groups in relation to progression and regression. Nuttman-Shwartz and Weinberg (2002) write that when societies regress, their dynamics become similar to those of a traumatised group. Under such conditions they believe it is appropriate to infer findings from the study of groups to the study of societies. Patterns of progression and regression of societies and the role of the leader in promoting such progression or regression are commented on by Volkan (2002). Volkan (2002) has drawn attention to the regression that can occur in large groups (such as ethnic, national, or religious groups), when a majority of group members share certain anxieties, expectations, behaviours, thought patterns and actions. This regression can occur after a society has faced a trauma, such as a war, battle, or humiliation by another group. A crucial factor is that a leader will either encourage progression or regression.

In sum, knowledge and insights into groups and group behaviour can enlarge our understanding of societies. This is relevant especially in relation to large groups in conflict, where 'chosen traumas' connected to ethnic, religious and national events can become reactivated and re-enacted. On the other hand, on a nation building level, the group as a base for a democratic society is of great importance in the current situation in South Africa.

Groupwork and South Africa

Groups and race The history of South Africa is one of identification of group to race, processes of homogenisation of the group-self, and attribution of general characteristics to the 'other' of another race. This ideology, reflecting the belief system of the dominant culture, drove the political process for 40 years. Group-based divisions were concretised through a system known as 'apartheid', which separated racial groups through legalised procedures and defined geographical areas of group separateness (Group Areas Act).

Discriminatory welfare policies This more recent past and colonial history also resulted in oppressive discriminatory welfare policies for the majority of the population. McKendrick (1990) traces the evolution of the welfare system in South Africa, with emphasis on the unique constellation of forces, historically and in the recent past, which defined the product provided by the system, as seen in the apartheid era.

Denial of social context Against the backdrop of nationalist government and apartheid policy, the social context was denied its relevance. In professional arenas, the individual, without reference to the broader context, or the socio-cultural concerns, was the primary focus of help. South African professional workers tended to rely primarily on intra-psychic interpretations of client problems, and in groupwork practice, this resulted in a focus on change within the individual through particular kinds of therapeutic group experiences.[23] Contextual issues were avoided in the treatment process. The inextricability and interrelated nature of the individual and society[24] was denied, or undeniably, minimised. In the socio-political arena however, the history of South Africa is embedded in the story of groups, which were instrumental in the development of liberation movements. Groups, small and large, were the contexts in which political movements to combat the apartheid government, flourished.

Changes post-1994 In 1994, a new political era was ushered in, which also ushered in a broader slant in groupwork practice. Gray (1998) writes on the changes seen in the welfare arena, the pivotal focus of which is on equality and social justice. This approach provided a base for an alternative approach to welfare, which broadened into a developmental welfare model that aimed to redress the imbalances of the past, and included a rights-based anti-discriminatory model of professional practice. Currently, major transformation of the society is in progress, following on the democratically elected government in 1994, and social developmental approach has become the framework of choice for the helping professions (White Paper for Social Welfare, 1997; Gray, 1998; McKendrick, 2001). Groupwork can play an important role in this developmental approach to facilitate the establishment of democratic societal structures, with goals of empowerment and advocacy. Models of community development drawing on a facilitative model of groupwork (Rooth, 1998) and linking social development and economic objectives (Gray, 1998) have been proposed, which aim to empower, build capacity, and have components of democratisation and participation transformation.

Group approach and ubuntu A group approach echoes the traditional African heritage of ubuntu, which is one of sharing and hospitality. It is the ethic that occurs in the extended family in Africa, where the group is seen as more important than the individual (Boon, 1996). 'A person is only a person because of other people' (31). The philosophy of ubuntu can be seen in this example of a Xhosa proverb: *Intaka yokha ngentsiba lenye intake* (translation: A bird builds its house with another bird's feather) (Boon, 1996: 32). This collective approach in African cultural life also means a focus on the group goal, rather than the individual goal, while in Western society the individual occupies the centre stage. Because of this African collective approach, there are ideally many available support structures in traditional communities. Currently however, with increasing urbanisation and change, the traditional coherence of many communities and the binding fabric of the support structures have waned. This has debatably contributed to individual and family problems, where timely assistance by the extended family and support structures could have prevented a crisis. This erosion of communities, especially in the urban areas, has not been replaced by alternative support structures.

Repercussions of apartheid In addition, 40 years of apartheid rule, when the vast majority of the citizens in the country were oppressed, left repercussions, which can be felt today. The apartheid legacy has become engraved on the consciousness of the population, and awareness of race and difference has impacted deeply on the national psyche. Importantly, while there has been a relatively peaceful transition to democratic rule, the country as a whole still carries the hallmarks of a traumatised society. Fragmentation of families, the abuse of women and children, the proliferation of gangs, violence as a way to resolve conflict, and crime, is rife. The containment structures within society are thin.

It is probable that some of the dislocation currently seen in communities and families is a reaction to the traumatised nature of the society as experienced during the apartheid years. As discussed earlier, society as a large group can hold events at a 'social unconscious' level, which can become acted out and cause regression in a society. The political leadership of the elected Head of State, Nelson Mandela, at the time of the transition in 1994, and the benign authority he held in South Africa assisted in preventing the development of regression as seen in Serbia after the collapse of Yugoslavia. Volkan (2001) has written eloquently on such regression, which can occur in traumatised societies. As we have seen above, the role of the leader is crucial is restoring a society previously traumatised. Mandela embodied for the nation a lost identity, now recovered. In addition, The Truth and Reconciliation Commission hearings (1998) allowed for some purification, which avoided the more destructive development of a true regression. This brings us to Hopper's statement (2001: 22) on the importance of openly working through past trauma:

> If space is not provided for working through traumatic events, they will never be worked through; and if space is provided, those in power will have to deal with threats to their authority ... traumatic events tend to be repeated over and over again, not only in societies, but also in organizations of various kinds ranging from large industrial firms to child guidance clinics ... I am reminded of Winnicott's statement that people in psychoanalytical treatment often get worse before they get better, ... and the sociological insight that revolutions occur just after there have been dramatic improvements in the standards of living of deprived sections of the population ... I would prefer to work with such possibilities than to suffer the repetition of catastrophes.

Groups transforming South African society Small, median and large groups are a microcosm of the country and respond to, and can affect, in a reciprocal manner, the macrocosm. When one studies groups, or works in groups, it is always contextual. Therefore, an important role for groupwork in South Africa is to see how groups can be used in social healing, to increase containment in the society, to empower, to facilitate indigenous leadership, to increase understanding cross-culturally, and to improve the holding function in society. In situations of transition, as seen in South Africa at present, with rural to urban moves, influx of migrants, and dislocation of communities, groups can be important small societies, and venues for containment, security and continuity, the working through of problems, personally and interpersonally, and the empowering of communities through participatory transformation and community development. Working with small, median and large groups can further the ideals of a democratic society, as it is within this context that there can be a focus on fostering interpersonal relatedness and mutuality, dealing with difference, conflict resolution, and transforming attitudes of prejudice. In promoting a theme of communication, sharing and togetherness, a start can be made in the direction of a broad healing of communities and society. A culture of caring can be promoted.

Conclusion

This chapter has highlighted the significance of groups and working with groups in South Africa. It has drawn attention to the history of groupwork as a modality, the origins of which emerged from demands for social change and individual healing. The broad parameters of groupwork typologies and its uses in professional intervention are outlined. This chapter also points out some parallels of group dynamics with societal dynamics. It comments that significant events experienced by groups and societies can be re-evoked and re-enacted, often generations later. It emphasises that the quality of group and societal leadership can be instrumental in encouraging group and societal progression rather than regression, with reference to change phenomena. Given the current situation in South Africa, one decade after the new dispensation, it comments that groups can be used to assist in building a democratic society with respect for diversity. Groups provide an immediate exposure to principles of interpersonal learning, mutuality and democratisation, which can permeate to the broader societal level, reflecting a true spirit of 'ubuntu'. In addition, as 'small societies', they can be containing structures, which can assist in cohesion and social healing, significant underpinnings in the transformational processes occurring in South Africa today.

Discussion questions

1 Can you identify the many ways in which we are connected to others and the importance of groups in our lives? Give examples from your personal and professional experience.

2 What can we learn from groups about understanding societies, and why is this important today?

3 How can groups be used in nation-building, social development, and social healing in South Africa? Think of a few areas where this could be pertinent in the local context.

Endnotes

1 Konopka, in Andrews, 2001: 52.
2 Cottes & Lewis-Williams, 1998, in Ettin, 2000: 238.
3 Kurland & Salmon, 1999.
4 Ibid.
5 Gray, 1998; Andrews, 2001.
6 In Brown & Zinken, 2000.
7 Foulkes, in Brown & Zinkin, 2000: 12.
8 Whitaker, 2001: 62.
9 Foulkes, 1964; Yalom, 1985; Bernard & MacKenzie, 1994.
10 Douglas, 1979; Toseland & Rivas, 2001; McDermott, 2002,
11 Cohen & Mullender, in Cohen, 2002.
12 Lieberman, in Ettin, 1999.
13 Toseland & Rivas, 2001: 16.
14 Schopler & Galinsky, in Encyclopaedia of Social Work, 1995: 1129–1142.
15 Foulkes, 1948: 29, in Brown, 1998.
16 Kaplan & Sadock, cited in Buchholz & Mishne, 1994: 4.
17 Freud, 1921, in Lonergan, 1994.
18 Freud, 1921: 78-79, in Dalal, 1998.
19 Freud, 1921: 79, in Dalal, 1998.
20 Foulkes, 1971: 212, in Dalal, 1998.
21 Winnicott, 1965; Pines, 1998; James, 2000.
22 Freud, in Nitzgen 2001: 335.
23 Drower, in McKendrick, 1996.
24 Foulkes, in Brown & Zinkin, 2000.

2 Thinking about groups

Lily Becker, Madeleine Duncan

Learning objectives

By the end of this chapter you should be able to:

- Reappraise the 'nuts and bolts' of groupwork in context.
- Think reflectively about the impact of theoretical orientations on group method, process and outcomes.
- Identify critical professional issues in group leadership and facilitation.
- Reaffirm the importance of ethical groupwork practice.

Introduction

There is a broad literature on groupwork with diverse approaches and seminal practice models.[1] Rather than reiterating what has already been documented, this chapter draws attention to the core elements of groups and groupwork in the South African context. The reader will be prompted to think about the fundamental 'nuts and bolts' of groups in order to appreciate afresh that groups and group functioning are not random events. There are multiple ways of identifying, explaining and responding to what happens in a group.

This chapter starts with a review of how modern and postmodern paradigms have influenced groupwork practice and argues for a reappraisal of these paradigms for the local context. It then addresses key elements of groups, the principles of setting up and running a group, and highlights issues of critical concern in group leadership. The chapter concludes by reaffirming the significance of ethics and human rights principles in groupwork practice.

Rethinking groupwork practice

We need to rethink group theory and practice given that society and the way in which we think about it is changing. Politics, art, science, economics, psychology, culture and education are experiencing shifts away from modernism with its rational and structural explanations of reality towards postmodern eclecticism, inclusiveness and multiple interpretations of reality. Postmodernist thought challenges hegemonic practices and perceptions of truth or reality. In so doing it addresses the marginalisation of 'other' perspectives, such as those of women and oppressed peoples. This is particularly pertinent in the multi-cultural South African society. It calls for us to evaluate local practice by challenging our assumptions about the universality of the human experience. While there has been a call in groupwork literature to consider alternative indigenous, culturally diverse interpretations of group processes (Ettin, 2000), little has been published about the application of culturally adapted group-work practice.

In South Africa, groupwork practitioners find themselves working with cul-turally heterogeneous groups. Practitioners, drawn from all races and cultures, run groups in different contexts and, given the eleven official languages, may need to make use of interpreters in order to engage optimally with group par-ticipants. The need for all groupworkers to be conversant with indigenous worldviews, idioms and practices remains the ideal.[2] The gap between limited literature and indigenous groupwork theory and the ideal of culturally rele-vant groupwork practice by practitioners from all language and cultural groups can be bridged. It requires commitment by stakeholders to adapt, or reformulate extant group theories to meet local needs. With this in mind, the following sections highlight critical elements of groups that deserve attention in context.

Getting a group started

Defining a group

Chapter One of this book includes examples of definitions of a group and groupwork. The language used to define a group reveals the ideology from which practice proceeds. For example, the definition of a group used for ther-apeutic purposes would include language that infers the group as an instru-ment for healing and restoration. On the other hand, the definition of a group used for community development, may include language that infers capacity building, social transformation and liberation. A group in an organization may be a team or work unit, and the language used may incorporate managerial constructs, such as human resources and strategic planning. The 'nuts and bolts' of a group such as its purpose, membership, leadership, duration and frequency of meetings, communication, interaction, goals, norms, culture and roles would be shaped by the definition that is adopted.

What can the group format offer?

What is intrinsic to the purposeful gathering of people that makes growth, healing, development and change possible? This question can be answered from different perspectives.

The **evolutionary** perspective reminds us that the ability to form groups has been significant for the survival of the human species. Humans congregate in groups to accomplish those tasks necessary for meeting basic human needs such as subsistence and protection, which they are unable to achieve on their own.

The **attachment** perspective highlights the need that humans have to connect and belong to each other. It suggests that these needs are initially met through early attachments in the primary caregiving milieu. In a groupwork format attachment needs can be met, re-experienced and renegotiated.

The **developmental** perspective argues that the individual is innately motivated to seek membership beyond the primary caregiving milieu, such as the peer group, the work group, and the community group. Structured groupwork experiences create opportunities for individuals to enact this innate motivation for connectedness.

The **existential** perspective points to the potential for individuals in a group to transcend themselves. The individual self becomes merged with the collective self and in so doing, the boundary of the self is transcended. The group becomes more than the sum of its parts.

From the group **analytic** point of view groups offer the opportunity to re-own projections and to renegotiate primary object relations. During groupwork, denied and split off parts of the self are discovered and opportunities found to reclaim and integrate defended dimensions of self.

The **critical emancipatory** perspective suggests that the group has the potential to empower itself against collective forms of oppression. Through the group format, group members develop awareness of social realities and use this conscientisation to participate in and transform society.

In essence, these and other perspectives about the group format suggest that it is a legitimate means for achieving a range of individual and social outcomes. Used either in a purist form, or in eclectic combination, these perspectives provide a theoretical foundation for the focus of groupwork.

Planning a group

The planning of a group may rest with the leader in therapeutic, organizational or developmental contexts, or may be owned by an existing group of people in a community who are embarking on a participatory action process to bring about change. Toseland and Rivas (2001) and Corey and Corey (1997) offer extensive directions for the group planning process. The essential domains of planning are briefly presented in the following section.

Composition

Whether careful assessment of composition is made or not will depend on the setting, type of group, the purpose and length of the group, and theoretical models used. In order to achieve certain outcomes, groups may need to balance homogeneity (similar characteristics) and heterogeneity (different characteristics) in composition. Alternatively the composition of the group may be predetermined and influenced by the context or culture, for example, in rural areas, the cost and availability of transport may make attendance difficult, or socio-cultural norms may dictate that mixed gender groups are inappropriate.

Issues of cultural homogeneity or heterogeneity may complicate the achievement of certain outcomes due to differences in fundamental world-views and values. This is true of groups generally, but particularly so in a country such as South Africa where the worldview and meaning-making of individuals of different cultures may be very diverse, and may be brought to the fore when members sit together in groups. Composition depends on the context and whether selection of group members is possible – for example, in an in-patient therapeutic unit patients may be expected to attend group therapy to address mutually identified psychosocial, behavioural or emotional needs. Therapeutic groups regard the selection of patients as an important factor in the successful outcome of therapy. For example, prospective group members may be assessed for their ability to work therapeutically, their interpersonal potential, their motivation, and the type and severity of their psychological and psychiatric difficulties as these factors can all affect the outcome of the therapy.

Educational groups may not require such careful selection, and community groups even less so. Support groups of various kinds, such as rehabilitation self-help groups, or adolescent support groups, have criteria for inclusion related to commonality of problem, while considering variability and hetero-geneity. On the other hand, the outcomes for community-based participatory action groups depend more on the affirmation and inclusion of existing informal social structures and groupings. To exclude someone on the basis of some pre-determined criteria, as may be the case in therapeutic groups, is to ignore the ethos of inclusivity and belonging inherent in the African philosophy of ubuntu, meaning 'humanness' (Shutte, 1993).

Clarifying the purpose of a group

The purpose of the group justifies its existence and should therefore be mutually defined between the leader and the members of the group. It is achieved through the short- and long-term goals of the group. These may include individual development and change, organizational output targets, or community and social transformation. While the goals are clarified early on in the life of the group, they become more realistic as the group develops, which increases motivation. The purpose of the group may have to be revisited in response to its dynamics, such as in times of conflict or group resistance. Reminding a group of 'why we are here' pulls the group back to task when conflict threatens to derail it.

Group size

The number of people in a group introduces different social dynamics: in the smaller group (5–9 people) there may be themes resonant with the recapitulation of the primary caregiving group; in a mid-size group (10–15), median groups (16–30) and large groups (30–60) (Ettin, 1999) themes resonant with cultural dynamics and a re-enactment of social or communal discourses such as ethnicity, gender, race and justice (De Maré, 2000) are seen. Groups in organizations can be large or small and can mirror the various social dynamics described above.

The assumptions however, about group size and dynamics may need to be revised given different interpretations of constructs such as 'family' and 'community'. For example, 'family' is interpreted in the African context as 'clan', 'village' or 'household' where members are not necessarily close blood relatives but are bound by ethnicity, traditions and cultural norms. Teffo (1999: 168) in discussing moral renewal and African experiences states that it takes a 'whole village to raise a child'. In the local context, awareness of alternative interpretations of reality such as these will inform the application of existing group theories about the interface between group size, membership, and process.

Duration and frequency of group meetings

Duration addresses the life-span of the group, and frequency the pattern and length of group meetings. The influence of duration and frequency of group experiences on individual behaviour and consequently on group process has been well documented.[3] 'Open group' implies changing membership. This influences the rate and depth at which the group process is able to unfold and therefore the type of goals that can be addressed. 'Closed group' refers to constant membership, which creates a stable forum for the emergence of group process and development.

The substantial human and financial resource constraints in the South African public sector may compromise the ideal duration and frequency of groups. However, short-term groups of all kinds, from support to therapeutic and developmental groups, have an important contribution to make in bridging resource constraints in all sectors. The group methods, whether applied in a single session or over an extended period of time, offer participants a range of benefits that may not otherwise be accessible.

Contracting

Contracting refers to a mutual participatory process between leader and group members through which the purpose and goals are formulated. The different procedural activities; logistics such as time, venue, length; boundary issues; the roles of the leader and members; and general expectations are all clarified. Contracting and the manner in which it occurs, helps to mutually define the work of the group and the roles and responsibilities of its members.

Both the group's and the individual member's perspectives have to be considered in the type of contracting that occurs. For example, in therapeutic groups, the individual member's ability to engage with contracting may be dependent on his/her intrapsychic readiness to embark on the change process. In task-oriented or support groups, contracting also helps in concretising the range of norms, roles and tasks of the group.[4]

In a community and/or multicultural setting, there may be additional considerations such as: who takes the lead in group negotiations and how contracting is done. The process of negotiation can have significant implications for the distribution of power and the affirmation of indigenous values. Teffo (1999), for example, states that '... some speakers in a community are said to be governed by rules of language restriction and avoidance during conversation. In some languages such as isiXhosa and isiZulu, these restrictive measures have allowed another type of idiolect to emerge, namely *hlonipha* language (that is, language of respect) ... the extralinguistic factors which warrant such semantic shifts in the context are rank, age and social standing relative to the person spoken to' (Teffo, 1999: 159). The careful choice and use of words and gestures such as curtsy, avoiding eye contact and cupping of hands in everyday communication carry emotive value. The tacit rules governing the distribution of social power based on respect for elders and other cultural specific rules of discourse may need to be considered.

A group unfolding

Groups always occur against the background of a social, political, cultural and economic context. This impacts on a group and its members because it forms the backdrop to the foreground of the group itself. Once a group has started its unique path, characteristics and dynamics unfold. These can be seen in different ways: levels, processes, dynamics and stages.

Levels of group

Groups consist of intrapersonal, interpersonal and group-as-a-whole levels of functioning.

Intrapersonal Based on the psychotherapeutic models of groupwork, individual members' intrapsychic processes, transference and countertransference issues, and defence mechanisms are considered either explicitly within the group or tacitly in the clinical reasoning of the group therapist. Members bring their anxieties, histories of interpersonal relationships, temperament and levels of motivation into the group. It becomes a contained space for working through intrapsychic concerns and unresolved conflicts.

Individuals may adopt different group roles, for example, the deviant, the joker, the gatekeeper,[5] which can reflect personal issues or be reactive to group interactions and themes. Some models of groupwork, for example Gestalt[6], focus on working with the individual intrapsychic material in the group setting while using the group as an audience capable of enacting or concretising dimensions of the individual's psyche or narrative.

These understandings of the intrapersonal level may not be congruent with indigenous knowledge systems for explaining and resolving problematic human behaviour. For example, Afrocentric worldviews may not separate the 'self' from the 'other' or from the ancestral world under certain circumstances.

What Western paradigms call 'illness or maladaptive behaviour' may be understood in Afrocentric paradigms as significant communication from ancestors requiring prescribed individual and group healing responses such as cleansing ceremonies. A multi-faceted lens is required in understanding the diverse realities of the intrapersonal dimension that are present in multi-cultural groups.

In a group of many cultures there is an opportunity to explore anxieties, commonalities, and differences at both the intrapersonal and the interpersonal level. The group environment, comprising of many different 'selves', provides a new relational backdrop from which to revisit and resolve intrapsychic inter-nalisations in the group, or to explore alternative meaning-making in different cultural realities.

Interpersonal The group is seen as an interactional space, with mutual exchange and dialogue between members happening in the 'here and now'. In psychotherapeutic groups, the linkages, commonalities, and communications between members are explored and may be seen as a re-enactment of primary caregiving issues (Yalom, 1985). Reparation and corrective emotional work is done based on the premise that the group process provides a 'matrix', which is the 'hypothetical web of communication and relationship in a given group' (Foulkes, 1964: 292). It is also seen as the 'common shared ground'[7] for con-taining, confronting and mediating intrapersonal, interpersonal and group-as-a-whole issues.

At the interpersonal level a restorative health-promotive climate can be cre-ated which would resonate in any cultural group and model of groupwork practice. For example, in the African culture, the concept of 'humanness' is a social ethic and a unifying vision enshrined in the Zulu maxim 'umuntu ngu-muntu ngabanye' ('one is a person through others'). The concept of humanness also includes compassion, which resonates with the Rogerian principles of unconditional positive regard, acceptance and non-judgementalism on the part of the group facilitator.

The group, as a meeting point for many cultures offers a forum of experience for sharing and finding commonalities in a world that can accentuate differ-ence. Within the safety of the group, entrenched barriers can be revisited and alienation explored.

Group-as-a-whole The group is seen as a coherent entity, a system, with properties and dynamics that are independent and more than the whole creat-ed by individual members and their various interactions. The progress and processes of the group itself are studied. In this way group-level themes, con-flicts and resistances are reflected and collective group identity confirmed.[8] Seeing the group as greater than the sum of its parts, as a system, is a dynamic way of understanding group functioning, in that one member's issues can res-onate at a group level. At a meta-level, the group as a whole will also express and be influenced by broader socio-cultural discourses, such as gender, race and power. The group-as-a-whole concept can be transposed to an organiza-tion. Within an organization-as-a-whole (Nitsun, 1998), the pooling of shared intrapsychic concerns may result in similar processes and dynamics as those that unfold in groups.

The demise of statutory apartheid in South Africa in 1994 did not result in the demise of systemic or attitudinal apartheid. In multicultural groups racial tensions and deeply embedded historical prejudices may play themselves out in group communication, as may culture-bound beliefs and values. An interpretive paradigm requires a deep appreciation of these systemic influences on the group-as-a-whole. Whilst the phenomenon of power and its impact may be universal, its manifestation will vary across contexts depending on situation-specific political histories.

The value of group therapy for group empowerment is well recognised by feminist advocates. Groupwork has been firmly established within the feminist movement as a method for consciousness-raising and mobilising women's strengths to effect social change.[9] By discovering commonalities and recognising that personal problems are embedded in social structure, women can begin to address the social basis of their oppression through the collectivity provided by the group.

Interpretations aimed at explicating possible group-as-a-whole dynamics should therefore emanate not only from knowledge of group dynamic theory[10] but also from an informed position about the socio-cultural experiences of members. A depth, psychoanalytic understanding of group-as-a-whole dynamics can be an effective discourse, which recognises the interaction of emotional, social and political issues.

Group processes and dynamics

Group processes refer to patterns, actions and properties of group behaviour. Group dynamics refer to the manifest and latent forces that result from interactive events in the group. The leader needs to follow the processes and dynamics to make meaning of, and respond to, group behaviour.

Group processes

While various theorists have developed frameworks to assist our thinking about and sense-making of group processes,[11] these frameworks differ in emphases and in groupings of characteristics. However, it is clear that a systematised approach to thinking about processes would include the following: interaction, communication, structure, norms, roles and status, goals, climate and group culture. These processes are interrelated, fluid and mutually influential.

The fundamental process is **interaction**, which is regarded as the whole of group behaviour. It refers to the reciprocal response and the mutual influence of people in the group. Patterns of interaction are influenced by factors such as emotional bonds, sub-groups, power issues, non-verbal behaviour, group size and composition (Toseland & Rivas, 2001). Interaction is founded upon the need of humans to make contact in the group (Foulkes, 1975). The essential means of developing interaction is through **communication**. This is the process by which people convey meanings to each other through the transmission of verbal and non-verbal signals. The vital role of communication has been emphasised by Foulkes (1975), in forming the group matrix.

According to Schlapobersky, 2000) the language of the group matrix appears in three forms: group monologue (speaking alone, with or without an audience), dialogue (a conversation between two people) and discourse (speech patterns of three or more people). Latent or manifest communications from the group in the form of themes can change as the group develops, and can also infer the focal preoccupations of the group, for example, the theme of authority.

The **structure** of the group refers to how **roles**, **status** and **subgroups** play out in a group. Structure is concerned with the perception of relationships and the recognition of positions that members hold in relation to one another in the group. **Roles** (the behaviour associated with a stated position in a social system) result from the interplay between individual, group and contextual forces, and are not always registered consciously. They could be limited, repetitive or varied and can determine the functions that individuals may fulfil in the group (Heap, 1984). Examples of roles are task roles (e.g. information-giver), maintenance (e.g. encourager), individual (e.g. blocker), and common roles (e.g. central person). An understanding of roles helps the leader to illuminate dynamics of communication in and for the group, for example, the scapegoat in a group (or outside of the group) can be the result of projected and disowned parts of a particular group.

Status refers to a differential social ranking within the group, often based on position (designated leader of an organization, or tribal chief), expertise (specialised skills), and social standing (age, economic resources); and is closely linked to power. **Sub-group formation**, which refers to alliances formed between members, can be based on similarity, support, or physical closeness and can be a source of strength and enrich the group. Sub-groups can also be problematic when they compete with the overall group or team functioning, for example, cliques.

Cohesion, the binding of the group as an entity into a sense of 'we-ness' (a group identity), produces a sense of affiliation. It is an indicator for a positive group experience. A cohesive group assists the preparedness of members to work towards individual and group goals, and reduces tension and negativity. **Group climate**, the prevailing atmosphere in the group, varies from being warm and supportive to hostile and defensive, and can affect the depth of mutuality and work done in the group. **Norms** are shared beliefs and expectations about appropriate behaviour in the group. They bring predictability, security and stability, and help to regulate the actions of members to conform to group expectations. Norms provide frames of reference for sanctioning behaviour in the group. **Group culture** is the sum total of the beliefs, values and knowledge which constitute the shared basis of the social milieu of the group. **Group influence** and pressure can be exerted on members to adhere to the culture and the norms of the group.

Goal formation and decision-making of the group are important processes which move the group to realise its aims. Goals are mutually agreed upon objectives to which the individuals and group-as-a-whole aspire. There is a dynamic amalgam of individual and group goals. The continual interplay of group decisions facilitates the attainment of various goals. Conflict, whether on a group level or an individual level, may interfere with the group reaching its goals and needs to be handled through various negotiations, such as conflict resolution and problem-solving techniques.

These group processes intersect and influence each other, and are closely linked with group dynamics. How these processes are manifested and operationalised is significantly influenced by the socio-cultural context in which the group occurs. For example, in some community settings, norms such as punctual and regular attendance are unlikely to be valued or owned by people attending groups in informal settlements. Lack of money to pay for transport and unreliable public transport may make it difficult for members to comply with attendance norms. Likewise, groups may only commence once those present and those absent have been acknowledged through singing and prayer. Sub-group conversations are also valued because they build community. Children may be breastfed in the group and their play behaviour accommodated in the midst of deep sharing amongst group members. Therefore, in the local context, a flexible appreciation of processes is necessary.

Group dynamics

An understanding of group dynamics involves attending to the impact of unconscious forces on human interaction. Combining the contributions of the classic psychodynamic theorists such as Freud (1922) and Klein (1946) with the contributions of the group-analytic thinkers such as Foulkes (1964) and Bion (1961) and revisionists such as Kohut (1977), Daelal (1998), Nitsun (1996) and De Maré (1998), the language and concepts of psychoanalysis is used to make sense of the 'hidden forces' determining the course of a group.

The analytic framework includes communicative constructs such as the common shared ground of the **matrix**; **projective-identification** (unconscious communication in which intolerable feelings are projected onto another person, who identifies with and enacts it); **transference** (repetition of significant past relationships in the present) and **countertransference** (leader's transference in relation to a member, and/or an affective response in the leader that links to latent group behaviour). **Defence mechanisms** (for example, denial, splitting, and projection) are unconscious mental processes that help the members and group-as-a-whole to deal with anxiety and other uncomfortable feelings.

Foulkes (1975) believed that psychological and psychiatric problems were due to interpersonal problems, and that relationships in a group setting could help to identify and clarify intrapsychic conflicts. He identified four interrelated domains of group communication that the leader helps the group to understand in order to bring about individual and group healing. These are: **current level** (the setting, identity of leader and members, and other practical features); **transference level** (the dynamics of relationships as discussed above); **projective level** (projection of part of the self or group self on others) and **primordial level** (the collective unconscious and archetypal shared images). Foulkes maintained that healing occurs as a result of the network of communications in the matrix of the group.

Bion's (1961) identification and description of the collective emotional states that can pervade groups has been particularly useful in understanding why groups cannot achieve their goals. When a group pursues its objectives in a rational, effective manner, Bion postulated that a 'working group' culture is present. However, at times it is clear that group behaviours are incompatible with staying on task and he noted regression into one of three emotional states (fear, helplessness, optimism) and subsequent emergence of a 'basic assumption' group. Bion identified three basic assumption groups. In the **dependency** group members act as if they are helpless and inadequate. They see the leader as omniscient and omnipotent and able to rescue them. The **flight/fight** group behaves as though it must flee from, or fight an enemy. The leader is expected to lead them into battle, or help them flee. The **pairing** group has expectations of being saved by a rescuer, or by an inspiring idea. Hope for the future is used as a defence against the difficulties of the task in the present and the group anticipates that the kind of leader they need, will appear. The dynamics of the group may be understood with reference to how it moves in and out of the security and safety of the work group and the 'valency' (affinity and tendency to congregate) of the various basic assumption groups. Any groups, including organizational teams, can be undermined by basic assumption mentality, and Bion's insights into group-as-a-whole behaviour have been particularly relevant in the field of organizational consultancy.

Yalom (1985) viewed group dynamics through the 'here and now' of the group interpersonal relationships. Members act out their conflictual relationships in the group and a corrective emotional experience occurs when they examine their behaviour in 'self-reflective loops'. Yalom's 'curative/therapeutic factors' (installation of hope, universality, information, altruism, corrective recapitulation of the primary family group, socialisation, imitative behaviour, interpersonal learning, cohesiveness, catharsis and existential factors) are essential ingredients for promoting restoration in and through the group.

The dynamics of group may also be understood in terms of its socio-cultural context, because the political (for example, gender, class, race) emerges in the personal (Blackwell, 2000). The dynamics of the group will inevitably include the 'social unconscious', which refers to the 'existence and constraints of social, cultural and communicational arrangements of which people are unaware' (Hopper, 2001: 10). Therefore, material emerging in the group arena needs to be understood on many levels.

Group development: Stages

The development of groups occurs through different stages, which may be linear, indistinct or cyclical. Group theorists categorise and name group stages differently, but irrespective of how they are understood the principle issue is that groups develop according to discernable characteristics over time.[12]

As a general guide three group stages may be discerned: beginning, middle and end. These stages are observable in short- or long-term groups and may also be identified in single-session groups. In closed groups the stages are usually more distinct, providing valuable direction to the work of the group. In open groups, with constantly changing membership, the development of the stages may be staggered, for example new, remaining and leaving members are each concerned with different issues.

Groups may revisit stage-specific themes in a cyclical pattern, for example, trust, which is a beginning stage theme, may be revisited at later stages. Some themes such as authority, or intimacy, may be struggled with repeatedly. As the group develops, it may return to such focal themes with greater depth.

The beginning stage **(orientation)** is concerned with the formation of the group as a unit. The themes are likely to be about trust, belonging, acceptance and dependency. Issues of being 'in or out' of the group play a role in its manifest (plainly evident) and latent (hidden or dormant) communication. Characteristic behaviours may include silence, scanning and superficial dialogue as members attempt to find their space in the group in relation to those present. Feelings usually include anxiety, apprehension, and uncertainty about their role and acceptability to the leader and other members. Collectively the group task has to be clarified and commonalities in the group identified. Communication in the group is mainly directed at the leader, who may be seen as an omnipotent parental or authority figure. The core function of the beginning stage is to establish the purpose of the group and to create a foundation from which to proceed with its work. A mutually agreed upon (verbal or written) contract between the leader and group members helps to promote a sense of common commitment by clarifying the tasks, logistics, roles and responsibilities and boundaries of actions and relationships.

The middle stage progresses through two phases: a **conflictual** phase (exploring and testing) and a **working** (problem solving) phase. During the conflictual phase the group wrestles with power, competition, rivalry, resistance and rebellion. 'Up–down' issues play a role in its latent and manifest communication. Group differences, for example gender, race, religion, social class, sexual orientation or other areas of potential prejudice and discrimination may be at the centre of the conflict. The group is also likely to be testing its boundaries, its own power and acceptability to the leader and each other in order to establish a collective identity. Distortions, denials, emotional contagion, splitting, scapegoating and sub-grouping are often present, as well as negative transference reactions to the facilitator and to group members.

Working through the conflictual phase has the potential to harness the positive forces of the group for its members. When the group is unable to resolve this phase, it could result in members dropping out, or the disbanding of the group. If sufficient, timeous attention is paid to the diffusion of tensions through conflict resolution strategies, the sustainability of group or community developmental initiatives may be ensured. Nitsun's (1996) concept of the anti-group reinforces the view that, although each group has negativity inherent in its very make-up, working through this releases the creative potential of the group members and the group-as-a-whole. The conflictual phase, once resolved, may resurface in milder forms in later developmental stages and be more easily negotiated due to strengthened group relationships.

The working phase is usually characterised by problem solving and consensus building leading to group action. Issues of 'near–far' tend to play a role in manifest and latent communication. Group action can occur *within* the group (for example, working on intra- or interpersonal problems), or *beyond* the group (for example, activism to address identified social concerns). The working phase within the group usually occurs in a climate of intimate sharing and mutuality, in which the purpose and the goals of the group become realisable. The working phase beyond the group, for example in participatory action groups, moves the focus outside the group boundary, where members are empowered by a sense of collective identity to address oppressive social structures or collaborate in community-building enterprises.

Certain group phenomena, for example **'groupthink'** (group pressure to think alike) and the need to conform, can promote or detract the group from effectively working towards its goals. 'Groupthink' may, for example, lead to mistaken decisions, because the influence of the group overrides individual interests and autonomous decision-making.

The ending stage **(termination)** refers to the completion of work as defined in the group purpose and contract. The latent and manifest communication at this stage is usually concerned with separation, individuation and ambivalence. Cohesion among members becomes diluted as they prepare to leave the group. The dynamics of past and current leavings are often re-evoked and re-visited as members share and work through feelings associated with termination and independence. The ending stage requires that the gains made and the obstacles overcome during the life of the group, are reaffirmed. The ending stage could also see a brief regression to themes of previous stages, for example, anxiety or testing out behaviour, or a resurfacing of unfinished focal concerns in the group, which need to be addressed.

The ending stage is likely to be successfully managed if termination is contracted and/or explicitly processed in the group. Without the working-through that the ending stage requires, both the person(s) leaving and those remaining are left with unresolved feelings. However, termination may occur prematurely through members leaving the group before engaging with the ending stage. In open groups, with staggered entry and exits, members' termination can trigger dynamics which require attention at a group maintenance level, in order for the group to remain focused on the task. A successful ending stage ensures that members are enabled to use the group as a positive point of reference for new beginnings.

Leading a group

Different names such as group leader, facilitator, counsellor, conductor or team manager, are used to describe the person who is responsible for guiding the work of the group. While there are some differences in orientation, this section focuses on commonalities within these different names and the term 'group leadership' will be used. Leadership is not exercised solely by the designated leader, as members too take on leadership roles as the group or team develops.

What is group leadership?

Group leadership describes the process of directing, facilitating, and conducting a group, helping to define its purpose, and assisting group members to reach individual and collective goals.[13] The place of the leader as 'out front or from behind' is not clearly agreed upon (Ettin, 2000). Ettin (2000: 235) writes that the British statesman Benjamin Disraeli quipped: I am the group leader: which way did they go?' The implication here is that leadership is about following the needs and directives of a particular group.

Boon (1996: 80) draws the following analogy between group leadership and firemaking. The ancient firemaker would hold a softwood stick under one knee and, using both hands, rapidly twirl a hardwood stick in a depression set in the softwood. The friction and dust caused from this drilling action would begin to smoulder and glow, and with gentle blowing and adding of tinder, fire could be created. Likewise, the group leader ignites the spark inherent in a group and fans its potential energy into a dynamic forum for change. Learning to be a firemaker or a group leader takes time. Shulman (2002) reassures us that the development of confidence and competence as a professional group leader is a process, and that group leaders grow by continuing to examine their work.

Functions of group leadership

The context of the group will determine which functions and responsibilities the leader needs to attend to. The functions of a group leader, as described by Yalom (1985), have a direct relationship to the outcomes of groupwork. The executive function requires the leader to set limits, to intervene when deemed necessary and to manage time. Through the caring function, the leader establishes a norm of support, warmth, acceptance and genuineness. The function of meaning attribution involves translating feelings into ideas and vice versa, clarifying communication, making interpretations and providing a cognitive framework for change. In small groups, the holding function may involve working with the affective component, while in the large group the leader may be tasked with holding on to thinking, in and of the group. In sum, group leaders' functions incorporate task (e.g. managing logistics) and maintenance (e.g. encouragement) dimensions to enable a group to proceed optimally.

Qualities of group leadership

The innate and acquired personal capacities of the leader are pivotal to the successful implementation of the leadership role. Corey and Corey (1997) provide an extensive overview of the personal characteristics of the effective group leader, such as self-awareness, inventiveness, sense of humour and openness. Harwood (2003) differentiates between the leader who is facilitative (promotes the group to become vitalised for their benefit) from the leader who is exploitative and charismatic (self-serving and uses the group to validate his/her power, authority and ideology).

In the circular space of the group many alternative experiences, realities, voices and emotions of the members intersect. The leader's ability and capacity to listen, receive, and contain the processes and dynamics within this space, will help shape the culture of a specific group. The culturally skilled leader has a readiness to affirm diversity and difference, having worked through his/her own belief and value systems.

Dimensions of the leadership role

Power Leadership is concerned with how power, influence, and control are exercised and managed in the group. Attributed power refers to the power that is given to an individual by virtue of his/her status, experience, education and other socially venerated attributes. Actual power refers to the available dynamic resources for changing conditions inside and outside the group (Toseland & Rivas, 2001). Both sources of power are generated by the historical, political and social context of the group. Structural determinants of power such as ethnicity, race, gender, socio-economic status and social class are inevitably mirrored and enacted within the group or team. According to Parry (1997: 5), 'it is power that determines what is real and attended to, what is emphasised rather than discounted, and what is ultimately silenced and ignored'. For example, in South Africa, racial dynamics can be enacted when issues of power and identity are considered in understanding interactions between multiracial group members or between racially or ethnically different group leaders and members. Essentially, the group leader must be aware of the effects of social forces and the possibility of the re-enactment of these consciously, or unconsciously, in the group situation.

In therapeutic, community or organizational contexts the leader accepts the attributed power because it embodies the containment that the group or team members wish for from him/her. At the same time, while they wish for a leader, group members may also be ambivalent about the authority that she/he represents. Given that groups inherently contain power, control, and status issues and that leader-centred groups intensify this potential (Rachman, 2003), it is particularly important that empowerment of the group itself occurs. Part of the work of the group is therefore to recognise and process the ambiguities and tensions generated by power. The role of the leader is to decentralise the power base and to mobilise the creative potential of the group as a self-empowering system.

Authority By virtue of his/her centrality in the group, and the fact that there is a mandate to lead the group and facilitate its progress, the leader carries a mantle of authority. Group leaders need to be comfortable in their role as authority figures. This implies that they have the right to exercise control for the benefit of the group by prohibiting harmful actions and limiting damaging behaviour in the group.

At times leaders struggle with being an authority figure, believing that it counteracts democratic principles of equality, or that it echoes authoritarianism. However, it is mandatory on their role that they assume responsibility for the group and are able to tolerate not being 'liked' in the group, when they assert an appropriate directive role. On the other hand, and not withstanding the authority mandate, they need to promote empowerment in the group and encourage mutual aid.

The skills and techniques of leadership

The skills of the leader can be subsumed under three broad headings: **relating skills**, **thinking skills**, and **action skills**. In brief, how must the facilitator 'be', what must she/he 'know' and what can she/he 'do' in the group.

Relating skills   The relationship of the group leader to the group is a vital component in securing a positive outcome, and is analogous to the relationship in individual psychotherapy. The group is seen as the client. In therapeutic, educational, developmental, participatory action or task groups, the quality of the relationship is important in the overall group experience because it is regarded as the key variable within which all other factors operate. The quality of the relationship is essential to the safety of the group. If the security and safety features of the relational encounter are not rapidly activated, then the group potential will not be maximised (Foulkes, 1964).

The environment for groupwork should be holding and containing (James, 2000). It should create an atmosphere of safety and security within which to explore thoughts, feelings and actions. For example, secure and containing environments are 'created for' troubled individuals in therapeutic groups in institutional settings such as psychiatric hospitals, mental health clinics, prisons or places of safety. On the other hand, such environments are 'created in collaboration with' people who share a common interest, aspiration and hope for a better future (for example a lobby group in the community for a socio-political cause). The ability of the group to withstand its own conflict provides either a healing or a conscientising and activation effect in the group and is dependent on the strength of the group relational field.

Thinking skills   The thinking of the leader is an essential tool for making sense of and interpreting group processes and dynamics. The leader must think at multiple levels about group phenomena by making sense of what is observed, heard and experienced in the group. Both group-as-a-whole and individual members' behaviours are scrutinised in order to discern links. What is relevant at the individual level resonates with the group as a whole and vice versa. The leader must also think through the impact of past group experiences on current group behaviour. A member may drop out in response to a previous unresolved group event. Due consideration should also be given to the influence of the context beyond the semi-permeable boundary of the group, such as influences related to socio-political unrest and poverty. In addition, issues which are in the realm of the 'social unconscious' such as the histories of individuals in the group, group and cultural history, and socio-political experiences. All these converging dimensions need to be thought through in making sense of this group in the 'here and now'. Using theory, the leader orders events in his/her thinking and predicts the likely outcome of actions taken in response to group events.

Action skills   Being a competent group leader requires a range of personal, interpersonal and technical skills. Basic counselling skills, for example listening, questioning, clarifying and summarising, as well as group action skills such as universalising, linking, activating the here-and-now, interpretation, modelling, confronting and blocking are useful in leading a group. Learning how and when to use these action skills is dependent on practice, feedback, supervised experience and the willingness to continue learning.

The skills of the leader should be compatible with a number of strengths-based approaches such as feminist, empowerment-oriented and self-directed models that emphasise the competence, hopes, talents and capabilities of members. The skills of mutual aid embrace the view that members are partners in the process of change. Mutual aid encourages inclusion and advances the common good (Steinberg, 2002). While mutual aid promotes a strengths perspective it may also promote a political perspective by people being conscientised as activists through group affiliation against oppression in all its forms. The group facilitator in the latter case uses skills of adult education. In the South African context, skills of language interpretation and working with interpreters may require additional training.

In the beginning stage of the group, the skills of the facilitator are aimed at providing safety. The group facilitator acknowledges the anxiety in the group, the newness of the situation and uses skills such empathising, listening, reflecting, supporting, and drawing out the commonalities in the group. The leader needs to work with group-level phenomena, as well as attend to and empathise with individuals to prevent them from feeling neglected because of the presence of other members.

In the middle stage (conflict phase) with the inevitability of conflict arising, the leader needs to be able to use a range of conflict-resolution skills. Kendler (2002) has delineated five techniques in addressing conflict in groups: (1) do not cut off confrontation too early before the members have arrived at the heart of the conflict; (2) do not allow the confrontation to go on too long, to the point at which members denigrate each other; (3) empathise with and validate the feelings of each member; (4) point out the commonalities in the group; (5) refer to the overarching purpose of the group. This last point is particularly pertinent in participatory action groupwork where the conflict must be negotiated in ways that lead to group action or activism. In this context, the group leader is seen to be a skilled resource person who promotes a culture of reflection, dialogue and self-assertion.

In the middle stage (working phase), the leader may use skills such as interpretation, confrontation, modelling and working with transference issues in the group. The use of specialised techniques such as role-plays, psychodrama, art, growth games, community theatre or drumming will require an additional range of skills from the group leader. As the working stage continues, the mutuality, intimacy and autonomy of the group increases. The growing competence of the group to conduct its own affairs allows the skilful leader to hold back as the group takes the lead. In the ending stage of the group the skills of the leader will be directed at enabling members to ventilate, share, reflect and reminisce about the group experience, and to review and integrate the gains that they have within and beyond the group.

Ethical base of groupwork

Groups can be used either for good or for harm depending on the morality and competence of the leader. Ethics are concerned with the values, responsibilities, duties, and obligations of behaviour and how we should act in relation to others. The moral obligation of the leader is to ensure that the negative potential of groups is restrained and that the positive dimension is advanced. Codes of ethics are outlined by different professions, which relate directly to codes of conduct of practitioners. While these codes offer specific guidelines for practice, there are situations where practitioners are faced with a choice from among alternative actions. Professional knowledge and judgement need to be applied to solve dilemmas where ethical codes are not always sufficient.

In revisiting ethics as an important aspect of groupwork practice, we direct attention to a number of issues that need vigilant attention, particularly because the group method is closely aligned with power.

For ethical practice, it is essential to consider the following issues:

Competent leadership

The ethical principles of **beneficence** and **non-maleficence** require that the group leader offers effective and competent leadership. This implies that the leader has the necessary theoretical knowledge of groups, has had supervised practice in learning to become a group practitioner, and can apply this knowledge to read the ongoing group processes and dynamics. Effective and competent group leadership includes personal characteristics such as empathy, sensitivity, good-enough maturity, self-knowledge, openness to learning, and flexibility. A reflective and reflexive stance in practice ensures that the leader remains objective, neutral and responsive to emerging group needs.

The role of leader is a powerful one, and the modelling inherent in this is a significant factor in promoting a group culture that is respectful of difference and affirming of the equality of those present. In South Africa, as in all countries with diverse cultures, this is a crucial factor in group practice. It implies having an understanding of different cultural beliefs, customs, meaning-making systems and metaphors in order to be attuned to the communications in the group. Group leaders must understand and be aware of their own beliefs about culture and difference, as attitudes and belief systems can influence leadership behaviour in an overt and covert manner.

Group pressure and conformity

Coercion and manipulation of members can occur, and group pressure towards conformity can conflict with the ethical principle of **autonomy** and **self-determination**. Group pressures can be very powerful, overriding individual morals and beliefs. While the emphasis in groups should be on mutual aid, interdependence and group problem-solving, undue pressure on members may occur. This may result in members foregoing their personal wishes and beliefs due to group influence. The ethical principle of non-maleficence requires the group leader to monitor the damaging potential in groups should group pressure, splitting and projection occur.

Safeguarding group psychological health

The leader needs to be protective of the group, especially regarding the vulnerability inherent in early disclosure of members before the group has attained sufficient trust and cohesion. This includes monitoring the affect levels with due regard for the dangers inherent in, for example, evocative techniques when the group does not have the necessary ego capacity to deal with the material that is evoked. The ethical principles of non-maleficence and beneficence guide the leader in safeguarding the psychological health of the group. The leader's awareness of the potential destructive processes and behaviours in the group would enable him/her to intervene timeously to protect members and the group as a whole by, for example, protecting scapegoated members.

Protection of group members

The leader is responsible for protecting group members through maintaining confidentiality, adhering to **informed consent**, allowing **freedom to withdraw** from the group, and monitoring the implications of **involuntary membership**.

The right to confidentiality is the right to maintain control over information that the group members choose to share, and includes the right to privacy (the right to keep certain information private). Limits to confidentiality in the group apply, for example, when a member's information poses a threat to others within or without the group, or to the member him-/herself.

Informed consent involves leaders making members aware of their rights and obligations and ensuring that the information offered is clearly understood by the members. The right of the freedom to withdraw from the group must be explained to members so that the locus of control resides with the individual members. Involuntary group membership needs to be handled with due consideration of members' fundamental human rights. While members are compelled to attend groups, they are offered the opportunity to exercise freedom of choice to select topics, and to control the extent of their participation.

The principle of **veracity** implies that the leader is faithful to the boundaries of professionalism. This would include avoiding dual or exploitative relationships with group members, perverse incentives, inappropriate physical contact, dishonesty with clients' money, and stereotyping.

Adhering to a rights-based approach

While ethics are concerned with norms of conduct and the morality of individuals, human rights are concerned with internationally agreed upon principles and legal frameworks for protecting individuals and groups against actions that interfere with fundamental human freedoms, equality and dignity.

A rights-based approach to groupwork refers to the processes of (1) using human rights as a framework for the development of people in the context of the group and (2) making human rights an integral dimension of the design, implementation, monitoring and evaluation of groups (WHO, 2002). This approach to groupwork offers the group leader a useful tool or framework within which to design, implement and evaluate service policies and programmes. It adds value to the processes and outcomes of groupwork by benchmarking excellence against an authoritative, constitutional standard, namely, the South African Bill of Rights.

At a practical level this means:

- Safeguarding human dignity and equality at all stages of the group process.
- Making the benefits of groupwork available and accessible to the most vulnerable citizens in society (for example, children; ethnic, linguistic and religious minorities; refugees; people with disabilities; prisoners, etc.).
- Being alert to gender differences and safeguarding against minority oppression within the group.
- Avoiding advertent and inadvertent discrimination in the planning and execution of groupwork.
- Ensuring free, effective and meaningful participation of groupwork beneficiaries, i.e. members of groups must be involved in decisions affecting them.
- Complying with service quality assurance principles (for example, explicitly benchmarking and articulating the rights and obligations of group members, group leaders and the group-based service itself against national norms and standards).
- Increasing transparency and accountability to all roleplayers at all stages of the group process.

(Adapted from WHO, 2002)

Conclusion

This chapter has reappraised the 'nuts and bolts' of groupwork. The principles of groupwork have been explained and applied to a range of contexts, with reference to different philosophical perspectives. Various forms of groups have been considered in order to demonstrate the relevance of this method in the South African context.

An overview of some essential dimensions of groupwork theory and its interface with practice provides the reader with a framework for thinking about groups. Understanding the key issues in starting and planning a group, as well as how a group unfolds through levels, processes, dynamics and development, offers the reader a systematic framework for appreciating group functioning. The role, functions, qualities, skills and techniques of group leadership are explained and the ethics of practice elaborated on in order to promote a critical, reflective stance to groupwork in South Africa.

Discussion questions

1 Why is it necessary to be cognisant of the context in starting a group? Think critically about the contextual issues you need to consider in the formation of a group in your local community.

2 How can group processes and group dynamics guide you in understanding group functioning? Give some examples to illustrate your answer.

3 Which ethical principles are useful to consider in leading a group? Discuss and give examples from your own experience.

Acknowledgements
We would like to thank Willem de Jager and Monica Spiro for their support, and thought-provoking participation in discussions on the content of this chapter. Their insightful comments on and contributions to earlier drafts are appreciated.

Endnotes

1 Bion, 1961; Foulkes, 1964; Douglas, 1973; Yalom, 1985; Corey, 1990; Whitaker, 2001.
2 Swartz, Gibson & Gelman 2002.
3 Heap, 1984; Corey & Corey, 1997; Toseland & Rivas, 2001.
4 Toseland & Rivas, 2001; Howes & Schwartzberg, 2001.
5 Heap, 1984.
6 Perls, 1973.
7 Barnes, Ernst & Hyde, 1999: 26.
8 Bion, 1961; 1962; Foulkes, 1964; Pines, 2000.
9 Home, 1991; Lee, 1994; Favor, 1994.
10 Bion, 1962; Pines, 2000; Whitaker, 2001.
11 Douglas, 1979; Yalom, 1995; Whitaker, 2001; Toseland & Rivas, 2001.
12 Tuckman, 1963; Northen, 1988; Toseland & Rivas, 2001.
13 Toseland & Rivas, 2001.

3

Community groups and 'peacebuilding from below'

Connie O'Brien

Learning objectives

By the end of this chapter you should be able to:

- Contextualise community groups within the South African NGO/civil society sector.

- Understand the juxtaposition between groupwork theory, community work theory, and a peacebuilding approach.

- Understand how community development/conflict resolution strategies contribute towards building peace.

- Adopt a critical perspective when working with community groups given the State/civil society relationship.

- Recognise some of the challenges that community groups face in the South African context.

Introduction

This chapter situates community groups within the context of the South African non-governmental organization (NGO) sector of civil society and considers the role of community groups and NGOs in the task of peacebuilding. The peacebuilding framework allows the 'micro' focus on community development/conflict resolution to be viewed in a macro context and as such it encompasses a developmental approach. For purposes of this chapter it suffices to say that community development has been used as a macro intervention (Gray, 1998). The notion of 'peacebuilding'[1] which will be discussed in more detail further on in this chapter, is relatively new in the field of conflict resolution or peace research. 'Peacebuilding from below'[2] has been largely spearheaded by theorists who have integrated the sociological/development dimensions of sustaining peace.[3] This chapter re-frames the purpose of community groups by arguing that community groups that are involved in capacity building, empowerment strategies, community peace-brokering and other community development and conflict resolution interventions are essentially engaging in 'peacebuilding from below'[4] and can be conceptually positioned within a multi-track 'peacebuilding paradigm'.

Furthermore, most of these community groups are groups that have been facilitated by NGOs, particularly those involved in conflict resolution and community development. Since these NGOs form part of civil society, understanding the challenges NGOs face involves examining some of the critical issues facing the civil society sector.

The South African context, NGOs, and civil society

Ten years after the first democratic elections, the South African government is still facing the rising tide of the HIV/AIDS pandemic, increasing joblessness, escalating criminal activities as well as widespread poverty. A noted South African economist, Terreblanche (2002, 419), suggests that the 'terms of the negotiated transition have trapped the poor in a situation of systemic exclusion' forcing the new government to pander to corporate/market demands and pay scant attention to the plight of the most needy. Terreblanche (2002) 'blames' the present socio-economic state of the country's poor on the particular brand of neo-liberal democratic capitalism that is being presently practised. Furthermore, in succumbing to the demands of the global economy, the new South African government has moved further away from its original political and socio-economic plans to address past injustices. Thus, for Terreblanche (2002), nothing short of a paradigm shift away from democratic capitalism towards social democracy is what is needed. However, a change in economic and social policy is not enough. It is vital that efficient administration and management systems are put in place so that much needed resources are effectively distributed to the neediest.

There will always be contesting ideological viewpoints as to how a truly just, equal, democratic and peaceful society can be reached. However, a naïve assessment of the various activities undertaken to achieve the goals of a so-called 'good/just society' could increase the very inequalities that exist in society. This becomes particularly important when one considers how many community group activities aimed at addressing vital issues have mushroomed all over South Africa. These activities fall within the ambit of the NGO sector of civil society. The NGO sector of civil society that operates largely through community group activities contributes towards social development in South Africa. Social development favours a holistic multi-sectoral approach to social problems. Ideally this approach involves both communities and the State seeking joint solutions. In 1998, there were over 98 000 NGOs active in various South African communities (Swilling, 2002). Some of these organizations have become increasingly bureaucratised and professionalised (Edwards & Hulme), making it difficult for facilitators/catalysts from such agencies to be truly empowering and facilitative of 'bottom–up' approaches with their community groups. Also, community-based grassroots organizations are being pressurised through subsidy arrangements/financial leverage to adopt strategies that may remove them further from 'grassroots approaches' and real social change.

According to Aall (2001, 367) NGOs may be broadly defined as:

> [P]rivate, self-governing, not-for-profit institutions dedicated to alleviating human suffering; or to promoting education, health, economic development,

environmental protection, human rights, and conflict resolution; or to encouraging the establishment of democratic institutions and civil society.

These NGO activities take place within the domain of civil society. The notion of civil society encapsulates all those civil activities that take place at a voluntary level outside the control of the state such as associations, clubs, and groups promoting various interests and/or religious perspectives or groups providing a range of voluntary services and so on. According to Chandhoke (1995), civil society should not be seen as an abstraction apart from the State since the State fashions many of the processes in this arena. This argument has, however, become considerably weakened with the post-1989 'resurrection' of the civil society debate and the emergence of a growing global civil society (Kaldor, 2003). Depending on the relative strength of any civil society it could play an even greater role not only in curbing the excesses of the State but through its global networking campaigns it could bring pressure on other states and multinationals.

In the case of South Africa, certain groups within civil society played a key role in dismantling an unjust system through its ability to mobilise the masses. Comparisons may be drawn with the East European velvet revolution, which as Vaclav Havel, the playwright who became president after the 1989 Czechoslovakian revolution, would attest to, was also largely brought about by ordinary citizens.

Presently, South African civil society appears to be more fractured than before as it struggles to articulate its stance in relation to the post-apartheid government. The NGO sector in particular is caught in a dilemma of wanting to make the new democracy work and yet not always being able to align itself with new policies that favour the growth of the economy above the basic needs of the people. Another factor that confounds this relationship between the NGO sector and the government is that some of the key leaders of the NGO/civil society sector have been absorbed into leading government positions. The expectation that there would be increased collaborative partnerships between the NGO sector and government is another factor to keep in mind. In some instances, NGOs have gone further than mere collaboration and may, in fact, have taken over some of government's functions (O'Brien, 2003).

These aforementioned factors could have resulted in certain sectors of civil society being co-opted into the power structure. Woodward's appraisal that the onset of democracy may have changed the nature of civil society, turning it into a 'civil society in power', partially describes what has happened in South Africa (Woodward, in Elias & Turpin, 1994: 228). Civil society could be acting more as handmaidens of the state rather than independent critics and watchdogs of the State.

It is, however, important to note that there is no one homogenous civil society as such but rather many 'civil societies' (Pillay, 1996: 345) coexisting in one society. Pillay (1996) also provides a loose classification of 'civil societies', namely: a 'progressive civil society' (those organizations that seek to democratise society); a 'conservative civil society' (those organizations that seek to entrench or reshape existing power relations); and 'reactionary organizations' that promote narrow ethnic/religious interests.

In our present South African context, a range of organizational and community groups are building alliances with the State for various purposes. Despite the fact that both the State and civil society could have elements that run counter to the democratic ideal, civil society is still entrusted with the task of holding the State accountable. Thus, it becomes an imperative that civil society retains its critical impartial stance. Community group leaders operating within the NGO/civil society context need to be aware of influences that shape their agenda along conservative, reform or social change directions. Nevertheless, from within this sector, citizens close to the grassroots have done much to hold communities together during times of conflict through providing emotional and practical support. Such groups play a critical role in peacebuilding, which will be discussed in the following section.

Background to peacebuilding

Peacebuilding is a broad overarching concept that bridges both development as well as peace activities and as such it provides the macro framework within which community development/conflict resolution activities undertaken at the grassroots can be understood. Furthermore, peacebuilding is a particularly crucial activity in post-settlement contexts.

South Africa could be described as a 'post-settlement' context. Post-settlement refers specifically to countries that have negotiated a transition to democratic governance through a peace settlement. Such contexts are characterised by various transitional issues that need to be addressed, such as dealing with increased criminality, the development deficit and community conflict amongst others. To consolidate the 'peace gains' made through the settlement, and to prevent a backsliding into conflict, peacebuilding initiatives aimed at reconstructing and developing the country are given priority. The RDP (Reconstruction and Development Programme) could also have been described as a 'post-conflict peacebuilding' strategy to sustain peace. In South Africa peacebuilding as a concept emanates from the field of conflict resolution and is linked to two other concepts, namely peacemaking and peacekeeping. Lederach (1997) suggests that peacekeeping, peacemaking and peacebuilding do not happen in linear, discrete phases but may overlap or occur in tandem. Peacekeeping is traditionally linked to the United Nations peacekeeping forces brought in to keep the peace and/or monitor the ceasefires whilst settlements were being brokered. However, ordinary civilians have also been keeping the peace through monitoring elections and carrying out inspection checks in their own communities. Peacemaking is commonly linked with official negotiations taking place at the top political level. At another level, however, 'community peacemakers' have also been brokering peace in their own neighbourhoods. Peacebuilding was initially conceptualised as those initiatives aimed at reconstructing war-torn societies (following peacekeeping and peacemaking) but later developed into an all-encompassing term that included building peace throughout the various stages of conflict in a country's history. Peacebuilding initiatives could include the following: confidence-building measures, prejudice-reduction programmes, building capacity in conflict-resolution skills training, addressing the range of development deficits such as enhancing leadership capacity, setting up intersectoral forums and empowering community groups to make their own land claims. In exploring community development and community conflict resolution initiatives, the notion of peacebuilding becomes a useful bridging concept especially if one recognises that there can be no peace without development. Significantly, 'peacebuilding from below' as advocated by Lederach (1997) resonates with 'human scale development' (Max-Neef, 1991), 'participatory development' (Carmen, 1996; Rahman, 1993) and empowerment (Friedmann, 1992). A people-centred, people-driven approach is central to change and transformation in the newly developing South African democracy. South Africa's past history of autocratic, top–down, segregated practices means that ensuring a more inclusive, participatory and democratic approach is a priority.

Peacebuilding through multi-track approaches

Lederach (1995, 1997, 2001), drawing on his extensive experience and knowledge gained both in the field of conflict resolution and development, suggests a framework for understanding how various multi-track approaches used synergistically could contribute to building a sustainable peace. Lederach (1997) indicates the kinds of leading actors and groups that could be involved in such an endeavour. His 'pyramid' diagram provides a useful lens through which to gain a better understanding of the dynamics of the different levels of leadership and group involvement across society when considering conflict resolution/peacebuilding initiatives. Track One refers to those negotiations that take place with an elite group of top-level leaders. Track Two refers to those group discussions that have been facilitated by middle-range leaders. Track Three refers to initiatives facilitated largely by grassroots leaders.

Three tracks in peacebuilding In a post-conflict, reconstruction and development phase, NGOs committed to meeting the needs of civil society and resolving conflict need to take a critical approach in peacebuilding, particularly as regards the nature of their relationship and level of engagement with the State.

The apartheid State failed to meet security and identity needs as well as a host of other developmental needs in communities, thereby prolonging social conflict in this country.[5] Against this past, it becomes all the more important in a new dispensation to empower community groups to resolve their own conflicts (Track Three initiatives) as well as lead their own development (human-scale, people-centred approaches). This does not preclude the State's support of these initiatives (Leftwich, 1994). Development has to be part of a State-led policy but it should be a policy developed from the bottom up.

Edward Azar's and John Burton's work have brought home the importance of 'Track Two' initiatives. The Track Two level of diplomacy addresses those issues that lie beyond the official bargaining framework of Track One's political diplomacy. Track Two approaches include pre-negotiation group meetings with influential middle range leaders and may involve citizen diplomacy and problem-solving workshops. The problem-solving workshops could entail bringing together influential leaders who have links to the broad-based constituencies (at the base of the pyramid) as well as access to the top political leadership. These workshops are specially designed discussions aimed at changing perceptions together with problem-solving exercises (Azar, 1990).

Lederach's pyramid (1997) provides a useful tool for understanding how multi-track approaches can operate in tandem. The importance of 'complementarity' of approaches has been highlighted by several authors[6]. The leadership roles at the various 'tiers' of the pyramid clearly suggest the range of influence these leaders could exercise should they work together synergistically. It is clear that top-level negotiations which do not have the support of the other 'tiers' will not be sustained in the long run. Furthermore, the development of leadership at the base (grassroots constituency) becomes an increasing priority. This chapter focuses attention largely on level three of the pyramid where community groups are being encouraged to initiate and/or collaborate in various peacebuilding activities. Before examining the roles of grassroots leaders as well as NGO leaders in facilitating peacebuilding initiatives at this level in four case studies, community groups is positioned within groupwork theory in the discussion below.

Further theoretical perspectives on community groups

Peacebuilding or social development?

This chapter has specifically adopted a peacebuilding paradigm in its discussion of community groups. Social development could be viewed as part of the peacebuilding canvass although both are macro concepts.

The so-called micro activities at the grassroots play an important role in shaping the decisions at the top government level of any society and as such the micro-macro dichotomy becomes problematic. If one wants to focus on understanding the nature of the community group (micro level) then clarification on a typology of groups would be helpful.

Typology of groups

This section draws largely on Corey and Corey (1997); Rothman with Tropman in Cox et al (1987); Toseland and Rivas (2001) and Weil (1988). Most group work/group therapy approaches are carried out with formed groups. Groups are formed for two broad reasons: to provide help and healing to the group members or to achieve a specific purpose that may impact beyond the group and achieve change at a broader level. According to Toseland and Rivas (2001) groups may be classified as treatment groups or task groups. This chapter focuses on formed groups that have specific tasks. Some of these task-oriented groups may also be meeting the 'therapeutic' and/or socialisation needs of their members. Conversely, some so-called treatment groups may also have a 'task-centred' focus. Toseland and Rivas' (2001) comparison of task and treatment groups offer some understanding of the major differences.

Comparison along seven dimensions	Treatment	Task
Bond	Members' personal needs	Task to be completed
Roles	Roles develop through interaction	Roles are assigned
Communication	Open	Focused on particular task
Procedures	Flexible/formal	Formal agenda/rules
Composition	Common concerns/ characteristics	Based on needed talents/ division of labour
Confidentiality	Usually private/kept within group	Private/public
Success	Based on members' treatment goals	Based on accomplishing tasks

Table 3.1 Comparing task and treatment groups
An adaptation from Toseland and Rivas (2001: 16, Table 1.2).

Toseland and Rivas (2001: 31–33) further provide a typology of task groups. They situate task groups predominantly in organizations/agencies where such groups are used to meet client needs, organizational needs and community needs. The emphasis in this discussion centres on community groups that have been formed as a response to community needs. According to Corey and Corey (1997: 9) the role of the task group specialist would be to 'assist groups such as task forces, committees, planning groups, community organizations, discussion groups, study circles, learning groups, and other similar groups to correct or develop their functioning'. Thus the skilful use of group dynamics serves the purpose of improving practice and achieving goal accomplishment (Corey & Corey, 1997: 9).

Community practice

In contextualising various task group approaches in community practice, Weil (1988) outlines five different models of community practice: community development; programme development and coordination; social planning; community liaison and pluralism; participation and political empowerment. Besides the core professional values that should underpin any intervention, Weil (1988: 136–137) highlights the importance of participation, social justice and social responsibility when engaging with community groups.

The **purposes** of these community groups cover a wide range of human development and security needs and include elements of social change tactics and strategies. The **leadership** often consists of both indigenous leaders and professionals. Sometimes the leaders would have been voted for and at other times they lead through consensus. The **focus** is largely on serving the community and social justice. At times it may include capacity building of members so that they can enrich the community. The **bonding** dimension is mostly connected to an ideological position, a sense of democratic participation and/or perceptions of justice. The group **composition** is made up of members who share a common interest about the change needed and/or members who want to make a difference to their communities. The **communication** patterns may be formal or informal depending on the purpose/focus. There also may be low-to-high member disclosure in relation to social problems. These selected group characteristics (purpose, leadership, focus, bond, composition and communication) have been adapted from a typology of task groups that serve community needs (Toseland & Rivas, 2001: 33).

Community strategies

This discussion on community groups straddles a number of disciplines and theoretical frameworks. When discussing community groups within a community organization/development framework, Rothman with Tropman in Cox et al (1987) highlight certain orientations, roles, processes and general strategies. These authors suggest that there are three broad strategies, namely social action, social planning and locality development. Ideologically, the frame of reference for engagement with these different approaches may vary. For example, the social action approach encompasses a strong social justice component which may call forth more adversarial roles such as activist advocate, negotiator and broker, and the tactics used for mobilising the community groups may involve direct action, conflict and confrontation. Indigenous leaders and/or professional leaders may work together for just ends. The issues of challenging the dominant power structure so as to obtain the needed resources and of securing a more egalitarian society are important to this approach. Those leaders/facilitators working with the social planning approach may espouse different roles such as analyst and fact gatherer and may be working within the power structure to secure the necessary benefits for the community. Problem solving of substantive community problems using a task-centred approach is central. In contrast, the social action approach focuses on the shifting of the power relationships and bringing about institutional change adopting both task and process goals. The locality development approach focuses on the self-help initiatives of community groups with an emphasis on process rather than task. In terms of roles adopted in this approach, the leader/facilitator is an enabler/catalyst and teacher of problem-solving skills. Rothman with Tropman (1987) emphasise that these need not be three discrete strategies but that the mixing and phasing of these strategies should be adopted in relation to the community's needs.

In conclusion, community groups can be conceptualised as part of a task/treatment typology, within a broader peacebuilding paradigm. Task groups can be seen in relation to Rothman with Tropman's (1987) three community strategies. Furthermore, Weil's (1988) emphasis on participation, social justice and social responsibility emphasises the core principles and processes that should underpin community task groups. Refer to Figure 3.1 for a diagrammatic summary of the theoretical perspectives underlying community groups, which enable these groups to be placed within a peacebuilding paradigm.

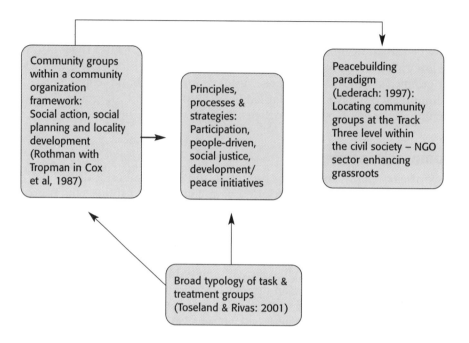

Figure 3.1 Peacebuilding framework for understanding community groups

These various theoretical frameworks, held together by the broader peacebuilding paradigm, provide the reader with the conceptual framework for understanding the various community group interventions.

The nature of these interventions that are being facilitated through NGO initiatives are described in the following case studies.

NGO-facilitated community groups[7]

Most NGOs carry out their activities through community groups or have facilitated networks, forums, or coalitions that bring groups together for social change purposes. Three of the fifty South African community development and conflict resolution NGOs that were part of the sample will be presented for illustrative purposes. These case studies are DELTA: A community development NGO; New World Foundation: A community development NGO integrating conflict-resolution strategies; and UMAC: A conflict-resolution NGO.

Most of the South African NGOs have undergone some transformation since 1994 and aligned their project goals and community group activities in keeping with the principles of the government's RDP (Reconstruction and Development Programme). Development should be a 'people-driven process'. This is one of the six principles of the RDP:

Our people, with their aspirations and collective determination, are our most important resource. The RDP is focused on our people's most immediate needs, and it relies, in turn, on their energies to drive the process of meeting these needs. Regardless of race or sex or whether they are rural or urban, rich or poor, the people of South Africa must together shape their own future. Development is not about the delivery of goods to a passive citizenry. It is about active involvement and growing empowerment. In taking this approach we are building on the many forums, peace structures and negotiations that our people are involved in throughout the land.

(African National Congress, 1994: 4–5)

For those working at the grassroots, community development has always been about building **people's capacity to drive their own development** and to procure the resources necessary to realise their potential. This principle resonates with Corey's and Corey's (1997) understanding of one of the purposes of a task group which is to enhance and develop the group members' functioning. Furthermore 'capacity building' would also be central to any participatory, development approach (Max-Neef, 1991; Freire, 1970). South African authors such as Hope and Timmel (1995) and Swanepoel and De Beer (1997), have also promoted this principle/process/strategy of 'development from below' thus placing empowerment through capacity building at the core of development. The central principle of community development is that development is not something that is 'done' to people, but something that people decide freely to do for themselves. This is summed up in the following statement.

Community development is about people development, it's not about roads, infrastructure, or housing first ... but people first ... we emphasise community participation ... in how people can help other people to participate ...

(Project Leader, DELTA)

Case study 1: Delta

Delta (Development Education and Leadership Teams in Action) is a community development NGO that focuses on empowering women.

The **Delta Women's Leadership Training Programme** links the notion of empowerment to the development model. The training focuses on education for economic independence and leadership in the development sphere. Since a significant cadre of women leaders were absorbed into parliament, leaving a lead-ership vacuum at the grassroots, DELTA focuses on addressing this vacuum and on widening the leadership base. The DELTA programme consists of three phases:

- **Phase One** – aimed at groups of women in township or rural areas who have limited or no education. Basic skills are imparted and the focus is on self-development.
- **Phase Two** – aimed at groups of women already working in community projects and who are potential leaders.

These women are exposed to further training in organizational and community development. They also are encouraged to network and share skills with other organizations.

- **Phase Three** – a community leaders' programme that basically trains the trainers. Women who have been through this programme are enlisted to run the Phase One programme in their own communities (Project Leader, Delta).

One of the models of community organization (Rothman with Tropman in Cox et al, 1987) is locality development. Delta's approach indicates this orientation. The focus of the training programme includes the principles and processes of participation, capacity building through skills transferral, and developing leadership. This programme also clearly depicts 'task-oriented community groups' in action (Toseland & Rivas, 2001).

Case study 2: New World Foundation

New World Foundation is a community development NGO that integrates conflict resolution strategies.

This NGO is situated in a community torn apart by gang warfare. Besides doing community development work such as empowering community groups through job creation projects and providing them with the education and training to have the capacity to transform their lives and the communities in which they live, this NGO is also **dealing with gang violence** by adopting a conflict resolution approach to its work in this area.

Lavender Hill has become stigmatised as a violent area ... there's a lot of gang warfare over the years ... people from outside areas are scared to come into the area and over the years we have been trying to change that ... we had a social worker who worked with the gangs...they could relate to him, he could relate to them. We assisted the gang members with the burial of their dead...no-one else wanted to do it. There have been various efforts to bring about peace and resolve the conflict. It's a different ball game ... everyone has guns ... they are so young ... now another peace process has started with the gangsters and the pastors. (Project

Leader, New World Foundation)

Part of this NGO's aim is to facilitate regular meetings with sectors of the community in order to monitor the 'peace process'.

So fortunately we have this peace process which we brokered. Every Wednesday, even if there hasn't been violence the gang leaders and the police meet with a representative of the pastors and various school principals. So because they meet on a weekly basis they keep an update of the violence. So if someone was shot on Saturday they would report who was responsible and our peaceworker works with that ... they are now accountable to this peace process. (Project Leader: New World Foundation)

Using Lederach's (1997) framework as a 'lens' to understand the group dynamics at work, it appears that a 'problem-solving' approach is being adopted within a context where grassroots leaders (gang leaders) (Track Three level) and middle range leaders such as the pastors, school principals, peaceworker and police officers (Track Two level) are working in unison to address the problem of gang violence. This case study shows how a community can be empowered to broker their own peace.

Case study 3: UMAC

UMAC is a conflict resolution NGO. UMAC, initially called the Urban Monitoring Committee, is an NGO that monitored urban violence, police activity and State activity in the apartheid era. It later expanded its work to include the 'demilitarisation of youth programmes'. UMAC, which is now an acronym for 'You Managing Conflict,' was instrumental along with other role-players in helping to build trust between the police and communities and working towards a new piece of legislation that regulated the relationship between the police and the community. The structure that was set up in keeping with this new policy was the Community Safety Forum that brought together representatives from other criminal justice institutions such as the courts, correctional services, prisons, police as well as welfare within a national crime prevention strategy (Project Leader, UMAC).

This NGO has thus played a vital role in facilitating this forum. Building coalitions, facilitating task forces, committees and planning groups all require group skills (Corey and Corey, 1997).

Umac also has a Women and Peacebuilding Programme that is aimed at empowering women to become leaders in the peacebuilding process in their own communities:

> The Women and Peacebuilding Programme ... the primary thrust is to identify women as change agents ... as peacebuilders in their community ... as a key constituency that could be trained and supported as peacebuilders. (Project Leader, UMAC)

UMAC's rationale is as follows:

> It's looking at conflict transformation, gender and development of the community ... we're changing the face of the community by training women ... we realised that women were not networked into opportunity ... (Project Leader, UMAC)

UMAC, alongside other NGOs, has a gender focus on women which is strategically aligned with one of the Millennium Development Goals for 2010. Women in South Africa have a crucial role in peacebuilding, which is seen as primarily linked to the satisfaction of basic human needs (McKay & De la Rey, 2001).

Building conflict resolution capacity at the grassroots level is vital for strife-torn communities. Besides training and capacity building, these NGOs also address particular social/human needs as part of a specific contribution to the transformation process in South Africa.

In bringing this section on case studies to a closure it seems that a variety of principles, processes and strategies have been adopted to achieve various aims. Most of the community groups were facilitated by personnel from the NGOs whilst at the same time growing indigenous leadership as was clearly demonstrated by Delta, UMAC, and the New World Foundation.

One could ask whether group theory, roles and processes have been subsumed into development and conflict-resolution strategies. In the aforementioned examples, theoretically, group processes, community development processes and conflict-resolution processes have mirrored each other. For example, community development processes such as capacity building and building social capital, can be compared with confidence-building procedures in conflict resolution and with trust building in groups; empowerment (community development) can be compared with working towards symmetry in contesting relationships (conflict resolution) and this can be compared with developing self-esteem and capacity as part of a group process; democratic procedures can be compared to the 'ground-rules' set up for conflict resolution or for a group process; the emphasis on 'process' rather than 'product' can be compared to process-oriented conflict resolution, community development or group dynamics. Some aspects of community development or group work could be termed conflict-management work and/or conflict-prevention work. Galama and Van Tongeren (2002) and Lederach (1997) would place all those services/activities undertaken by these community groups within the peace-building framework.

The challenges that lie ahead

At a macro level, in dealing with ethnic conflict in Africa, Amoo and Odendaal (2002, 1320) stress Burton's (1990) notion that intractable conflicts have their roots in the frustration of basic human needs. These authors suggest that the frustration of these needs lie enmeshed in the cultural, social and political structures that need transformation. The work being done by the NGOs referred to in this chapter bring home the transformational capacity of various community groups and the influences that they can exert on their surroundings. In this regard, McKay and De la Rey (2001) suggest the use of consciousness-raising groups as an intervention strategy against gender oppression. Other commentaries on social change and citizen action, advocacy and empowerment through social action groups and the use of group work techniques to resolve inter-ethnic conflict (Vinik & Levin, 1991) have contributed to a greater awareness of the importance of using groups for facilitating social change, promoting development and building peace. Community groups can address the problems at the coalface since they are close to the grassroots. The challenges that lie ahead are linked to unmet basic needs, scarce resources, lack of capacity, unemployment and the HIV/AIDS epidemic. On a cautionary note these community groups are not being offered as the panacea for the country's problems but they do provide a creative citizen force that could, in partnership with organizations, business and the State make a real difference to the quality of life in communities and in South Africa as a whole. These community groups operating at the micro level capture the African essence of ubuntu through the manner in which they generate that social capital of networked relationships serving the good of the whole and thereby enhancing the individual's potential at the same time. The ubuntu philosophy essentially points out that a person is only a person in relationship to other persons.

The stability of South Africa's democracy is centrally linked to the social and economic development of its peoples. Development takes time and can lead to more conflicts and tensions that need to be resolved from the 'bottom up'. Peacebuilding 'from below' via community groups, presupposes that people have the skills and capacities to participate, make informed decisions and resolve their own conflicts. The synergy that is already taking place in the field needs to be applied much more consciously and deliberately as integrated strategies. The networking that already exists through the variety of partnership arrangements, coalitions and consortia can be a conduit for facilitating integrative conflict-resolution/community development practices. These same networks could become channels through which movements for non-violence and human scale development can be promoted.

Discussion questions

1 Weil (1988: 136–137) highlights the importance of participation, social justice and social responsibility when engaging with community groups. What do these concepts mean in actual practice? What are the factors that make participation and genuine empowerment problematic?

2 What is the State's role in meeting basic needs/service delivery in comparison to the voluntary sector? What do you think about the State/NGO/civil society alliance?

3 Group characteristics such as purpose, leadership, focus, bond, composition and communication have been adapted from a typology of task groups that serve community needs (Toseland & Rivas, 2001: 33). Which other characteristics play a role in a society undergoing transformation?

4 Reread the case studies and try and analyse them by adopting a 'particular lens' through which they could be assessed.

Endnotes

1 Galtung, 1996; Lederach, 1995, 1997, 2001.
2 Galama & van Tongeren, 2002; Lederach, 1997, Reychler & Paffenholz, 2001.
3 Azar, 1990; Burton, 1987, 1990; Curle, 1971.
4 Galama & van Tongeren, 2002; Reychler & Paffenholz, 2001.
5 There is sufficient evidence to link distorted patterns of development, communal discrimination and protracted social conflict (Azar, 1990; Burton, 1987).
6 Bloomfield, 1997; Keashley & Fisher, 1990, 1996; Lederach 1995; 1997.
7 This section draws on actual data gleaned from in-depth interviews undertaken with NGO personnel in the Western Cape which formed part of a larger doctoral study that focused on: 'Community Development and Conflict Resolution: An examination of the potential for complementary strategies in post-settlement contexts, with special reference to Northern Ireland and South Africa' (O'Brien, 2003).

4 Groups and organizational life

André de V Smit

Learning objectives

By the end of this chapter you should be able to:

- Explain the nature of organizations and how they function.
- Identify the role of groups in organizational life.
- Identify the various types and functions of organizational groups.
- Describe the role of management toward achieving organizational goals.

Introduction

In order to achieve that which cannot be achieved by individual effort alone, individuals pool their efforts to achieve a collective outcome that is greater than the sum total of each individual's effort. Such a pooling results in the formation of a group with a structure, specific goals, and behavioural norms. While such a group can constitute an organization, most organizations are larger and consist of a number of groups, called organizational groups. These groups are formed primarily to perform given tasks and form the building blocks of the organization. The discussion in this chapter is applicable to different types of organizations from companies to NGOs to religious organizations.

This chapter introduces the concept of organization by briefly tracing the history of organizational activity and by defining organizational purpose and characteristics. The structure and function of the various types of organizational groups are identified and jointly they portray the central role that groups occupy in the structure of organizations.

Given that vast resources are allocated annually to social service delivery the importance of effective and efficient management of these resources is highlighted. Apart from dealing with the concepts of effectiveness and efficiency, the chapter briefly refers to the functions of management and their relationship to organizational groups. The distinctions between leadership and management and their respective pivotal roles in organizational goal attainment are briefly discussed.

The chapter concludes that in order to achieve organizational goals, the management of that organization needs to have a sound understanding of the structure and behaviour of organizational groups as well as of the influence of leadership and management on organizational life in general and on organizational performance in particular.

Organizations and organizational behaviour

Organizations and goals Human behaviour is goal directed. However, many goals that individuals aspire to cannot be met through individual behaviour. For example, an individual who wishes to earn a living from making a product or providing a service but lacks the expertise to design, market and sell the product or service or to manage the finances, may team up with other individuals who have the requisite expertise in order to form an organization that generates the required income. In this way, individual goals are achieved by meeting group goals and the whole (organization or group) is worth more than the sum total of the individual contributions; this is often referred to as *synergy*, a biological term.

Organizations, like groups, exist primarily to achieve that which a person cannot achieve on his or her own. Individuals form organizations to engage in specific goal directed behaviour, such as making a profit, providing welfare service or spreading a religious faith. Organizations can make things happen that individuals cannot do on their own: 'They pursue goals and objectives that can be achieved more efficiently and effectively by the concerted action of individuals *and* groups' (Gibson et al, 1988: 5).

History of organizational theory For centuries humans have relied on organizations to achieve organizational goals in order to satisfy their individual needs. Many examples describe early organizational life. Way back in 1491 BC, Jethro urged Moses to delegate authority hierarchically (Exodus 18v25 in Schafritz & Ott, 1987: 20). Similarly, in 500 BC, Sun Tzu in *The Art of War* identified the need for hierarchical organization, communication and staff planning (Ibid, 10).

Organizations play a central role in the daily life of all human beings. While the chronology of organizational life and writings thereon dates back centuries, the formal study of organizations emerged about a century ago. Organizational theory (or organizational behaviour, organizational/industrial psychology) is a relatively new field of study. The study includes the behaviour of individuals, groups and organizations and the influence exerted on these by organizational structure and processes such as among others, decision-making, communication and performance appraisal.

Theories on organizations also took cognisance of the influence of management on organizations. As early as 1910, Louis Brandeis argued that railroad increases be denied as substantial savings could rather be effected by improving management (Ibid, 11). Subsequently, many theories (Frederick Taylor's *Scientific Management*, Henri Fayol's *Administrative Management*, Max Weber's

Bureaucracy, Elton Mayo's *Human Relations Movement*, and Douglas McGregor and others' *Human Resources Movement*) have informed this field of study. More recent theories include **systems**, **contingency** and **management science** theory. [See Gibson et al, Hellriegel et al and Griffin for more information about these theories and approaches.]

There being no peopleless organizations, many of these theories highlight the human side of organizations and stress the importance of human resources. A sound understanding of human behaviour (individual, group and organizational) in the workplace is thus fundamental to organizational goal achievement.

Organizational behaviour   According to Orpen (1981: 13), characteristics common to organizations include formality (rules regulations and procedures), hierarchy (control and command structures), duration (lives longer than individuals), staff replacement (constant movement of staff), location (factory, business, campus), complexity (large membership), specialisation (division of work) and rationalisation (rational grouping of persons).

Organizations are not inanimate objects such as buildings and factories; rather they are a social collective that have particular organizational goals. In order to attain such goals, organizations have plans (strategic, programme and operational) to meet such goals. To give effect to plans, organizations employ people and position them in organizational structures – which involve positions or jobs and how they relate to each other. Leadership and various organizational processes (communication, decision-making, and performance evaluation) ensure that individual, group and organizational behaviour give effect to plans.

Groups as organizational building blocks

In order for an organization to be successful, i.e. to meet its organizational goals, it must be structured so that the groups within the organization can perform optimally. Groups are thus key building blocks of an organization as they contribute to the attainment of organizational goals. For example, traditionally an army organizational structure will reflect various groupings in a hierarchy, the lowest and smallest being a section, which consists of a few soldiers. A number of sections form a platoon, platoons form a company, companies form a battalion, battalions form a brigade, brigades form a division, divisions form a corps, and corps form an army.

Individuals and groups   The success of the army's efforts is thus dependent on the successful effort of the various groups, down to the successful effort of the smallest unit, the section. In turn, the section's success depends on the successful efforts of its individual members. Many organizations, be they government, non-government or for profit, are similarly structured. Figure 4.1 indicates the relationship of individuals, groups and the organization: individuals form groups and groups form the organization.

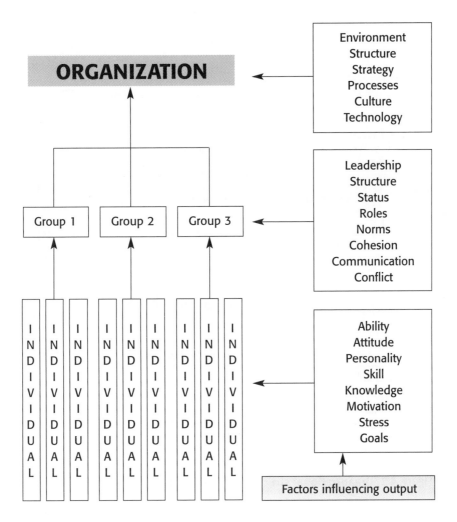

Figure 4.1 Individuals, groups and the organization, and factors influencing effectiveness

Organizational structures Unlike time-bound therapeutic groups, the dynamics of organizational groups, determined by organizational size and structure, can be very complex. In an organization, the leader of a group becomes a member of a group of leaders; the leader of the group of leaders becomes a member of a group of group leaders and so on. For example, in the organizational structure reflected in Figure 4.2, the social work supervisors (each a leader of a group of three social workers) together with the deputy director of Social Services form a new group. Similarly the three deputy directors, each representing a group, constitute yet another group. In this way leaders of groups link their groups to others that they serve in.

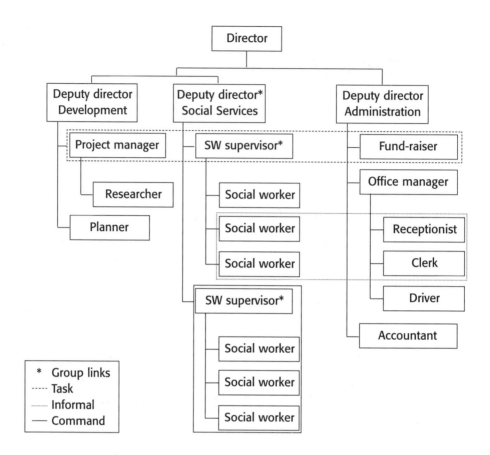

Figure 4.2 Organizational structure and types of organizational groups

Organizational dynamics   It stands to reason that the greater the number of groups and their grouping into departments or divisions within an organization, the greater the variation and complexity of potential relationships. The larger the number and the greater the diversity of the groups, the greater the number of potential relationships managers have to contend with. Managing five groups performing exactly the same repetitive task will be much less onerous than managing ten groups each having very different tasks. As such, the management structure becomes a central determinant of functional or dysfunctional group performance.

Furthermore, unlike most other groups (including therapeutic groups), organizational groups exist almost exclusively to perform a given task in order to achieve organizational goals. Groups within an organization often compete for resources in order to meet their goals and thus the potential for conflict between groups. This conflict is compounded if the task and desired outcomes are not clearly articulated in group and organizational goals. In organizational groups management is typically more concerned with 'task' or production-related issues than with 'maintenance' or people-related issues. [See Chapter 2.]

The concentration on task at the expense of dealing with the people issues can make membership of an organizational group stressful. Such stress often manifests itself in anger, withdrawal, apathy, resistance and can negatively influence individual, group and hence organizational performance.

There are also a number of factors that influence successful behaviour at individual, group and organizational levels as reflected in Figure 4.1. For example, it cannot be expected of an individual to perform a given task successfully if the person does not have the ability or the motivation to do the task. Similarly, its leadership style (authoritarian or participative), communication patterns (top-down or unrestricted) and forms of conflict (constructive or destructive) could influence a group's effectiveness. Further, the environment (political, social, economic and technological) in which it operates and the technology it employs influences the organization's structure and hence its goal attainment. For example, a computer manufacturer which operates in an environment where technological advances are extremely rapid will adopt an organizational structure and use manufacturing methods that are responsive to the constantly changing market.

Certain environments such as those of schools, municipalities and correctional facilities remain relatively stable and these organizations' structures and outputs do not change much over time. Organizations can be positioned on a continuum that reflects a mechanistic structure (stable and formal) as opposed to the less formal organic structure that is more responsive to an unstable environment (Burns & Stalker, 1961). Mechanistic organizations such as correctional facilities typically have highly specialised tasks, hierarchical control structures and are highly formalised. Here one can think of a typical bureaucracy (*bureau* being desk and *cracy* meaning rule – thus the rule from the desk) with rigid systems in place.

On the other hand, unstable environments require organizational structures that are very flexible and that can react to rapid environmental changes – IT (information technology) organizations being a good example of the organic type. In an IT organization, as in other organic organizations, structures are flexible, control is exercised through networks, jobs are less specialised and individual input is more highly valued. It follows that the nature and type of organizational group will be influenced by the organization's structure.

Type and nature of organizational groups

The type and nature of the groups that make up the organization will depend on its organizational structure, which in turn is determined by the organizational goals. For example, a social service organization providing a child welfare service will firstly have to identify child welfare needs and develop specific programmes to address such needs (i.e. educational, developmental, residential, foster and adoption). These programmes will identify the tasks and other parameters (i.e. intensity, frequency, standards, financial) that have to be performed and met. These tasks and parameters inform the group (or team – to be discussed in more detail later) formation process and the selection of group members in terms of skill, ability, knowledge and other characteristics.

Organizations consist of many types of groups in order to achieve primarily output goals (normally a product or service). Apart from each group contributing to organizational output, they meet a host of other psychosocial needs typically associated with group formation such as interpersonal attraction, security, affiliation, esteem, goal achievement and importantly, also economic gain. With a few exceptions, the reasons for both group and organization formation are similar.

The typology of organizational groups varies – some refer to groups while others refer to teams. Groups identical in structure and function often use different terminology. Table 4.1 reflects a summary of the more traditionally found organizational groups.

FORMAL GROUPINGS (mandatory and sanctioned in terms of structure and policy)

– **Functional groups** (have specific tasks and are not time-bound)
  • Command/work (supervisor & subordinates reflected in structure)
  • Autonomous work group (group that is self-regulatory)
  • Standing committee (deals with same issues, e.g. fund-raising committee)
  • Board (mostly policy formulation and regulatory, e.g. management board)

– **Task groups** (have specific tasks and are time-bound)
  • Task force (multi-disciplinary group, i.e. to design new service programme)
  • Ad hoc committee (expert group, e.g. to review new legislation)

INFORMAL GROUPINGS (voluntary and not part of organizational goals/structure)
  • Social group (members who gather voluntarily, e.g. weekly group lunch club)
  • Interest group (members with similar interests, e.g. jogging at lunchtime)
  • Friendship group (attracted by similarity, e.g. singles)

Table 4.1 Summary of the more traditionally found organizational groups

Formal groups

Primarily, organizations consist of **formal** and **informal groups**, with subgroups in each of these categorisations. The formal groups form an integral part of the organization's structure and are composed specifically to meet organizational goals. For instance, the group of social workers and their supervisor identified as a **command group** in Figure 4.2 is a formal group constituted to perform a given social work function – therefore also sometimes referred to as **functional groups** as they perform the functions for which the organization was established. Such a group, also known as a **work group**, is the most commonly found formal group. Typically, it has a formal leader (the supervisor) and subservient followers (the social workers), hence the term command group – it represents the traditional hierarchy found in mechanistic-type organizations.

If the three social workers did not have a supervisor and functioned autonomously, sharing leadership or facilitation of the group and rotating responsibilities, it will be known as an **autonomous work group**. While still concerned with providing the same social work service as the command group, it has more freedom and flexibility that comes with self-regulation.

Another formal group, the **standing committee**, is found in most organizations. These committees are constituted to perform a particular or a more general function typically represented by for instance the fund-raising or budget review committee or more generally, the executive committee.

Boards are to be found in many organizations; typically business and non-profit organizations have a board of directors and there are the well-known school and hospital boards. These boards normally assist in determining policy and perform a regulatory function in ensuring that organizational goals are met.

All the above-mentioned formal groups are of a more permanent nature – membership is stable and longer-term. Once a particular task has been completed they do not disband. For example, once a command group of teaching staff has completed the year's curriculum they do not disband, rather they will continue with the following year's teaching duties. Similarly, once a major fund-raising event is over, the fund-raising committee will continue with the next event.

Task groups

Unlike functional groups, task groups are not stable and membership is not long-term. While they are also constituted to contribute to organizational goal attainment like other formal or functional groups, their tasks are more specific and are time-bound.

Typically, the task group is formed to transcend the confines of a highly formalised structure with its attendant and restrictive vertical command and communication patterns. Such groups are often multi-disciplinary and are formed to undertake a specific, time-bound task. The task group attempts to draw members from across formal command groupings and thus also serves to integrate otherwise independent units. In Figure 4.2 the task group consists of members from three distinct and independent units, namely the project manager from the development division, the social work supervisor from the social services division and the fund-raiser from the administration division.

Much like autonomous work groups, task groups are usually self-regulatory and leadership or facilitation of the group is shared irrespective of position or rank of individual members. For example, should the director (Figure 4.2), two social workers, the planner and the office manger form a task group, the director is not assured of the leadership as the task group determines its own leadership – for instance, it could very well be a social worker or the planner.

Given their multi-disciplinary nature and cross-structural performance ability, task groups are particularly well suited to be creative in developing new services or trouble-shooting within organizations.

Ad hoc committees are another form of a task group. As the name implies (ad hoc meaning *for that purpose*) the committee's life is also of short duration. It is established to perform a specific task and when the task is completed, it disbands. Such committees are established to address once-off or infrequently occurring issues. Typically, this is the legislation or policy review committee, a staff selection committee, or a committee established to prepare for an organization's anniversary celebrations.

Informal groups

While formal groups are created and sanctioned by organizations as being crucial to organizational goal attainment, informal groups are not formally created or necessarily sanctioned by organizations. While organizations recognise the benefits of informal groups, their existence is not crucial to organizational output. In some cases, they are frowned upon or discouraged because of the negative influence they exert on group and organizational performance.

Informal groups consist of organizational members who constitute on a voluntary basis in order to meet given social needs such as recognition, affiliation, security and communication; to pursue particular non-organization related interests; or to share that which is common to all members. The membership of informal groups is not limited to the formal relationships imposed by the formal structure. Thus in Figure 4.2 it will be noted that, irrespective of division, two social workers from one formal command group and a receptionist and clerk from another command group constitute an informal group. Similarly rank or position is not a criterion for membership – the director or any other senior member of staff could conceivably join the group.

Social groups accommodate workers outside of the work confines imposed by formal groupings. They may serve a purely social function such as going to lunch once a week. **Interest groups** are formed to accommodate the particular interest of its members. Typically, such a group could foster a particular sport, religion, hobby or other interest such as music or art. **Friendship groups** serve to allow those that are attracted to each other because of similarities (age, politics, sexual orientation) to commune with each other.

Much as formal groups are the building blocks of the formal organization, informal groups contribute to the creation of the informal organization. Informal group behaviour can either enhance or impede organizational output. An informal group could for instance solve a work-related problem over lunch or while out hiking or improve communication across formal command work groupings. However, an informal group could spread malicious rumours (through the informal grapevine found in every organization) about the organization that could affect staff morale.

Management is also wise to the benefits of using informal groups and often use the grapevine managed by informal groups to sound out how staff will react to proposed ideas or plans. Should management wish for example to reduce overtime pay, they communicate this via the informal network to test the reaction thereto. Should the reaction be favourable, management can communicate the message through official channels; if the reaction is negative, management simply dismiss the message as a rumour or information not officially released.

Team vs. group   Thus far, the term 'group' rather than 'team' has been used. It should however also be noted that many prefer the term 'team'. It is an increasingly popular term and is rapidly replacing the term 'group' in the working environment. The term somehow exudes the warmth of a collective that is closely knit, clearly focused and highly energised. This is probably thanks to its association with sports teams that rely on its coach (a form of mentor) rather than on formal or autocratic leadership. It seems a more cosy term, lashed with loads of bonhomie and all things good; the common perception is more positive than negative, as are the many of the associated terms such as 'A-team' or 'winning team'.

Given that 21st century organizations are struggling to meet the demands of globalisation in an increasingly unstable environment, the move from the mechanistic to the organic model of organizational structure will favour the 'team' rather than the 'group' approach. This is not too dissimilar from the term 'management' replacing the popular understanding of the term 'administration' during the previous century.

While conceptually similar, some authors argue that there is a difference between a work group and a team, Lumsden and Lumsden (1993: 13) in referring to Kinlaw, state: 'A team starts out as a group, but … it reaches a new level of quality, it develops special feelings among its members, it creates critical work processes, and it reflects leadership for its own development and performance.' They continue to define a team: 'A team is a diverse group of people who share leadership responsibility for creating a group identity in an interconnected effort to achieve a mutually defined goal within the context of other groups and systems' (Ibid, 14).

Stoner et al (1995: 500) state that some modern-day groups have characteristics of both formal and informal groups; they are the 'superteams' or 'high-performance teams'. Inherent in these posits is the notion that the team is somehow a group, but one of a higher order; it does not always subscribe to all the formal processes and characteristics common to a formal task group. It is somehow imbued with a greater wisdom, creativity and energy.

However, is a team really a 'wundergroup' or is it simply a group that is infused by the elixir of inspirational leadership?

Managing organizations through groups

Social services in South Africa are rendered in the main by a partnership between the government and the private sector. The country has a very vibrant and extensive non-profit sector that provides a substantial portion of the social services. The 1998/99 study by Swilling and Russell revealed this to be a R9,3 billion industry with some 98 920 non-profit organizations employing 645 316 workers and utilising some 1,5 million volunteers (2002: 15–20). Given the vast public resources that are poured into social services annually, it is crucial that such resources are optimally employed through effective and efficient management.

Effectiveness and efficiency

Central to any organization's success and long-term survival are the key companion concepts of effectiveness and efficiency. An individual, group or organization is effective when the intended outcomes of individual, group or organizational behaviour are achieved. Efficiency is achieved when resources are optimally employed to achieve intended outcome, be it individual, group or organizational. However, effectiveness without efficiency or vice versa, will adversely affect individual and group, and hence organizational, output. Being both effective and efficient constitutes excellence – Hodge and Anthony (1984: 301) capture the concepts in the following dictums:

Effectiveness – doing the right things.
Efficiency – doing the right things.
Excellence – doing the right things right.

In order for groups that constitute an organization to be effective and efficient, individual contributions to group activity have similarly to reflect efficiency and effectiveness, and thus excellence. The cardinal contribution to effectiveness and efficiency by individuals (IE = individual effort) and groups (GE = group effort) and the effect on organizational excellence (OE), is conceptually depicted in Figure 4.3.

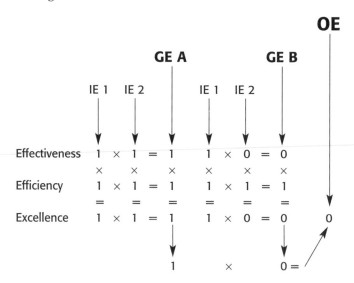

0 = No
1 = Yes
IE = Individual effort (individual 1 or 2)
GE = Group effort (Group A or B)
OE = Organizational effort/excellence

Figure 4.3 Individual, group and organizational effectiveness and efficiency
Source: Smit, A. de V. (1992). Managing for Effectiveness and Efficiency, *Welfare Focus*, (27/1) p 7.

Functions of management

Managing effectiveness and efficiency at individual, group and organizational levels involves managing the interdependent and complex relationships that individuals have within a group and that the group in turn has within the organization. Should some individuals in a group be ineffective and/or inefficient, it not only influences the group effectiveness and efficiency but will also negatively influence the motivation of productive individuals within the group. Thus, in addition to meeting the task requirements of the group, the manager/leader must also address the 'people' or 'maintenance' issues, notably motivation.

Motivation is, however, intrinsically linked to the four basic functions of management: planning (identifying goals and developing plans to achieve them), organizing (structuring of jobs, grouping of jobs and attendant relationships), leading (style and nature of leadership) and controlling (monitoring match between effort and intended output).

The four functions of management are applicable throughout the life of the group from inception to goal attainment and constantly have to take cognisance of complex prevailing group characteristics and dynamics – see Figure 4.4. Managing an organization is thus a very complex task.

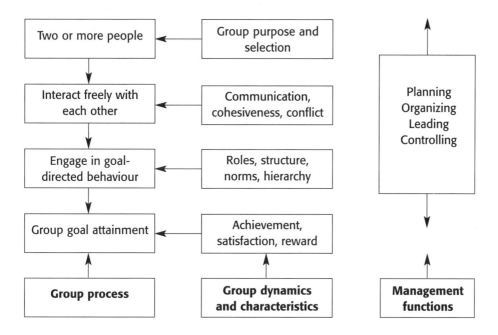

Figure 4.4 Group process, dynamics and management

Apart from interpreting the organizational canvas on which the external environment and other macro issues such as culture and technology are sketched, management is expected to understand the influence that group and individual characteristics exert on individual and group behaviour (see Figure 4.1).

To ensure that organizational groups function optimally, management is also responsible for the following:

- Providing direction through clear goal setting.
- Selecting members for the various formal groups.
- Ensuring that communication flows smoothly.
- Fostering functional cohesion.
- Ensuring that conflict is not dysfunctional.
- Ensuring that appropriate norms are established and conformed to.
- Assigning tasks and roles that are clear and acceptable.
- Ensuring that roles are not overloaded or in conflict with each other.
- Providing a structure that is conducive to optimal performance.
- Ensuring that the group hierarchy and statuses are clearly understood and respected.
- Recognising and rewarding successful task completion.

Planning   Planning, the first management function, is crucial to individual, group and hence organizational performance. As human and group behaviour is goal directed, the absence of goals and/or poorly articulated goals can lead to poor performance.

Effective planning ensures that there are clear objectives (measurable statements of accomplishment desired) and plan of action (identified tasks, performance standards and role players) to achieve these objectives. It means looking at what one has, what one wants, and what one has to do in order to get what one wants. Van Breda (2000: 13) points out the importance of strategic direction (planning) by stating that '… social workers who are familiar with and seek to execute the organization's strategy also enjoy their jobs more, have more energy and motivation for work, feel more committed to the organization and perceive their clients to be more satisfied with their services.'

Organizing   A clear understanding of what the objectives are and how they are to be met is pivotal to organizing – designing jobs (or positions) and their relationship within a structure and appointing staff to do the jobs. 'The behavior of individuals and groups in organizations is affected in significant ways by the jobs they perform. The job itself provides powerful stimuli for individual behavior' (Gibson et al, 1988: 429).

The organizational structure represents the relationships of jobs (or positions) within an organization – it reflects formal functions, groupings and authority and communication patterns. Organizing consists of the following steps:

- Identifying and specifying the work to be performed in order to attain organizational goals.
- Dividing the work into tasks (individual and group).
- Rational and efficient grouping of similar tasks.
- Co-ordination of individual and group tasks.

Leading: Role of the leader   The role of leadership is critical to group and hence organizational performance. The leader has to provide direction (planning), provide structure (organizing), provide support and motivation (leadership) and make sure that group and organizational behaviour is appropriate to meeting group and organizational goals (control). Stoner et al (1995: 470) defines '… managerial leadership as the process of directing and influencing the task-related activities of group members.' Further, they imply that it involves others, the followers, an unequal distribution of power and the ability to use power to influence follower behaviour.

Leadership power is variously sourced and leaders, depending on the situation, rely on some or all the power bases available to them. French and Raven (Hellriegel et al, 2001: 284) identified five sources of power:

- Legitimate – attached to position and formally sanctioned by formal structure.
- Reward – based on the leader's ability to reward followers.
- Coercive – based on ability to punish followers.
- Referent – based on personal characteristics/charisma.
- Expert – based on expertise in a given area.

While many examples of good and bad leadership abound through many centuries, various approaches to the formal study of leadership only started during the first half of the previous century. The first, the **trait approach**, consisted of identifying the traits commonly associated with successful leadership. Such traits commonly included assertiveness, intelligence and so on. The second and more scientific **behavioural approach** was based on studies conducted at the universities of Michigan and Ohio State (Griffin, 1987: 426–427). This approach was further expanded by the development of the Leadership Grid by Blake and Mouton (Stoner et al, 1995: 479). Essentially this approach looks at what the leader does (behaviour) rather than what the leader is (traits). It analyses behaviour on two axes: that directed at getting a task done and that directed at meeting followers' psychosocial needs – the 'task' and 'maintenance' leadership functions common to most groups. This approach posits that high scores on both axes are desirable.

The third or **contingency approach** holds that there is no ideal leadership behaviour common to all situations. Rather, the situation will determine the type of leadership behaviour required. Thus for example in the military, an autocratic and task-driven rather than a participatory leadership style is more apposite. According to Fiedler organizational conditions such as the task structure, leader–member relationships and the leader position power will determine the type of leadership required – task-oriented or relationship-oriented (Hellriegel et al, 2001: 290–291). Leadership style is thus contingent on the situation. Various theorists such as Fiedler, Hersey, Blanchard, House, Vroom and Yetton contributed substantially to the development of this approach.

The fourth and more recently developed approach is the **transformational and charismatic leadership approach**. This approach argues that the existing approaches do not account for exceptional leadership that is reflected in political, business and other fields. A very good example of this type of leadership is Nelson Mandela, whose enchanting persona sways great influence not only in South Africa but also in the international arena – often referred to as the 'Madiba Magic'. 'Transformational leaders' influence rests on their ability to inspire others through their words, visions, and actions. In essence, transformational leaders make tomorrow's dreams a reality for their followers.' (Ibid: 299). It is this form of leadership combined with an organic-type organization that is particularly suited to addressing the rapidly changing demands of the 21st century.

Leading: Role of the manager   To what extend do managers lead? Are they too concerned with keeping the system operational rather than providing future direction that enthuses and energises followers? Kolb et al (1995: 330) provide an interesting distinction between leadership and managerial behaviour – a modified summary is contained in Table 4.2.

Leadership	Management
Establish vision	Plan and budget
Create, generate ideas	Process and systematise
Align people to vision	Organize and staff
Motivate and inspire	Control and problem solve
Produce change	Produce order/predictability

Table 4.2 Leadership and managerial behaviour
Modified from: Kolb, D., Osland, J. & Rubin, M. 1995. Organizational Behavior – An experiential approach. Englewood Cliffs: Prentice-Hall Inc., p 330.

From Table 4.2 it is evident that leadership is primarily responsible for direction, motivation and change whereas management is more preoccupied with processing, organizing, stability and controlling. While helpful, care must be taken not to label either leaders or managers based on this juxtaposition. Many leaders are not visionary or inspirational whereas many managers are. Similarly, leaders can have good management acumen and managers can provide inspirational leadership.

However, the previously asked question relating to teams being a 'wundergroup', is probably best answered by looking at the role of the leader as reflected in Table 4.2 that also closely resembles the transactional and charismatic approach to leadership. 'Wise and seasoned leaders are guided more by their own lights than those of others' (Smit, 1990: 308). The super team leader is up front leading but is also sufficiently behind the front ranks to inspire, support and develop those who follow.

Controlling   The last management function, management control, is directly linked to the first, namely planning. It serves to measure the degree to which intended output (determined by the planning function) is being realised through

individual, group and organizational task behaviour. Management control refers to the various measures adopted to ensure that organizational goals are attained. Control is focused on physical resources (assets, materials), information (policies, client feedback), human resources (staff) and financial resources (cash, investments). The control process consists of the following steps:
- Determine the performance standards for identified tasks or jobs.
- Measure individual, group and organizational performance.
- Compare the measured performance to the determined standards.
- Evaluate results and if needed, modify objectives or action plan.

While the emphasis thus far has been devoted to the formal groups (chiefly task-focused groups) and informal groups that constitute the organization, mention must briefly be made of the beneficial role that therapeutic groups can exert on organizations. Many organizations employ a range of professionals (social workers, psychologists, nurses) commonly known as EAP (Employee Assistance Programme) staff to facilitate such groups. Examples are quality-of-work-life groups that attempt to improve social conditions in the workplace or groups that address a number of issues which influence employee performance such as alcoholism, drug addiction, child care, and recreation (Walker, 1988: 110). Various other groups address the stress and trauma that is often part of organizational life: death, retrenchment, retirement, rapid change and technological innovation.

Conclusion

Once individuals pool their efforts to achieve mutually agreed upon communal or group goals, an organization exists. The manner in which individuals perform will depend on the type of group in which they are, the design of their job, the organizational structure and the influence that leadership and management exerts.

Hannibal managed to get elephants across the Alps and man has landed on the moon. Organizations can achieve virtually anything once the power of group effort is harnessed. Understanding the dynamics of organizational groups and the role that management has in employing groups in the attainment of organizational goal attainment can therefore not be over emphasised.

Discussion questions

1 Why do organizations exist?
2 What is the influence of individual and group effort on organizational output?
3 How do organizational groups differ from therapeutic groups?
4 What are the different types and roles of organizational groups?
5 Identify management functions and their effect on group performance.
6 What is the influence of management and leadership on group motivation?

5 Group analysis and groupwork

Assie Gildenhuys

Learning objectives

By the end of this chapter you should be able to:

- Present group analysis as technique, providing a setting, and scientific attitude.
- Describe the development of the interpersonal and communicational network in groups.
- Discuss the role of the therapist as conductor, commentator and consultant.
- Identify a restrictive group quality and the related restorative action by the therapist.

Introduction

This chapter focuses on the theory and practice of **group analysis**, the framework of which radically departs from general group practice. The first section, 'Group analysis and the social context', builds the case for group analysis by outlining the social significance of groupwork and going on to offer a broader definition of the role of the group practitioner. This overview presents groupwork as a field within which group analysis has a clearly defined role to play. Group analysis as a model is then presented in detail, referring to theoretical shifts and adaptations to practice.

This chapter goes on to discuss the central constructs and their implications for conceptualising the small-group analytic therapeutic group. These constructs provide a framework for creating the group (formative aspects) and the position for interrogating group, intrapersonal, interpersonal, and transpersonal dynamics in the network of relations (Foulkes, 1982). Some of the guiding principles for broadening participation and communication in the group will also be discussed. Next, an overview of the group analytic framework will be given, identifying some commonalities with other practices but also highlighting technical differences relating to the stance of the leader and the remedial processes in the group.

This limited overview cannot give credence to the full extent of the practice of group analysis but will hopefully stimulate thinking in groups and find some relevance in training and supervision of groupwork.

Group analysis and the social context

Contemporary society in South Africa is in rapid social transformation and grappling with issues such as education, gender matters, socio-cultural and political concerns, all of which have relevance to the field of groupwork. Given the centrality of social issues in the lives of individuals, it follows that the concern of groupwork should not only focus on treatment but also on working with and improving interpersonal relations and social relations.

Recently, Swartz, Gibson and Gelman (2002) have argued strongly that psychodynamically informed practices can contribute significantly in addressing complex societal, and historically contextualised, mental health problems as seen in the South African context. Group analysis is such a practice in that it offers a therapeutic framework that gives prominence to the experiential world of the group, thereby responding to the social complexity in South Africa. The dual importance of the small group has implications firstly for treatment context and secondly for the social significance of the group.

In the South African context we are confronted with overwhelming demand reflected in the government's *Strategic Priorities for the National Health System, 2004–2009*. The government is aiming at making mental health care more accessible as well as addressing the specific health concerns like HIV/AIDS which further tax delivery of the professional services. Groupworkers need to address the remedial and delivery capacity by thinking in new ways. For example, focusing on practice and utilising new formats of training could help to adapt mental health programmes to accommodate local needs on the various community and service delivery levels. As well as addressing psychosocial concerns there is an important role for the small group in establishing, developing and maintaining social order and personal integrity.

The broadening role of the group practitioner   The role and function of the group practitioner extends further than the therapeutic function, as groupwork itself encompasses a wider frame of reference than the therapeutic setting. It involves attending to a 'symphony' of voices from different fields and dramatic events within the group that are related. The practitioner needs to formulate the relevance of the behaviour for the group in a dynamic way. Such a formulation can include some links to events in the group and the individual contributions, the history of the group, the external events, and the issues raised in relation to her role and the group's response to both the conductor and the set aims of the group.

Setting out evaluative principles

The group practitioner as therapist needs to get clarity on her role and identify the focus of her observation in the group. This involves identifying firstly the **stance** and secondly the **scope**. Stance refers to the manner in which the therapist engages with the group. This will be informed by a particular theoretical framework. Scope refers to the range of elements and phenomena that the group practitioner chooses to observe and conceptualise. It specifies the width, depth, and types of exchange that will be noted. In a therapeutic framework certain aspects need to be highlighted as a whole and not in isolation. These aspects are leadership, role, membership, the group-as-a-whole and sub-grouping, which are always dynamically interrelated in the running of a group.

Group practitioners participate best by being reflective and descriptive. Participation in groupwork is research-in-action. This requires not only an extension in the practitioner's role but also a widening of conceptual scope in addressing the layered social events embedded in the constitution of the group.

The following principles might be helpful in assessing and formulating the group practitioner's critical stance to obtain a coherent view of theory and practice. These criteria address the theoretical formulation and application of group analysis but also govern the process of critical assessment and comparison. The group analytic model attempts to:

- **Give a coherent system and a consistent frame of formulation:** This refers to how broad the constructs are and the integrity with which various theoretical contributions fit into the conceptual system and 'frame' or applied context of practice.
- **Map psychosocial development:** This indicates the critical developmental path of individual growth in relation to the 'other' in the socio-cultural context. This implies the normal social development having to cope with the ever-widening circle of people (other) – from the mother–infant pair to the citizen.
- **Apply and accommodate:** This implies the established practitioner's culture of verification or confirming of group phenomena and expansion of constructs and technique. Such a culture accommodates developing ideas and change.
- **Incorporate transportability:** Indicating the ease and clarity in transforming constructs into practice and use of clinical evidence from practice in order to refine and redefine constructs.
- **Be culturally attuned:** This refers to the degree that the therapeutic frame incorporates and integrates social and cultural contexts.

Why group analysis?

The group analytic approach was from its inception attuned to the social embeddedness of the individual. Problems were seen as not only personal but always conveyed the dilemmas of society at large. This important contribution has led to group analysis positioning the group within its immediate and wider social context.

In order for groupwork to achieve the level and type of theoretical formulation and practice relevant to the South African context, it is necessary to adopt a stance that accommodates both the observable events in the group but also relates these to the wider social context and personal group-associated history in as much as it becomes part of the mutually created history of the group in progress. It is here that group analysis has a part to play.

As a form of psychotherapy it applies concepts derived from various fields aiding the group to form a social learning environment. It utilises various levels of communication addressing not only the presenting problems but also the wider adaptation to social and cultural living. It provides a broadly based theoretical framework and group therapy model. The practitioner using group analysis is conscious of the social dynamics of the context and institutions. This could allow for the development of a remedial format which is free from social and institutional politics.

Group analysis offers a paradigm where the work in the group is offered to the group itself by gradually making the various experiences more accessible so that the group can participate in formulation and interpretation. In group analysis a radical new 'culture' is established, whereby members need to find their own 'voice' in the group. This means that the group practitioner does not make the visible problem within a group the focus but instead allows the group to develop a free-floating discussion in which a variety of themes can be offered and connected with by other members. Group members are encouraged and positively supported to acknowledge their own ability to participate and contribute to the growing culture of understanding and awareness. It allows the group to become a major contributor to its own capacity to formulate and integrate the various aspects of the common, shareable events. Gradually group members start to link this approach to their personal lives and social world and offer new ways in which group life can be made 'civilised'.

Who uses group analysis? Group analysis can be utilised by two sets of groupworkers. The first is the novice groupworker or student who starts to form a working model of the various approaches in therapeutic and remedial group application. The other is the more experienced practitioner who has encountered various group events that challenge common understanding and invite further investigation. These models guide the practitioner in setting up groups and assessing the leader's role in creating a supportive and remedial environment. For students the relevance lies more in the basic structural elements in running a group. The more experienced practitioner may be more concerned with the layers of events in the group and how to support the interactive flow between them.

Group analysis as a framework for learning and change

History of group analysis theory In general the formulation of new practice follows a radical shift in theory, facilitated by the work of innovative thinkers responding to specific life events. One such major shift in groupwork, group analysis, was made possible by 'a new scientific paradigm, that of the move from the study of the single entity, the item, the individual to the study of the relationship between an entity and the field of forces in which other entities are encountered' (Pines, 1981: 276). The founder of group analysis, S H Foulkes (1898–1976)[1], a psychoanalyst who emigrated from Germany to the United Kingdom in 1933, initiated a psychoanalytically informed group approach. His contribution was original, radical, and influential. He made the small group an instrument of scientific investigation (Foulkes, 1964b: 91). Not only did it initiate a new approach and way of thinking about small therapeutic groups but his work generated lively interest that lead to the establishment of the Group Analytic Practice (London) and an internationally acknowledged training programme at the Institute of Group Analysis in London.

Another invaluable outcome was the establishment of the journal *Group Analysis*, first published in 1967. This is the journal of The Group Analytic Society (London) which is an academic and professional body that offers a wider international forum for the exchange of ideas. They host scientific meetings and organize conferences and workshops in London and abroad. The journal provides articles allowing for continual international debate and refinement of theory and practice.

Contributing theoretical fields In group analysis diverse and rivalrous sets of meaning are tolerated. As a model it incorporates various other theoretical contributions as long as they are consistent with the basic framework. This allows for a vibrant growth (Pines & Hutchinson, 1993). Fields contributing are systems theory, object relations, self psychology and attachment theory (Brown, 1998b). The **psychoanalytic** premises of this framework underscore the unconscious, dynamic communicational and relational network

What is group analysis? Group analysis is a truly group-oriented view propagating a scientific study of group (Foulkes, 1964d). The group analytic frame brings the disturbance in the members' relationships to the fore and supports the gradual re-establishing of rewarding emotional ties. Foulkes describes it as a shift 'from the individual and the group to the individual in the group' (1964a: 58).

Group analysis extends the role of the therapist to consider socio-cultural, institutional and individual development in formulating an understanding of group events. The traditional role of the practitioner to determine and maintain the setting in the small therapeutic group is familiar. Foulkes shifted the focus from the individual to the relations in the group, including the therapist (Foulkes, 1964f) and the group as a whole. Foulkes described group analysis as 'psychotherapy by the group, of the group, including its conductor' (Skynner, 1984: 101).

Experience in the here-and-now is highlighted and analysed and can lead to re-establishing ties and relations. Members respond to the context through their interaction and relationships in a multiperson network. This reconnection of ties and relations spans time frames and is re-enacted in the here-and-now, making links and awareness to past relational contexts possible. These processes are all underpinned by the communication, and the capacity of the individual to convey the internalised meaning to others.

Establishing the therapeutic frame of group analysis

Therapeutic groupwork requires a specific learning environment; **therapeutic frame** implies more than the relationship as it includes the wider social pres-

entation like gender roles, sub-grouping, family development and current relations. The individual's development is always associated with belonging and
relating to others. Foulkes refers to this as the 'first basic problem of social life'
(Foulkes, 1964a: 58) indicating the relationship to others and the group-as-a-
whole (or the 'social fibre' of individuals' encounters with others).

Foulkes built his formulation on the dynamic therapeutic pair (which was
the initial frame that Freud created), and one in which the social reality was
somewhat excluded. The dynamic therapeutic pair refers to the standard practice of the analyst and patient comprising the therapeutic relationship.
Emphasis is placed on the reliving of the emotional conflict of past relations
reactivated in the free-associative flow of relating to the analyst referred to as
transference. Foulkes made the conceptual shift to include the 'other' stated as
the 'group of three' ('model of three', Foulkes, 1964c: 49), which became the
model of formulation. This therapeutic frame, by incorporating the entity of
the third into the relationship, acknowledges that the one-on-one relation
changes to one of being observed by a third that can provide a commentary on
the exchange of the other two. This model allowed not only an awareness of
the communication as process, but also a 'locating' of the disturbance. Any
group event can be understood within the total network of relations and communication. Using the Gestalt principle the event (foreground) becomes
understandable within the 'ground' of the configuration (background).
Configurations can be observed and operate within the whole (Foulkes, 1964e;
Foulkes, 1973).

The group is an 'active learning environment' not only of the individual and
his relations but how individuals respond to the social reality of the moment.
The group provides a stage for action, reaction and interaction. Within this psy-
cho-dramatic and socio-dramatic environment the inner integrative capacity of
the individual is being activated and reformed. Foulkes referred to this as 'ego
training in action' (Foulkes, 1964e: 82).

In the following section the various aspects relating to the therapeutic frame
will be expanded under the following headings: the total situation, levels of
communication, group as space, and holding and containing.

The total situation   Foulkes referred to the 'total situation' (1968: 443),
which suggests that the conductor observe the group development and communication as part of the individual development, the group's shared history
and the wider social context.[3] More specifically, the small group generates the
context in which the original patterns of the family context can be re-enacted
and made accessible for comment and interpretation.[4] Viewing group members
and the group itself as part of a wider social context constitutes a new therapeutic frame. Pines (1981: 275) describes the significance of Freud's contribution
by quoting Milner (1952): 'The frame marks off a different kind of reality that is
within it and that which is without it; it also marks off a special kind of reality
of a psychoanalytic situation, and in psychoanalysis it is the existence of this
frame which makes possible a full development of that kind of creative illusion
which we called the transference.'

The therapeutic frame creates a setting and defines the relationship between participants, to the whole and to the conductor. The therapeutic frame defines fore- and background in evaluating the prominence and 'clustering' of specific events. This takes into account the whole situation and how the constellations within the network can be viewed from various perspectives, i.e. from the foreground or background. Creating and maintaining this frame becomes the main therapeutic alliance. Group analysis allows the group to enlarge this frame to accommodate various levels of communication. [Refer to following section for a discussion on levels of communication.] Pines refers to the developmental aspect as the 'therapeutic society' (1991: 276) in which the individual becomes part of the 'movable changeable context' (De Maré, cited in Pines, 1998b). The group including the conductor sets its own frame of reference every time (Foulkes, 1964f).

How extensively is the frame enlarged? The following quote illustrates the difference between individual treatment and group treatment as regards how much the outside world brings to bear on the treatment: 'Group treatment is the resolve to take a larger part of the external world and of the persons associated into a field of direct observation than is the case with individual treatment' (Foulkes, 1964, cited in Pines, 1981: 276). Broadening the conceptual and observational field has theoretical and practical implications. In the group analytic setting the shared experience provides 'common sense', the sense of the community. Gradually the group develops the capacity to take more into consideration, to widen its own enquiry and develop an open stance to what Neri (1998) describes as the 'common field', which refers to the shared evolving reality of members' awareness in the group.

Arguably the frame offered by group analysis differs from the interactional frame normally operating in group therapy. In the interactional frame the primary emphasis is placed on the interpersonal learning in the here-and-now, and the significance of the immediate awareness generated between members. In comparison group analysis introduces an unfamiliar group structure in which a culture of open exchange and free-floating discussion (Foulkes, 1964a) is made the central focus. This process is verbal or non-verbal, conscious or unconscious. The group has limited structure and no given task, allowing for greater freedom to introduce material and relate to each other. This leads to the development of the group matrix.

Levels of communication   Foulkes (1964) distinguished between the **manifest** level and the **latent or primary** level. The first refers to the contemporary adult level of interaction and the latter to processes and mechanism that are primarily unconscious.

The latent level manifests in here-and-now participation that at times might seem uncommon, threatening and unintelligible. Allowing and supporting the effort by the group members to work with unfamiliar and painful realisations becomes the occupation of the group. Combining the gradual restoration of communication in the supportive group environment, members can reintegrate and own the defended and anxiety-provoking parts of their experience. This happens in collaboration with and in the presence of others, forming the working method of group analysis.

Communication can be viewed from four levels of events (Anthony, 1968). The first being the **current level** of reality that is observable by all the members. This includes the physical environment and social events of being together in a group The next is the **transferential level** where there is a link between the different individual's internal psychological organizations, referring to individual personality development founded in the family structure, manifest in the group relations. At this level organizational and representational features (such as one's perception of authority, sibling envy, or a sense of trust) are relayed from one system to another, between intrapsychic and interpersonal to the group-as-a-whole, between members and to the therapist. In general group therapy practice these two levels of events are attended to. The third level is the **projective level** where there is a movement of parts of members' intrapsychic systems (as parts of self; part-objects) and their relocation within the network of the group. This is where members unconsciously assign and respond to certain emotions and beliefs which they hold as belonging to other members in the group. The fourth is the **primordial-collective unconscious level** of communication. This presupposes the collective unconscious level that forms part of the social unconscious and was formulated by Jung.

The **matrix** is the term used by Foulkes to describe the communication and relational network developing in the group. Foulkes differentiated between the **dynamic matrix** and the **foundation matrix** (Foulkes, 1968). The first term refers to the network of relations that develops in the group, 'elements brought into the matrix by interactional, transpersonal processes during the life-span of the group' (Ahlin, 1985: 116). This is ever shifting and brings about a psychological organization, or framework of assumptions and expectations, which forms the backdrop against which the individuals rectify their perceptions. This is based on the working through of their transference relations and working on new ways of engaging and responding in the group. 'Just as the individual's mind is a complex of interacting processes (personal matrix), mental processes interact in the concert of the group (group matrix)' (Foulkes, 1973, cited in James, 1994: 68).

The foundation matrix is the shared bedrock of collaborative human social development. It refers to subconscious or preconscious elements such as cultural, ethnic and linguistic patterns and concepts (Ahlin, 1985). Ahlin summarises (1985: 117): 'The matrix, being the basis, atmosphere and main source of group behavior, also encompasses elements of primary human existential and cultural beliefs, concepts, fears and myths about men, women, society, life and death.'

The communicational and relational network (Neri, 1998) provides a multidirectional and multidimensional frame in which the shared history in group and personal relational histories are being held. This process of communication is central to group analytic work. Foulkes (1964f: 97; 1964e: 80) stresses that although the members might have much difficulty in communication it is the basic urge 'to relate' that upholds the group. Group members are encouraged to explore blockages in communication and this forms an important part of the therapeutic function of the group. Progressively a more flexible and adequate network of communication develops that allows for more subtle and increasingly complex patterns to emerge and be tolerated. This evolving therapeutic capacity of the group ensures greater permissiveness for more primitive and elementary sources of disturbance. These are associated with the pre-verbal period of development and are essentially related with the primary relation with the mother-object. Group analysis promotes the notion that each member of the group, and indeed the group as a whole, is endowed with therapeutic potential (Behr, 1990).

Group members are individuals who experience themselves isolated from meaningful encounters. They communicate their isolation through symptoms, which demonstrate their wanting to be attended to in an exclusive manner. The individual must develop ways in which the inner conflict can be 'translated' (Foulkes, 1964e: 81) into understandable language and this is a central part of the group's achievement. This translation holds the key for moving from the position of exclusion to inclusion. It is the group analytic equivalent of 'making the unconscious conscious'.

The members gradually learn to appreciate the potential of the open flow in the discussion allowing them to voice various emotional contents. These can start to be offered as the members become accustomed with the spontaneous, uncensored discussion. Feelings and attitudes towards others can be shared and are essential to the broadening clarification of the group. These are the learning opportunities, including learning about oneself and other.

Group as space   The individual cannot be conceptualised without the other and the group. In this sense the group always represents ' . . . both physical space and psychological space, and the circle is a space bounded by members of the group' (Pines, 1981: 279). The implication of this social and psychological space is that we need to develop models that can encompass a multi-bodies psychological formulation (Pines, 1975: 303). Group analysis emphasises the multi-body functioning in presence of others. This is the important move from the intra-psychic, to the pair (mothering pair) to the acknowledgement of the family and socio-cultural context which is where the individual gains a multi-bodies formulation).

The group-analytic circle holds the potential for development, which includes the sharing of experiences within the group. The open flow of communication and developing relations allows members to contribute in their unique ways. The interplay between the group providing the space and the member gradually redefining personal boundaries, leads to greater freedom for the group as a whole. The space that develops is neither only the subjective world of the member nor the objective reality but rather something in between (Schlachet, 1986: 40) and allows for cultural experience (James, 1994: 71). The primitive autistic symptoms (at that point not transferable into language) are being modified by the more advanced mental processes and become articulated in the interpersonal network of the group.

Holding and containing   The object relations perspective has emphasised the significance of the other and the notion of object seeking for survival, development and maturation (James, 1994). Various authors (Pines et al,

1993; Roberts, 1991; James, 1984) developed ideas around the 'holding' (Winnicott) and 'containing' (Bion) functions of both the group and the conductor. James (1994) shows how the holding represents the notion of the total situation whilst containment refers to the developing mental capacity of the group. These two functions are attributes of the group but the conductor plays a central role in maintaining these functions. Roberts (1991: 103) stresses the conductor's containing ability.

The group analytic practice

The analytic group setting outlined above will have an episodic life with varying themes related to dependency (on the group experienced by group members) and counterdependency (the phenomenon where group members behave as if the group is not important – to cope with the hurtful feelings that are evoked by being dependent) and maturation (but these can very easily be activated with change in the group's life, for instance a holiday break). One of the central tasks of the group is to encourage members to move away from dependence on leadership and authority and toward engaging with the group on their own terms in a more mature way. Foulkes outlines the 'group-analytic situation' (1964c: 50) as a face-to-face situation, with an informal structure which is not bound by set programmes. This structure is without usual censorship and members engage in free discussion. The group therapist reflects the open attitude by encouraging active participation. Initially the members find this format anxiety provoking but the group therapist should resist the dependency needs and defensive patterns.

The term used for the group therapist in group analysis is the **conductor** (Foulkes, 1964b; Kennard, Roberts & Winter, 1993) (discussed below). The conductor needs to be aware of the group-as-a-whole and how members respond to the group as an entity. The here-and-now referring to the face-to-face reality of the group does not only refer to the immediate and observable events in the group, but is intimately woven into the events outside the group.

Format of the group analytic therapy group   The group analytic therapy group is generally a slow-open, stranger group consisting of between seven and nine members that contract to attend the group for an extended period of time. Slow-open group refers to the practice of continuing the group by adding new members when others have completed or left for other reasons. In general practice, the members of the group do not know each other socially and are encouraged not to establish social ties during their attendance in the group. The group meets regularly and has clear rules confining communication among members in the group setting. The group without a clear task should not become too occupied with its own process (Foulkes, 1964c) but should share in free group association referred to as free-floating discussion ('free group association', Foulkes, 1982). Foulkes illustrates the idea of free-floating discussion with the example of strangers travelling together in a coach or train compartment and where the discussion will freely and loosely flow from one topic to another. In a group the associative link will bring together some shared reality but will also be individually based. Hopper (1984) gives an extensive case study relating how the group members of a well-established group discuss the exterior and interior of his practice but at the same time they all engage in thoughts about the conductor and their fantasy that he is in a very privileged position.

Psychosocial development Inhibiting forces, such as anxiety provoking and fearful expectations that members have about the group and specific group members are recognised in the group. Psychological development is a continuum of critical relational events, and primary emotional material stemming from previous significant relations in childhood and thereafter can be introduced in the group. These emotions are intense (like hatred or remorse about losses) and the participant might even fear that he or she or even the group will not be able to tolerate the intensity. Material shared can link to primary relations and contains intense anxiety. The introduction of object relations constructs provides a framework (Pines et al, 1993) in which we can understand the intensity and consequence of sharing primary emotional material. Introduction of the multi-bodied psychology to our thinking has allowed us to incorporate not only the internal structures and development but also the acknowledgement of the complex process of achieving a sense of self.

The therapeutic group offering little of the social constraints will certainly evoke intense emotive responses. These can manifest in ways that hamper the development of the group. Nitsun has introduced the 'anti-group' construct to show how the group can be inhibiting and not achieve the potential of open shared exploration. He has elaborated (1996) on the importance and dynamics of these counter-developmental aggressive forces towards the small group. He argues that inherent to the group experience are many fears and regressive forces embedded in the matrix of the group. The anti-group should be seen as a process and not an entity (Nitsun, 2000). These aspects should also become part of the group's experience as they contain the negative influences of the family and institutional realities. The phenomenology of the anti-group reveals the complex family-relations development. By acknowledging these forces, addressing their impact and accepting the fears underlying them can become an integrative potential for the group.

The conductor will aim at balancing the tension in the group. Although bringing to the fore intense 'uncommon' unconscious material impacts, it must be balanced by the group's increasing level of tolerance and acceptance based on its own strength. It is for this reason that the group therapist conveys inherent trust in the group in achieving the higher but more difficult level of functioning by relating to them in an adult manner.

The conductor:[2] Therapeutic leadership as practice

Group analysis requires conductors to uphold the analytic attitude of non-intrusive attunement in a supportive environment. Therapeutic leadership defines the relationship with the group and also incorporates the person of the conductor. The conductor creates the group and is aware of how the group becomes an object of transition and how the individual members will relate to him. The conductor becomes available to the group on the manifest and latent levels of participation. This awareness is essential to conduct and remain the instrument of the group; to be observing in the group and to reflect on the group between sessions.

Role of conductor   Let us now focus on the role and function of the conductor. The conductor creates a democratic relationship. He establishes the culture with the following attitude: 'He treats the group as adults on an equal level to his own and exerts an important influence by his own example' (Foulkes, 1964a: 57). Foulkes refers to this as 'not leading' (1964a: 56) using the term 'directing' or 'conducting'. The therapist does not assume active leadership but conducts the group. It is described as providing some 'leading' to the group but being available to assist the group in forging its own direction. The conductor's 'attitude of dynamic neutrality' (Foulkes, 1964c: 51) allows the dynamic matrix to be generated. It is in this respect that the notion of conducting becomes significant as it indicates the manner in which the conductor enables members to participate in leading the group and facilitating communication.

The group members need to find and voice their own position in relation to the conductor and these will alter depending on the mood, events, needs and content offered in the group. Interventions by the conductor will be directed at the group. Although such intervention might be directed to the individual, it will also be a communication giving multipersonal and multilayered commentary. Initially the role of the conductor is central (crescendo) and gradually becomes less prominent (decrescendo) (Foulkes, 1964a: 59).

The role is described as being reserved, observant and liberating. 'One could say that the conductor aims at a 'tolerable imbalance' between constructive and disruptive tendencies, or upsetting and supporting influences, and that he has continuously to assess their proportions (Foulkes, 1964a: 58). This is the **analytic attitude** (Foulkes, 1968).

Response of group   The group responds in a collusive and collective manner towards the conductor. This relates to what Foulkes had described as the latent level. It is the unconscious fantasy of the group that puts him in the position of the primordial leader who is omniscient and omnipotent. Foulkes does not see this as only part of family dynamics and therefore part of family transference relations, but primarily a redefining of the relationship to authority. The conductor activates and energises the underlying (latent) intent and helps in analysing the content and interpersonal implications. Foulkes calls this the 'second basic experience' as the adjustment of the relationship between the leader and the group (Foulkes, 1964a: 60).

The conductor accepts whatever position the group confers on her. It requires that she never actively assumes the position or acts within it, but does not deny it either. This allows the group to use her as an instrument of its own needs and allows group members to reintegrate the aspects projected. One of the best examples of this is the idealised view in which the group is seen only as a good and supportive experience with members centring their expectations primarily on the conductor to provide comfort and exclusive leadership. The conductor should take every caution not to respond to these expectations by not challenging the group's own abilities to engage and face the challenges of the new group. As a general rule it is very helpful to the group when the conductor gives and invites commentary about her role and members' perception of what significance this has for the group. Foulkes refers to this function as providing security and immunity that emanates from the conductor's authority (1964a: 61) and also provides the opportunity for him to abdicate any of these positions. This is the process of replacing the leader's authority by that of the group.

Dual functions of the conductor Pines and Hutchinson (1993: 39) describe the dual role of the conductor as being the **dynamic administrator** and the **analyst-interpreter**. The first function is related to the following aspects of the group: selection and maintenance of boundaries, upholding therapeutic norms of tolerance and nonjudgmental acceptance, provision of atmosphere of safety, support, containment, increasing participation and range of expression, and enhancing communication in articulate and shareable language. As the analyst-interpreter (1993: 41) the conductor 'makes the group the instrument of its own therapy'. The analyst-interpreter's concern is to make the group a working environment with members achieving much of this through their own effort. In a similar vein, Anthony talks about the 'tailman' leading from behind and allowing the group a sense of their own achievement (1991). Foulkes describes the conductor in this way as being' . . . the first servant of the group' (Foulkes, 1964b: 89).

Being aware of the manifest level of interaction at the same time as the latent level and helping the group to cope with both can be likened to listening to music on two wavelengths. To conduct is to identify themes, to recognise patterns, and to bring into play elements that contribute to the group process (Pines et al, 1993). The conductor maintains a participatory stance in the group and is open to and reflective of even the unfamiliar thought. These examples include situations where she might start to feel bored or distanced from the group. This material then becomes an alternative questioning perspective aiding the conductor herself but ultimately the group to face present difficulties. By acknowledging her own inner response the conductor becomes part of the communicational process and is then more able to transform the difficulty in the group process to become accessible and workable.

Group analysis: A model of transformation

This limited review of group analysis has given an indication of its contribution to groupwork practice. This model does not only focus on the individual and the problem addressed (personal gain) but by making the group central, a new type of 'temporary institution' for learning is established. It is seen as an instrument that facilitates the re-integrating of the individual into his relations and social systems.

Tables 5.1 and 5.2 give a synopsis of the framework applied to practice. Table

5.1 focuses on transformation and supports the idea that the group is inaugurated with a very specific stance in mind. Without the group analytic setting and guarding of the **group analytic attitude** the objectives will not be reached. The conductor's stance is described as 'contracting'; this refers to the respectful manner in which the conductor reminds the group of their own capability as well as the way in which the conductor is 'contracted' to achieving the group's objectives.

In sum, group analysis provides a multi-faceted view of the group. It focuses on the small group to which various theoretical models (one-, two- and three-person psychologies) may be applied (Pines, 1998a; Schlapobersky, 2000). The small group can also constitute the family group constellation. The group is also a transformational (learning) space. The members with the assistance of the conductor are able to observe and transform events, thoughts and feelings in the process of relating to each other, to the conductor and to the group-as-a-whole in the social context. The transformational space includes the conductor's response to the individuals, the members, and the group.

In Table 5.1 some aspects of the process of transformation are outlined. On the left-hand side key issues are presented. These have theoretical and practice implications. In the first column these key issues are defined as restrictive because they hinder psychosocial healing. The underlying idea is a developmental continuum. Implied is the potential for positive growth and integration.

The second column indicates an understanding of the psychological significance of group relations and interactions (psychology of connectedness, Nitsun, 2000). Although the table gives a limited overview of these themes it will be easy to extend the scope. This gives some direction of the manner in which the events can be defined in a broader manner to illustrate the difficult historical constellations (family, peer, and socio-cultural groupings) that each individual had to negotiate and has to revisit in the group context.

The third column refers to potential. It indicates the direction and shareable quality of the experience of re-engaging with the inhibiting aspects. It gives the group an analytical view on both the conditions and attributes that the group can develop when it is assisted by the conductor and by greater containment. Containment refers to the developing capacity in the group to become more reflective and integrative of the experiential reality in the group. This dimension provides the practitioner with the shared frame and helps to 'hold' the diverse and confusing material.

The fourth column portrays the specific stance of the conductor in the group analytic setting. 'Contracting' portrays a certain intention. The multi-levelled approach in attending to the group is implied. It should not be read as 'technique' but as the stance that will instill the culture of the group, in which communication and relations within the matrix will be supported. This emphasises the 'culture of interconnectedness' (Pines, 1991).

In Table 5.2 the group practitioner, the practitioner's contracted stance as given in the first table, can be refined further. The first column, depicting the conductor, is divided into role and function. Role refers to the formal aspects that relate to setting up the group and the professional status of being a therapist. The role of the conductor is expanded to include the commentary and

	Restrictive group qualities	Psychological significance	Restorative capacity	Contractual engagement and establishing culture
Key themes in the group analytic setting	Unconscious dynamics	System of events – levels of communication	Translation	Analytic attitude of the therapist Attention to constructive and destructive patterns and the wider social context and social unconscious
	'Model of three' Three-body psychology	From the individual to the pair to triangulation and the other in dialogue	Co-establishing meaning	Supportive and liberating; fostering culture of group's own capacity
	Psychology of the family group and the social life Original constellations	Complex relational dynamics Re-establishing ties Envy and rivalry and parental representation	Permissive and reflective transformation of emotional relations	Projective and transferential material
	Isolated autistic position	Restoring the original position	Engaging with the original context	Being attuned to the transitional space of the group
	Communicational network i.e. matrix	Relational network and group-as-a-whole	Gradually allowing more understandable communication and group becoming the agent of own achievement	Experientially based conviction of the group's restorable capacity to broaden communication by continual reflection on the process and levels of communication
	Clustering of group events	Series of discernible interconnected transactions	Attentive to content, process and structure	Analysis of content and process in inferred relation to any other, other to one and to the group as a whole
	Connectedness	Psychology of connectedness	Free-floating exchange	Maintenance of open flow by actively addressing constrictions
	Transformation in here-and-now	Ego training in action	Gradual regaining sense of self and others	Building culture of tolerance and encouragement of self-affirmation
	Leadership	Centrality and authority on primary level	Development of varied view of central person and development of personal and authority of the group	Development of own sense of established autonomy (crescendo and decrescendo)
	Anti-group	Tension between creative and destructive forces	Allowing dialogical interplay and acknowledgement of social and institutional interference	Countertransferential responses and acknowledgement of personal anti-group reactions
	Inhibited communication	Locating the disturbance	Analytic capacity, reflection, and translation	Affirming individual's and group's role in establishing links

Table 5.1 Model of transformation – from restriction to exploration

consultative function. The therapist views and participates in the group from various positions. In the table these functions are separately presented for illustrative purposes. The presentation illustrates how the interchangeable roles present the group with a variety of opportunities.

Commentary leads group members to formulate their own thoughts which are shared with the rest of the group. The commentary is intended to support this reflective capacity but also to strengthen the member's ability to offer his or her own comments. This is an engaging process in which comments generate new thoughts and loop back as tentative notions for the group to work with.

The third column shows how the conductor responds in the broader group analytic frame. The conductor attempts to make the wider social and institutional context accessible to thinking. Formulations can be critically scrutinised

		Conductor	Commentator	Consultant
Contracted engagement	**Role**	Dynamic administrator – Inauguration of the group	Engage participant Verbal and gestural engagement	Inquiry about the group in progress Inside-directed scientific stance
		Analyst interpreter	Inner reflection	Creating and utilising learning opportunities: supervisory, academic seminar discussion
	Function	Location of disturbance	Creating a contextual awareness Socio-cultural and social unconsciousness	Close scrutiny of both the 'institution', 'constellation', 'frame' and the 'group as object' in the cultural sphere
		Addressing blockage of communication	Offering contra-positions in establishing links and significance of emotive states and collective responses	Verification by the group through a process of group validation
		Drawing together	Questioning commonality and differences	Offering group wide and specific open-ended ideas
		Positioning within the constellations and relational matrix	Own countertransferential responses (sub-groupings themes and anti-group)	Availing oneself to both the group and the wider social context
		Binding together to form nexus	Interconnectedness and connectivity and connectedness	Being both revolutionary and non-prominent
		Affirming the group's capacity to develop their own understanding by creating links and establishing ties	Attuned to the group analytic setting	Being sensitive to the institutional and organization wide events impacting on the group
		Object of transference and projections	Group-specific factors Balance between integrative and analytic forces	Keeping an open mind for the dramatic flow of the group process
		Anti-group forces Active management	Containment and transformation	Reflective thinking on the inhibiting forces and tolerance for ambiguity

Table 5.2 The group practitioner

in the therapy group or during supervisor or academic discussion. By allowing the intent and the thoughts to become part of the frame the conductor can become a consultant to the group in progress but can also enrich a discussion on groupwork or institutional processes.

Facilitating change

The social significance of groupwork informs that it is not only used as a remedial environment but also offers diversity of learning about context and institutional life, as well as offering opportunity as research in action, for research opportunities. Group analytic thinking can contribute in training and supervision programmes. The model provides a framework that approaches training as a collaborative enterprise making the training context a developing matrix.

Groupwork can be introduced without an exclusive focus on skills training and formulating remedial goals or focusing on case management. Although all of these are critically important, scope will be allowed for the process and context of training within a specific institutional environment to become part of the training framework. All training institutions are tied to group processes that can be transformational or destructive (Nitsun, 2000).

Acknowledging the group-related experiences that shape one's view is an important first step in exploring alternative formulations. Participation is a here-and-now event but both the group and the individual have a developmental history that will show restrictive and restorative qualities. The group (including the conductor) can become aware of the constellations embedded within social development.

Another important area is the practice of experiential learning. It is accepted practice that groupworkers take part as members in groups. Although there are many pitfalls this practice is highly valued. Planning and setting up of such groups can benefit from these principles.

Extending the frame

The group analytic framework has also been developed and adopted to practices outside the domain of the small therapeutic group. De Maré (1989; 1991a; 1985) transformed the approach to apply it to larger groups. His work opened the possibility of making cultural experience accessible and allowed new work in the transcultural field (Hearst, 1993; Le Roy, 1994).

Institutions and organizational groups have been other areas of application. In these contexts group analysis enables the groupworker to make a contribution in understanding processes that seem to undermine organizational functioning through providing an evaluative and consultative framework (Nitsun, 1996, 1998).

Another interesting contemporary development is the application of ideas in analysing virtual group formations. Internet discussion groups as social phenomena and group presentations have become a new social presence (Weinberg, 2002; Davidson, 1998; Weinberg, 2001; Hynes, 2002). These practitioners are presenting pioneering ideas that may lead to new applications.

Gordon Lawrence (1998; 2000) has initiated an innovative application of groupwork. He developed a technique where members present dreams, with the assumption that groups develop a new way of relating in the dream matrix. This is generating further ideas and understanding of social complexity (James, 1994). Dreams have also been used in supervision (Hahn, 1994) and in group therapy (Neri, Pines & Friedman, 2002).

A group analytic stance has been adopted in therapeutic communities in the running of a whole therapeutic unit or hospital (Kennard, 1998). Much of what has been outlined in the model becomes part of the day-to-day running of affairs, allowing patients and staff an equal opportunity in establishing the therapeutic matrix and maintaining the frame.

Conclusion

The group analysis model has outlined the transition and psychosocial development in a group as well as the diverse positions of the conductor in establishing and maintaining the therapeutic frame.

In the wider context, the group analytic approach in groupwork can contribute substantially in normalising society. It can provide the opportunity for people to connect in a meaningful manner with their own inner tensions and become empowered to share and give opportunity for others to participate. In such a manner the alienating and isolating tendencies of our highly mobile, competitive and transitional society can gradually become addressed on a level that will re-establish emotional and relational ties. Group analytic work does not propose a set norm but allows participants to develop a more open system through communicating both their inhibiting and supportive relational awareness and therefore making it accessible to the group as a whole.

If group analysis as practice and intellectual tradition becomes part of the wider debate on change and social integration, it could be applied creatively in many contexts in South Africa. It can contribute, for example, to some pressing issues in our society, such as restoration of the family context, assisting in transcultural and social understanding and healing of individuals and communities. Social transformation, alienation and the process of societal change can be contemplated, and the value of creating new relational constellations using the small group format can be utilised.

Managed change by direct institutional or organizational intervention seems the order of the day but groupworkers need to maintain the reflective space. Many of these institutional programmes do not give enough support to participants who are often left disillusioned. The contribution of the group analytically oriented practitioner can be valued in practice, management, organizations and training.

In sum, group analysis can assist in developing a '**community-based restorative paradigm**'. Such a paradigm will focus on the total situation, acknowledge the complex developmental history and social injustices in this country, but will also move towards creating a containing frame. Such a paradigm will have to offer critical principles and allow the socio-cultural, political and economic domains to become part of the developmental programme. An open flow of communication should be the intention but full appreciation and a healthy respect for both constructive and disruptive forces should be upheld. Acknowledging the negative shared history and mistrust in groups that is part of our country's history, opens these issues and makes them part of the work of the group. We need to create an environment that is research in action and to translate the significance of understanding relations to the complex social context, and the wider field of human relations that includes society, culture and organizational realms.

Discussion questions

1 Formulate some ideas on the process of individual experience becoming accessible.
2 Formulate ideas on developing the capacity to share and communicate.
3 Foulkes had very high expectations of the group becoming a democratising environment. Is this opinion too optimistic?
4 How do you understand the inhibiting and destructive dynamics in small groups?
5 Group therapy should ultimately help the individual. Does group analysis in your opinion cater enough for this?

Endnotes

1. 1982; 1975c; 1976; 1975a; 1975b, 1964g; 1968; Foulkes & Anthony, 1973.
2. In group analytic thinking a distinction is made between the male and female functions. The group-as-a-whole represents the female holding function whilst Foulkes' discussion of the conductor centres on his own experience as male conductor. He defined a very specific type of leadership and the term conductor is gender-free. When he discusses leadership it will ring true for both male and female conductors. Referring to his works the male form of addressing will be maintained. In the general discussion I resort back to the female form.
3. The significance of this point has been conceptually expanded in the work of Hopper (1984; 1997) focusing on the social unconscious, De Maré (1985; 1989) large societal group context and Brown (1987) and Le Roy (1994) in the transcultural field.
4. Some very significant work has been done investigating this primary constellation (Skynner, 1986; Neri, 1998; Nitsun, 1994) and allowing for sibling relations (Brown, 1998a) to be acknowledged and reintegrated in the present context of the analytic group. Pines and Hutchinson refer to the 'corrective family group experience' (1993: 33).

6 Groupwork to facilitate empowerment in the context of HIV/AIDS

Sandra J Drower

Learning objectives

By the end of this chapter you should be able to:

- Outline the impact of HIV/AIDS in South Africa.
- Describe the needs of people affected by HIV/AIDS in South Africa.
- Explore how groupwork may be used in the context of HIV/AIDS.
- Identify the roles and intervention strategies which may be used by the group facilitator in the context of HIV/AIDS.
- Present a case example of how the group may be used to facilitate the empowerment of people affected by HIV/AIDS.

Introduction

It is no longer possible to live in South Africa and not be aware of the HIV/AIDS epidemic. The media provides extensive coverage on a range of HIV/AIDS-related issues including newspapers reporting the spread of the disease; debates on television and radio on its causes and effects; and magazines and billboards providing educational information. Increasing numbers of South Africans are confronting the personal experience of grief and loss through witnessing the deteriorating health and death of family members, friends and work colleagues. All areas of life are being intimately affected by the ravages of this disease.

Statistics On a global level, and according to the Human Development Report (United Nations Development Programme, 2002: 27), 'by the end of 2000 almost 22 million people had died of AIDS, 13 million children had lost their mothers or both parents to the disease and more than 40 million people were living with the HIV virus – 90% of them in developing countries, 75% in sub-Saharan Africa'. These are frightening figures indeed. But, what do they mean for South Africa?

South Africa forms part of sub-Saharan Africa and is a developing country. The estimated total population of South Africa in mid-2001 was 44 560 644

(Editors Inc., 2002: 16). At the same time it was estimated that 7 million South Africans were infected with HIV (Editors Inc., 2002: 53). The Human Development Report (United Nations Programme, 2002: 27) estimates that, as a result of the HIV/AIDS epidemic, life expectancy in South Africa will decline from 64 years to 45 years during the period 2000–2005.

Response to the epidemic A common response to the magnitude of the epidemic is to ignore the figures and hope that the problem will 'go away'. However, this is not a helpful reaction from people involved in human service delivery. It does not address the devastation which this disease is increasingly having on social, economic, and political life in South Africa. Groupwork is one of the methods used in human service delivery to facilitate people building their capacity and to becoming empowered to meet the challenges in their lives. Given that the HIV/AIDS epidemic is the central challenge facing South Africa today, it is important to explore the potential contribution of groupwork to addressing this challenge.

Destruction of societal groups Membership of 'groups' is a shared human experience. It is through the 'group' that the newborn is introduced into society and begins a process of socialisation into his/her cultural, religious and societal heritage. 'Groups' fulfil important functions in providing protection, meeting basic human survival needs, and identity formation. Throughout life they play a central role in meeting the individual's need for support, nurturance and a sense of belonging. For these reasons the various 'group' formations found in society, for example family groups, peer groups and community groups, may be regarded as the building blocks of society itself.

The HIV/AIDS epidemic is threatening these basic building blocks of South African society. The impact of the epidemic may be seen at the level of the family where poverty and the number of child-headed households increases with the illness and death of the breadwinner; at the level of the community, where traditional community support structures and coping mechanisms are placed under severe strain; and at the societal level, where the economy is disrupted through the illness and death of members of the most economically active population, and health and welfare systems are unable to meet the demand for services.

This chapter begins with a general description of HIV/AIDS as a life-threatening disease and then goes on to discuss HIV/AIDS in the South African context. Next, some of the implications of an HIV+ diagnosis for individuals and their families are explored. This section is followed by a discussion of the use of groupwork in the context of HIV/AIDS. Emphasis is placed on working with people's strengths, building capacity and facilitating people to empower themselves. An example of the use of groupwork to build capacity and facilitate empowerment amongst HIV+ people living in an informal settlement in Gauteng is presented. The chapter concludes with a summary which highlights central aspects of the contribution of groupwork in addressing the HIV/AIDS epidemic. Study questions are provided at the end of the chapter to assist with further study.

Overview of HIV/AIDS

What is HIV/AIDS?

'HIV' refers to Human Immunodeficiency Virus, which is the virus widely accepted as causing AIDS. 'AIDS' refers to Acquired Immunodeficiency Syndrome. Whiteside and Sunter (2000: 1) explain the term AIDS as follows:

- **A = Acquired.** This means that the virus is not spread through casual contact such as 'flu. In order to become infected with HIV an individual has to do something, for example have unprotected sex, or have something done to them, for example receive infected blood which exposes them to the virus.
- **I and D = Immunodeficiency.** The virus attacks the individual's immune system (the system which fights off infections) and makes it less capable of fighting infections, i.e. the immune system becomes deficient.
- **S = Syndrome.** AIDS is not just one disease. It presents itself as a number of diseases that arise as the immune system fails, for example tuberculosis and pneumonia, i.e. as a syndrome.

How is HIV transmitted?

Five main ways in which HIV is transmitted from one individual to another, and in order of importance, have been identified (Barnett & Whiteside, 2002: 38):

- Unsafe sex/unprotected vaginal or anal intercourse.
- Transmission from an HIV+ mother to her child.
- Use of infected blood or blood products.
- Intravenous drug use with contaminated (unsterilised) needles.
- Bodily contact involving open wounds.

Underlying each of these means of transmission is the exchange of bodily fluids, especially semen and blood, from an infected to a non-infected individual.

Course of HIV/AIDS

In order to exist Human Immunodeficiency Virus (HIV) has to enter a cell in the body and insert itself into the cell's DNA where it reproduces itself (Whiteside & Sunter, 2000: 2). The blood tests which are used to determine whether or not an individual has HIV detect the antibodies to the virus rather than HIV itself. If these antibodies are present the individual is diagnosed as HIV+. During the early stages of the infection, the antibodies may not be detected through routine blood tests. This time, between infection and the detection of HIV antibodies, is referred to as the 'window period'. However, the infected individual is infectious to others during this period and may experience a short period of illness. This period of illness is a result of a rapid multiplication of the virus and an equally rapid response from the body's immune system in which each attempts to destroy the other. In time the virus destroys the immune cells more quickly than they can reproduce themselves. As the immune system weakens new 'infections occur in increasing frequency, severity and duration until the person dies. It is the(se) opportunistic infections that cause the syndrome referred to as AIDS' (Whiteside & Sunter, 2000: 9).

Wide disparities in the length of the incubation period amongst infected people in the developed world as opposed to the developing world have been noted (Whiteside & Sunter, 2000: 9). In developed countries people live for at least 10 years before becoming ill and the normal period from the onset of AIDS until death is a further 12 to 24 months. In Africa, the incubation period has been estimated to be between six and eight years, and the period between the onset of AIDS until death, up to one year. A wide range of socio-economic factors contributes towards this situation. In South Africa these include high unemployment; gender inequality; poor education; prevalent substance abuse; crime and violence; and the historical legacy of centuries of colonialism and apartheid.

HIV/AIDS and the South African context

Why are South Africans particularly susceptible to HIV?

A number of reasons have been put forward to explain why South Africans seem to be especially susceptible to HIV infection. These include (LoveLife, 2000: 6):

- Established epidemics of other sexually transmitted diseases which act to increase the likelihood of transmission of HIV.
- Disrupted communal and family life to which apartheid, migrant labour, and poverty contributed.
- High mobility which has facilitated rapid movement of the virus in the southern African regions.
- Resistance, based on cultural and social norms, to the use of condoms.
- Gender inequality, in society in general and in heterosexual relationships in particular, which makes it difficult for women to protect themselves.
- Social norms, particularly amongst men, which accept or encourage large numbers of sexual partners.
- Social norms that do not permit open discussion of sexual matters, and thereby limit the sex education available to children and adolescents.

Government responses to HIV/AIDS

In 2000 the Department of Social Development (2000: 61) described HIV/AIDS as 'the single most important phenomenon that will shape future demographic and development trends in South Africa'. While it is thought that HIV was already in the country during the 1970s (Department of Social Development, 2000: 62), its rapid spread has occurred parallel to the development of South Africa's democracy. An immediate challenge for the first democratically elected government in 1994 was to put in place social and economic policies which would begin to address the mass poverty, and inequalities of income and access to resources, inherited from the past. Development of the skills, capacities, and resources of all of the people of South Africa, and the mobilisation of all sectors of South African society – economic, educational, health and welfare – to address these issues became the State's priority. It is against this background that the devastating consequences of HIV/AIDS should be viewed.

In its annual report for the period 1 April 2000 to 31 March 2001 the Department of Social Development (2001: 29) identified HIV/AIDS as one of its six priority areas for the period 2000/2001 to 2003/2004. In this regard three goals were noted:

- To lessen the social and economic impact of HIV/AIDS on vulnerable groups, i.e. women, youth and children.
- To contribute to reducing the occurrence of HIV/AIDS amongst vulnerable groups.
- To develop sound policies and programmes on HIV/AIDS through research and the use of information on population and development.

In order to identify how groupwork may be used within the context of HIV/AIDS in South Africa it is important to explore the relationship between the needs of people affected by HIV/AIDS and the qualities and characteristics of groupwork.

Implications of HIV+ diagnosis

The needs of people affected by HIV/AIDS

People in South Africa who are most vulnerable to infection with HIV are the poor, women, young adults, adolescents and children. HIV/AIDS aside, individuals belonging to each of these vulnerable groups are confronted with a range of distinct life tasks. For example, the poor confront the central task of daily survival with respect to food, shelter, clothing; women face the gender inequalities in society which today demand that they are both home-makers and active in the economy; young people are concerned with establishing new families and securing employment; adolescents attempt to establish an independent identity, often through a process of experimentation which may involve risk taking in sexual relationships and use of drugs; and, depending on their age, children meet a range of challenges during this period of the most rapid physical, emotional, intellectual, social and spiritual growth in the human life cycle. If these are some of the 'normal' challenges faced by people in society, what are the additional challenges which people living with HIV/AIDS may meet?

Psychosocial issues

Ross (2001: 21–26) identifies a number of psychosocial issues which arise for individuals and families living with HIV/AIDS:

Family structure   HIV/AIDS impacts on basic family structure. Many people no longer live in what used to be regarded as traditional family structures. Of increasing concern is the phenomenon of the child-headed household. This family rearrangement often means that the traditional functions of the family are no longer fulfilled.

Misunderstanding   There is often misunderstanding concerning the causes and course of HIV/AIDS. When an individual discloses his/her HIV status to family members he/she may receive a range of responses, including anger, rejection, fear, guilt and acceptance. The response received affects how the infected family member manages his/her HIV status. Guilt may be particularly acute when mother-to-child transmission of the virus has occurred.

Financial burden   There is a physical, psychological and financial burden in caring for a family member whose health status is deteriorating. This burden is often beyond the capacities of the family unit, especially when more than one family member is affected by the virus.

Stigma   A stigma is attached to HIV+ status should the individual choose to disclose his/her status. While stigmatising others may free some members of society from addressing the complexities of HIV/AIDS, for the stigmatised individual it may result in rejection, isolation and a decrease of support.

Discrimination   HIV+ people face discriminatory attitudes in the community, at school, in the workplace and in health and welfare services. Often these attitudes are due to ignorance and fear of the disease on the part of service providers.

Emotional responses   The course of HIV/AIDS and the inevitability of death evoke many negative emotions. Similar responses to those triggered by other terminal illnesses, for example cancer, may be experienced by providers of health and welfare services, and family members. Frustration, powerlessness, anger and depression are common emotional responses which serve to further drain the personal resources of those who are caring for individuals with HIV/AIDS.

In the face of the range of challenges presented by the HIV/AIDS epidemic there is a message of hope. With the development of effective antiretroviral therapies, people infected with HIV can expect to live for a longer period of time, and there is the possibility that AIDS may become a manageable disease (Whiteside & Sunter, 2000: 9). This suggests the need for an increased focus on enhancing the quality of life of people affected by HIV/AIDS.

Groupwork and HIV/AIDS

Functions of groupwork

Toseland and Rivas (2001: 12) define groupwork as:

> *goal directed activity with small groups of people aimed at meeting socio-emotional needs and accomplishing tasks. This activity is directed to individual members of a group and to the group as a whole within a system of service delivery.*

The following aspects of this definition are particularly relevant to a discussion of groupwork and HIV/AIDS:

Groupwork is purposeful It is not a haphazard gathering of people but rather a meeting of individuals who share a common concern, issue or experience which is the reason for them coming together. Group purposes within the context of HIV/AIDS may include:

- To provide support for people living with HIV/AIDS.
- To educate adolescents about safe sex practices.
- To facilitate the empowerment of women to negotiate their relationships with their partners.
- To raise awareness amongst men about the nature and course of HIV/AIDS.
- To increase the self-esteem, social integration and sense of control of people living with HIV/AIDS.
- To develop and strengthen community networks in the face of the HIV/AIDS epidemic.

Meeting individual needs Groupwork is directed toward meeting individual needs and accomplishing tasks. In the context of HIV/AIDS individual needs may include the need for support, information, and skills; tasks may include fund-raising for home-based care of people with AIDS, social action to increase access to resources of people affected by HIV/AIDS, and HIV/AIDS education for employers.

Group-as-a-whole Groupwork is concerned with the individual members of the group and the group-as-a-whole. Whether the group is directed towards meeting individual needs or accomplishing a particular task, the facilitator is always aware that the success of the group in meeting its purpose is related to the extent to which she mobilises the resources of individual members for the benefit of the group, and the extent to which the group as a whole meets the needs of individual members.

Service delivery Groupwork takes place within a context of service delivery. In South Africa the context of service delivery may vary considerably when the focus is on HIV/AIDS. For example, the context of service delivery may be an informal settlement, a church, a school, a recreation centre or a workplace.

Both the purpose of the group and the 'agency'/ 'organization' which renders the service, for example a health facility versus a faith-based organization, influence the context of service delivery.

Advantages of groups in the context of HIV/AIDS

Groupwork has a particular contribution to make in addressing the various challenges presented by HIV/AIDS. A number of groupwork theorists (Corey & Corey, 2002; Lee, 1994; Toseland & Rivas, 2001; Yalom, 1995) discuss the advantages of using the groupwork method to address individual and community needs. Amongst these advantages, and of particular relevance for groupwork and HIV/AIDS, are the following:

Groups challenge loneliness   Groups challenge the sense of isolation, separation and aloneness which is frequently experienced by those affected by HIV/AIDS. In addition groups provide immediate support, and a safe environment in which members can try out new ways of dealing with a range of situations in their lives. For people affected by HIV/AIDS such life situations may include disclosing HIV+ status to a partner, challenging discriminatory responses from community members, and negotiating condom use with a partner.

Sense of belonging   Groups provide a sense of belonging, may enhance self-esteem, and challenge feelings of powerlessness. For people affected by HIV/AIDS to live positive and full lives, it is important that their sense of worth is maintained and that they are provided with the knowledge and skills to challenge the sense of disempowerment which the course of the disease may precipitate.

Mutual aid   Groups provide an opportunity for members to help each other to form mutual aid systems. Mutual aid is a powerful means to raise self-esteem and overcome isolation. For both individuals and families affected by HIV/AIDS, particularly those in poorly serviced areas, a mutual aid system may become especially important outside of group meeting times, for example when crises occur.

Creating hope   Groups are powerful means for creating hope. In the context of HIV/AIDS a sense of hope is relevant for infected and non-infected people alike. Infected individuals are able to see first hand how others with the virus live productive lives and manage family and community responses to their status. For non-infected individuals, the group may be a powerful educational tool in challenging the stigma and myths associated with HIV/AIDS.

Social action   Groups with a social action focus are an important vehicle in facilitating the empowerment of individual group members. The Treatment Action Campaign (TAC) is an example of how infected and non-infected people have been able to work together to increase access to treatment options for the former. Through its activities it has facilitated the reclaiming of power of a marginalised and stigmatised section of the population.

Democratic ideal   Groups can be a powerful instrument in furthering the democratic ideal through emphasis on the democratic participation of all members. Again, this can be a powerful experience for group members who come from stigmatised and marginalised sectors of the population, for example those affected by HIV/AIDS.

While groupwork has many advantages in addressing the challenges of HIV/AIDS there is need for caution. The main disadvantage of the use of groups in this context concerns the issue of confidentiality. While the form it takes in different traditions may vary, in South Africa particular value is placed on the privacy of people. Indeed the right to privacy is enshrined in Article 14 of the Bill of Rights contained in the South African Constitution (Act No 108 of 1996). Most human service professionals in this country, for example, doctors, social workers and nurses, are bound by codes of ethics which, as one of their functions, set the parameters as to how professionals should manage the personal information to which they have access during their work. However, members of groupwork groups are not bound by the same ethic and as individuals may have very different ideas as to what is 'personal' information and how such 'personal' information should be handled. It is the responsibility of the facilitator to ensure that the boundaries of confidentiality are carefully negotiated with the group. In the context of HIV/AIDS and where knowledge of an individual's HIV status may have serious wider implications with respect to family relationships, work opportunities and community attitudes, this responsibility of the facilitator should never be underestimated.

Points of departure

The following five points form broad parameters from which an underlying orientation and intervention strategies for groupwork in the context of HIV/AIDS may be explored:

Causes and course   The facilitator should be fully informed about the causes and the course of the disease. This is crucial so as to ensure that myths about HIV/AIDS are challenged and that people affected by HIV/AIDS are encouraged to live their lives to the full.

Normal needs   The facilitator must be able to recognise and differentiate between the 'normal' needs of people living with HIV/AIDS, i.e. those shared with others at a particular life stage and living in a particular community, and those which directly result from the disease, for example treatment options, stigma and concerns relating to disclosure.

Legal status   The facilitator should be aware that people living with HIV/AIDS have the same rights to continued employment, social benefits, and privacy as all other members of society. Should these rights be infringed, the facilitator has an obligation to alert the appropriate authority accordingly.

No cure   The facilitator has the challenging task of supporting people affected by HIV/AIDS to face the realities of this disease and to maintain a sense of hope as they do so.

Stigma   The facilitator needs to acknowledge the stigma attached to HIV/AIDS and the broader implications of this stigma for the individual, family and community. In doing so the facilitator will need to explore his/her own fears and misconceptions about the disease.

Underlying orientation

The nature of HIV/AIDS as a life-threatening disease, the implications of this diagnosis for individuals and families, societal responses to HIV/AIDS, and the developing nature of South Africa suggest an orientation to groupwork in the context of this disease which is informed by:
- the strengths perspective;
- empowerment practice; and,
- capacity building and human resource development.

The strengths perspective   The strengths perspective has been described as:
> *'an orientation in social work and other professional practices that emphasises the client's resources, capabilities, support systems, and motivation to meet challenges and overcome adversity. This approach does not ignore the existence of social problems, individual disease, or family dysfunction; it emphasises the client's assets that are used to achieve and maintain individual and social well-being'.*
>
> (Barker, 1999: 468)

In the context of HIV/AIDS the strengths perspective requires that the group facilitator identifies the personal resources which individual members bring to the group, and is able to mobilise these for the benefit of individual members and the group as a whole.

In working from the strengths perspective it is helpful for the group facilitator to keep in mind six underlying assumptions of this orientation (Saleebey, 1992a: 5–7):
- People's strengths should be respected.
- People have many strengths.
- Motivation is based on strengthening people's strengths.
- The facilitator is a collaborator in the helping process.
- People who ask for/need/receive help are not victims.
- All environments are full of resources.

The strengths perspective is well suited to address the issue of HIV/AIDS in South Africa. Lack of material resources, limited formal services and in many areas poor infrastructure suggest that the primary resources available are people themselves. The strengths perspective demands that the 'helper' has a firm belief in the capabilities of individuals, groups and families (Saleebey, 1992b: 41), and is able to recognise and harness these human resources.

Empowerment practice   'Empowerment' is a concept central to the strengths perspective. It has been defined as:

> *'the process of helping individuals, families, groups and communities increase their personal, interpersonal, socioeconomic, and political strength and develop influence toward improving their circumstances'.*
> (Barker, 1999: 153)

In empowerment practice the 'helper' does not 'hand over' power but facilitates people to claim their own power. 'Real power is not gained through delegation' (Adams, 1990: 125).

Either through their medical status or by association, people affected by HIV/AIDS are members of a stigmatised group. People who are stigmatised are 'related to in a way that disempowers, excludes, and controls them' (Gibson et al, 2002: 42) . In other words they are marginalised. Marginalisation and exclusion of people affected by HIV/AIDS has taken many forms, for example avoidance of contact with people known to be HIV+, denial of places in schools for children who are HIV+, and blaming HIV+ people for their status. While the South African Constitution is clear as to the legal status and rights of people with HIV/AIDS, fear and ignorance often leads to these rights not becoming reality. When an individual with HIV/AIDS is poor, i.e. is a member of another marginalised and stigmatised group, their isolation and exclusion is compounded.

Lee (1994: 13) identifies three interlocking dimensions of empowerment which inform practice from this perspective:

- The development of a more positive sense of self and belief in one's own power.
- The gaining and development of knowledge and the ability to critically understand the various social and political realities that impact on one's situation.
- The development of resources and strategies, and competence for meeting both individual and group goals.

Similarily, Gutierrez (1990: 150) emphasises increasing self-efficacy, developing group consciousness, reducing self-blame and assuming self-responsibility as critical to facilitating the empowerment of people.

For people affected by HIV/AIDS these dimensions suggest that the group facilitator working from an empowerment perspective should:

- Utilise intervention strategies that build self-esteem and a positive sense of self-worth, and facilitate members' ability to gain control over their lives.
- Be mindful of how the 'professional' role may serve to disempower members.
- Be comfortable with sharing, and letting go of, the power vested in the 'professional'.
- Provide information and educational material that challenges members' previous perceptions of themselves and the world around them, and facilitates them to think critically about circumstances which have contributed to their present situation.

- Identify resources within individual members and their communities which may be mobilised to address the issue at hand.

Building capacity and human resource development   The White Paper for Social Welfare, published in 1997 by the Ministry for Welfare and Population Development, describes 'the development of human capacity and self-reliance' (Ministry for Welfare and Population Development, 1997: 15) as part of its vision for a new welfare system. Building capacity and developing self-reliance are concerns of both the strengths perspective and empowerment practice, and in groupwork involve the facilitator in similar activities, for example:
- Challenging the group to identify the strengths and resources of its members and their community.
- Facilitating the group's access to information and their sharing of knowledge and ideas about the issues at hand.
- Co-ordinating group activities and the information members have gathered.
- Linking members with key resources and facilitating their skill in accessing these.

Intervention strategies, techniques, and skills

'Strategies' are 'carefully designed and implemented procedures an individual or group uses to bring about long-term changes in another individual or group' (Barker, 1999: 467). Techniques are 'the knowledge-based skills, methods, and procedures purposefully used to achieve explicit goals' (Barker, 1999: 482). A group approach which emphasises strengths, builds capacity, facilitates empowerment, and has as its ultimate goal the reclaiming of members' sense of control over their life events, demands that a particular stance is adopted by the facilitator and that particular strategies and techniques are used.

Strategies   Groups are the optimum medium for empowerment. However, 'the empowering potentialities of the group are only realised by the (facilitator's) skill in defining empowerment as group purpose, challenging obstacles to (the) work, and enhancing (the) group processes that develop the group's power as a group' (Lee, 1994: 209). Here two strategies of the facilitator are pertinent:
- She must regard the group members as the experts in their world, must be comfortable about learning from group members, and must be able to relinquish the role of 'expert'. Ultimately she must be comfortable with the group assuming its own leadership. Unless the facilitator is herself living with HIV/AIDS she does not know the day-to-day emotional, physical, social, and spiritual challenges of doing so. Her intervention should provide members with the opportunity to develop skills and capacities which serve them after her termination with the group.
- She must firmly believe in the existence of strengths and resources in each individual group member and the potential for the group as a whole to mobilise these resources to address shared concerns. This approach

requires that the facilitator moves from a position which emphases 'deficits' to one which emphases 'resources'. Without denying the unique needs and concerns that an HIV+ diagnosis presents for individuals, families, and communities, affected individuals share the same sources of stress and joy as the rest of the population. Empowerment practice challenges the facilitator to bridge the gap between similarity and unique.

Techniques   Lee (1994: 29) underlines the notion of partnership between the facilitator and the group members by identifying a number of empowering roles which the former may assume.

She emphasises that these invariably make use of the prefix co-, for example 'co-teacher', 'co-investigator', 'co-builder', 'co-activist' and 'co-worker' (Lee, 1994: 29). The facilitator purposefully places her strengths, knowledge, skills and perspectives alongside those of other group members. In this way she validates members' experiences and resources, aligns herself with their concerns, and adds strength to the group. The facilitator serves as an 'ally' within the group of which she is an integral part.

The function of the facilitator is to support the development of group identity, through emphasising commonality and encouraging inter-member communication. The group becomes a mutual aid system in which members are facilitated to lend their resources and strengths to each other. Problem-solving and decision-making become shared learning experiences. The group as a whole and its individual members are both the means to and the ends of growth and change. Empowering group practice requires that the facilitator helps the group to increasingly develop its autonomy until her presence is no longer needed (Lee, 1994: 209).

Skills   Many of the skills utilised by the facilitator are generic to all practice with groups and are discussed by various groupwork theorists (for example, Garvin, 1996; Middleman & Wood, 1990; Northen, 1988; Shulman, 1999). However, four groups of helping processes and skills, with special significance for empowerment group practice, are identifiable (Lee, 1994: 32–37). These empowering skills have the following functions:

- To bolster motivation, for example gaining resources, attending to presenting problems, accepting the member's definition of the problem, facilitating the member to name and own personal strengths; enlisting the members' energy in changing events.
- To maintain psychic comfort and self-esteem, for example externalising sources of oppression, facilitating members to share and validate each other's experiences, reducing self-blame by focusing the member outward.
- To enhance problem-solving and to promote self-direction, for example facilitating the group to brainstorm alternatives, co-teaching/sharing possible solutions, challenging members' strengths and creativity, maintaining equality in the problem-solving process, and sharing information.
- To promote social change, for example making a clear, mutual contract that bridges the personal and the political and includes a social change focus, establishing the common ground and common cause among members, and reaching for each member's maximum participation in the process.

The Young Adults' Group

The following case study provides an example of a groupwork service which was informed by the strengths perspective and which aimed to facilitate the empowerment and build capacity of group members in the context of HIV/AIDS. It alerts the group facilitator to three issues for practice in this context:

- making flexible use of the group in meeting human needs;
- consciousness of the inter-dependence of the group and the environment; and,
- balancing hope and fear in the face of seemingly overwhelming challenges.

Setting of the group

The group was held under the auspices of a community-based, non-profit organization which aims to support people living with HIV/AIDS, their families and their caregivers. The underlying philosophy of this organization is that all South Africans are affected by HIV/AIDS and that everyone has a contribution to make in addressing the epidemic. It facilitates people to develop their own skills to meet the challenge of HIV/AIDS, and does so by supporting people with HIV/AIDS; providing training and support for caregivers; providing material care; and, facilitating the development of income-generating projects.

The group took place in an informal settlement approximately 25 kilometres south of Johannesburg. This community is poverty stricken, has a high unemployment rate and little formal infrastructure. Its main social problems are child abuse, child prostitution, substance abuse, rape, and, increasing numbers of child-headed households. The group met in one of the two churches located in the area. In close proximity was another church, a school, a crèche, a clinic and some shops. These constitute the formal local resources. Group membership was drawn from the local clinic which is run on a daily basis by five nursing staff and volunteers from the local community who assist with the distribution of medication to tuberculosis patients. Approximately 80% of the people attending the clinic are HIV+.

Community members' lack of confidence in the extent of confidentiality at the clinic, and their fear of rejection and isolation should their HIV status become known, were concerns of the clinic which were noted by the facilitator prior to group formation. Lack of open discussion meant that the unique needs of those affected by HIV/AIDS were not addressed, and that education of the broader community was curtailed. In turn, psychological isolation and a sense of marginalisation amongst those affected increased.

The origin and purposes of the group

After a failed attempt to initiate a support group for HIV+ people who were attending the clinic – none of the patients wanted to be associated with such a group – the facilitator initiated a community meeting to gauge whether or not community members, both HIV+ and HIV-, were interested in establishing an income-generating project to assist people living with HIV/AIDS. Eleven volunteers from the clinic committed themselves to this project and formed a task group to explore income-generating activities. The task group identified three priorities for its work:

- Starting a food garden at the clinic to ensure nutritious food for people affected by HIV/AIDS.
- Developing an income-generation project to support the food garden.
- Organizing an awareness campaign for the community with a special focus

on substance abuse, teenage preg-
nancy and HIV/AIDS.

The project was based on the belief that
by helping community members to take
action in the face of a seemingly overwhelming challenge, their sense of self-
worth and control would be increased,
and they would be empowered to take
further action, on their own behalf and
that of others.

After a number of meetings of the task
group, the community work project had
started to progress, and its members
expressed the need to have a separate
group in which they could learn more
about HIV/AIDS and be encouraged to
give each other support in the face of the
epidemic. As the initiator of the income-
generation project and the only social
worker in the area this presented a dilemma for the facilitator. How could she be
the facilitator for the income-generation
project and of an HIV support/education
group simultaneously when membership
of the two groups overlapped? To clarify
the needs of the group, and the expectations of potential members, the facilitator
conducted individual interviews with
potential members. Common themes
emerged. All of the potential members
had been personally affected by HIV/AIDS,
all wanted to gain greater knowledge
about the disease, and all wished to gain
support from others in their community in
order to be equipped better to meet the
challenges presented by the disease.
However, none wished to share their HIV
status with members of a group. The facilitator identified two tentative aims for the
group from these meetings:

- **Education:** To facilitate the dissemina-
  tion of knowledge and increase understanding of HIV/AIDS; and, to develop
  skills and facilitate the empowerment
  of group members in responding to
  the impact of HIV/AIDS on themselves,

their families and their community.
- **Support:** To provide support and to
  develop a mutual aid system in the
  group through members exploring
  their own fears of HIV/AIDS; and, to
  identify different ways of coping with
  the challenges presented by HIV/AIDS.

The group process
The group comprised nine members – two
men and seven women. All were members
of the income-generation task group. Their
ages ranged form 23 years to 45 years. The
group met for 10 sessions, each session of
two hours' duration, over a six-month period. All of the members of the group had
first-hand experience of HIV/AIDS – five
knew they were HIV+ and the remaining
four had witnessed the deaths from AIDS
of immediate family members. At the com-
mencement of the group these details
were known only to the facilitator. The
group members were among the same
community members who had declined to
become part of a group which openly
identified itself as an HIV/AIDS support
group. Thus, the group presented here as a
case study became known as the Young
Adults' Group.

Sessions 1 & 2
Themes of the first two meetings focused
on defining the boundaries of the group
through a group contract, developing trust
in the group, and sharing knowledge and
information on HIV/AIDS. Lack of trust
and ambivalence about sharing were
raised at the beginning of both sessions.
Explaining why she wanted to be in the
group one member in Session 1 said: 'I
have a particular reason why I am in this
group and I know that in time I'll be able
to share it. L (the facilitator) knows why,
but I prefer that she does not let anyone
know. I feel I should be the one to tell.'
Similarly Session 2 began with another
member reaffirming the value of confi-

dentiality: 'I want to say that what we discuss in this group should not go out of this meeting. It should end here in this room.' All agreed. The need for members to share their existing knowledge of HIV/AIDS was raised in the first session as one of the members openly wept about the death of his brother from AIDS and expressed confusion about 'what this illness does'. Sharing information about HIV/AIDS was pursued further in Session 2 when the facilitator encouraged members to talk about their understanding of the disease and to help each other to fill in gaps in their knowledge. During this discussion members acknowledged that they had never spoken to their children about sex or HIV/AIDS and agreed that their immediate task should be to share the new knowledge they had gained in this session with their children. They decided to tell each other how they had managed with this task at the next meeting of the group.

Sessions 3 & 4
Sharing of the experiences members had had in discussing sex and HIV/AIDS with their children brought a number of issues to the fore in Session 3. Members felt very uncomfortable discussing the issues with their children, they were disturbed that they had not been able to answer all of the questions which their children had asked, and they felt 'bad' that their children were so ignorant about the issues. During this discussion two members disclosed their HIV status to the group. They said that while it had been hard to do so they had felt that their children should know their status. They felt strongly that without this knowledge their children would not be able to learn to accept 'their situation'. The group agreed that they needed to find ways of telling their children about their status in order to prepare them for the future. At the same

time they thought that, as community members, they should be engaged in preventive action, particularly amongst schoolchildren. The fourth group meeting explored what the group might do by way of prevention amongst schoolchildren. The group explored the idea of an HIV/AIDS Awareness Day at the local school. Members became energised and enthusiastic as they started to identify the various tasks which could be involved in such an exercise. The first absences from the group occurred in Session 4 – one of the members, Thandi, was ill, while another had to look after her sick child. At the end of the meeting the group decided to visit Thandi.

Sessions 5 & 6
The fifth group session began with the group talking about the health status of Thandi. One of the members said: 'I do not think she will be able to come back to the group.' This opened up a discussion of members' own fears about dying and death, and the future care of their children. The immobilisation this caused was challenged by one of the group members who emphasised the need for them 'to do something' and 'not forget' about their plan to organize an HIV/AIDS awareness day at the school. Once again the group became energised as members reviewed their previous ideas and began to share amongst themselves the different tasks involved. Concern with Thandi's health was expressed again in Session 6 when members discussed their experiences of their visits to her home. Dying and death remained group themes and members voiced their sense of hopelessness and helplessness in the face of the HIV/AIDS epidemic. Here the facilitator reminded the group that the HIV/AIDS Awareness Day which they were planning demonstrated their wish to take action. This helped to refocus the group's attention.

During Session 6 the facilitator raised the issue of her own termination with the group after another four sessions. Members were distressed at this prospect and said that they would then 'no longer be able to serve the community'. The facilitator pointed out the extent to which they were already working independently both in and outside of meeting times and that she believed that they would be able to continue with these initiatives after she had terminated with the group.

Sessions 7 & 8

Termination was the main theme in Session 7 with members expressing sadness and loss. While acknowledging their feelings, the facilitator encouraged members to continue with their projects after she had left the agency. This challenge was taken up by two group members who emphasised the need for the group to make things happen on their own – 'unless we do something no one will'. The discussion then turned to planning for the HIV/AIDS Awareness Day. Similar themes were pursued in Session 8 which opened with members reporting back on their visits to Thandi and voicing concern as to who would look after her children when she died. The group agreed that the last group session should be held at Thandi's home. Powerlessness was challenged by group members as they reported back on the progress of the planning for the HIV/AIDS Awareness Day. Again, the termination of the facilitator was discussed. However, this time it was raised by the group, and members explored the need to expand group membership in order to share the skills they had learnt with other community members, and to ensure that the initiatives the group had started continued.

Sessions 9 & 10

Session 9 was concerned with finalising the activities and responsibilities for the HIV/AIDS Awareness Day and the arrangements for the group's termination party at Thandi's home. Members were confident about managing the HIV/AIDS Awareness Day. All had been involved at some level in organizing the event and all expressed their sense of achievement. This confidence also emerged in discussing the termination of the facilitator. While the group expressed sadness that she would no longer be part of the group, they said that they now knew about other resources in the community which they could use with their projects, and that they were now much more skilled and confident about doing so. Session 10 was held at Thandi's home. After reviewing the success of the HIV/AIDS Awareness Day, but before party celebrations began, the group constructed a group memory box. Each member put their thoughts about how they would like to be remembered by their family and friends on paper and then placed them in the box. Some members cried quietly as they did so. The members supported each other in this process and, with the facilitator, shared their sadness at 'endings'. The group decided that the memory box should be placed on the clinic's reception desk, and that it should be decorated with red ribbon as a way of raising the consciousness of people about HIV/AIDS. While termination was a recurrent theme, the group expressed confidence in members' capacity to continue with their various projects. As one member noted: 'the group is terminating but not the friendships or the projects'.

Summary

Groups are a natural part of human life. It is through various kinds of groups that human needs are met. Groupwork, as an approach to helping people solve their own and their community's problems, and as a means to developing their own and their community's strengths, is well suited to address the wide range of challenges arising from the HIV/AIDS epidemic. This chapter has provided an overview of the use of groupwork in response to HIV/AIDS in South Africa as a developing country. Explanations of the cause and the course of HIV/AIDS as a life-threatening disease were outlined and its human, social and economic implications described. The threat that this disease poses for the broad development of the country, and indeed the whole southern African region, should not be underestimated. HIV/AIDS is an issue which deserves the attention and concern of all South Africans.

Groupwork may be used to provide support for and to develop mutual aid among people affected by HIV/AIDS; to raise consciousness of people about this disease, emphasising that it is an issue which warrants the attention of all concerned community members; to challenge the stigma and stereotypes associated with the disease; and to facilitate empowerment of individuals and communities in addressing the impact of the epidemic on individuals and communities. However, to be able to use groupwork for these purposes the facilitator must adopt a unique stance towards the group with which she is engaged. In particular, she must have a firm belief in each member's innate strengths as well as the strengths of the group as a unique entity; she must be mindful of her role as facilitator of the members' and the group's empowerment of themselves as opposed to being the delegator of power to the group and its members; and she must be open to learning from the group.

The case study described in this chapter raised some of the issues which the facilitator of a group with a special focus on HIV/AIDS should bear in mind. These included:

- Confidentiality as central to defining the boundaries of the group, demonstrating respect for members, and allowing members to be in control of the process of self-disclosure.
- Self-reflection on the part of the facilitator in order to work constructively with an issue which triggers considerable emotional pain, and makes heavy demands for acceptance and non-judgementalism.
- Pacing the work of the group in order to ensure that the needs of individual members and those of the group as a whole are met.
- Balancing hope and fear by acknowledging the reality of HIV/AIDS as a life-threatening disease, but also the potential for people to take collective action in efforts to address this reality.
- Mutual aid as a means to facilitate empowerment and mobilise human resources in the face of the challenges presented by HIV/AIDS.
- Flexible use of the group and the role of the facilitator in acknowledging that groups which have a contribution to make in addressing HIV/AIDS may have varied origins and locations.

HIV/AIDS is an emotionally laden issue. It may lead to defensiveness, blame, denial, avoidance, helplessness and immobility. This chapter has attempted to illustrate that HIV/AIDS is not only an issue which leads to enormous human anguish and suffering but also one whose management challenges the potential for united human action. Groupwork as a method of helping is well placed to respond to this challenge.

Discussion questions

1 What do you believe are the principles which should guide the facilitator in running groups with people living with HIV/AIDS?
2 This chapter has identified some of the uses of groups within the context of the HIV/AIDS epidemic in South Africa. What other ways do you think may be used to address the wide-ranging impact of this disease?
3 Identify the qualities of the group which have special relevance for work in the context of HIV/AIDS.
4 What do you understand by the concept 'empowerment'? What implications does empowerment practice have for the role of the facilitator of a group which focuses on the needs of people affected by HIV/AIDS?
5 This chapter describes a groupwork service which developed through a community work project, with both initiatives running concurrently. What are the implications of such a situation for the group members and for the role of the group facilitator?

7 Group therapy with young adolescents

W de Jager, Ben Truter

Learning objectives

By the end of this chapter you should be able to:

- Outline the psychodynamic approach in group therapy and the limitations of its application with children and adolescents.
- Explain the impact of the psychodynamic model on the adolescent group.
- Describe the structure and stance group therapists need to adopt in order to assist adolescents in working through their presenting issues.

Introduction

Childhood as a distinct phase In a similar way that groupwork is an effective and valid method of helping and treating adults, it can also be used with those individuals struggling through the initial dilemmas of adolescence. During the previous century childhood became a more distinct and valued life phase, a highly differentiated period that became a major area of study that evolved into a sophisticated science (Santhrock, 1998). Adolescence became a life stage separate from childhood. However, fundamental changes were occurring in what it means to be a child or adolescent during the last two decades of the 20th century. On the one hand, the influence of outcomes-based educational paradigms, the impact of the media, the mass availability of electronic communication devices, the ethos of consumerism, the role of rights-based child laws and the changes in family structure have lead some to speculate that we are living in an era where the boundaries between adulthood and childhood have become less categorical and that childhood will cease to be a recognisable entity (see the work of Postman, 1983). Conversely, the refinement and delineation of theories, models, and revisions that are a consequence of research into all aspects of child development have lead to an acknowledgement that the broad categories of both childhood and adolescence need to be understood as complex and that clear sub-phases exist for both (Remschmidt, 2001). For adolescence, the psychosocial task of forming an identity has received much attention since its initial description by Erikson (1968). However, it is now generally acknowledged that the developmental tasks of the pre-, young and older adolescent differ from each other. The implications of the struggle of the younger adolescent, and the consequences this has for groupwork with this age group, is the focus of this chapter.

Group therapy and adolescent identity   As adolescents begin the process of identity formation by disengagement from parents and from internalised parental images, the peer group becomes more important, acting both as container of the resultant anxiety and as stage upon which future roles can be experimented with. The Zulu saying 'we are, therefore I am', which is an expression of the African worldview of collectivism, also expresses the concept that identity is a result of our belonging to a group. In light of this knowledge, group therapy, which allows for and uses peer group identification, has become the treatment of choice for pre- and young adolescents (Rachman, 1975). Group therapy is particularly relevant in the South African context, where the process of the 'self becoming' has to occur against the background of a society devastated by its past, traumatised by the unleashed consequences of change, and wracked by the ravages of poverty and AIDS. It is important for our youth to connect and belong.

In the following section, literature on group therapy with children and adolescents is reviewed. The chapter goes on to discuss the impact of the **psychodynamic** model on adolescent groups. This model concentrates on intrapsychic processes, focusing on the tensions between conscious and unconscious motivations and current relationships (Robertson, Allwood & Gagiano, 2001). The psychodynamic approach is then reappraised and suggestions are made for modifying its application to adolescent groups. Finally a case study is presented which illustrates the particular problems which adolescents present to the group therapy encounter as well as the limitations of the psychodynamic response previously mentioned. The chapter ends with conclusions pertaining to modifications in the psychodynamic approach, drawn from the events of the case study.

Review of literature on child and adolescent group therapy

History of group therapy with children

Therapeutic group treatment with children dates back almost 70 years. Many different terms have been used to describe this work, such as 'training', 'work' and 'therapy'. So how do we distinguish between all of these terms? An overview of relevant literature through the century reveals that group psychotherapy generally refers to interventions that are geared towards heightening the child's emotions and self-awareness in order to effect psychological and behavioural changes – a noble intent. Despite the breadth of this definition, it

provides a crucial clue as to how 'group psychotherapy' with children was conceptualised.

In the 1920s and '30s therapists in Europe and North America first began to
use the group context as a means for treating children with behavioural and
emotional difficulties. Slavson's work in the 1930s with delinquent adolescents
is generally seen as the pioneering group therapy done with children, and
although the emphasis in his groups was on activity, he approached the group
from a psychodynamic viewpoint, providing analytically oriented interpretation to the children's activity. There were several reasons for using the group as
the context of treatment: some of these were purely practical, in that more children could be 'treated' at once, but it was also hoped that the group treatment
of adults could be generalised to children and adolescents.

Perhaps more significantly though, Slavson and others were influenced by
the pre-eminence at the time of the **psychoanalytic approach**, and they
believed that children's own experiences of themselves would shift and develop as they became more aware of what motivated their behaviour. According
to the psychoanalytic approach it was thought that the patient would act out
parts of early relationships (different roles or attitudes or feelings) in relation to
other members of the group and the therapist, who would then interpret these
inner feelings and desires to the child and the group. In keeping with the primarily Freudian thinking of the time, the focus was mainly on the relationship
that the patient developed with the therapist, this interpreted from a parent-
transferential perspective.

Since Slavson's (1944) pioneering work, the difficulties of applying a model
used to explain adult pathology and with no developmental weighting have
continued to arise in the psychotherapy group run with children. This lead to
many group therapeutic endeavours not producing the envisaged results and
the current situation is such that groups have been embarked on with trepida-
tion and much anxiety by therapists and available literature is scarce (Canham
& Emmanuel, 2000). The use of the group therapy milieu for adolescents and
pre-adolescents however, continued to evolve against a backdrop of the predominant developments in adult group psychotherapy.

Group psychotherapy with adolescents

Pyschotherapy and psychodynamics Inherent to most current adolescent
psychotherapy groups is that they operate, at least to some degree, within a
psychodynamic framework (Moss-Morris, 1987). Whilst the behavioural/
cognitive and interactional approaches are the other major orientations to
group therapy in general (Reid & Kolvin, 1993), historically it is the psychodynamic approach that has found more ready application in the adolescent group
(Scheidlinger, 1985).

The use of groups to work with adolescents cannot be separated from developments in group psychotherapy with adults. In the early 1940s the work of
Foulkes, with his insistence that an individual cannot be separated from the
society in which he or she lives, began to garner support. Foulkes (Foulkes &
Anthony, 1957) believed that it was in the group that this very phenomenon

could be observed, and that group members would bring their societal roles and expectations into the group. At the same time Wilfred Bion's (1961) leaderless approach (with the therapist as passive observer) to the process of the group emphasised the importance of the unconscious dynamics for the group-as-a-whole.

The psychodynamic therapist   In essence these two theorists laid the groundwork for the psychodynamic orientation in the group context, where the therapist's non-intrusive and passive manner would allow for the group's process to evolve and develop. The primary form of intervention in the life of the group by the analyst was by the making of interpretations. In so doing, group members' own experiences of themselves in earlier developmental stages can shift and grow, as they become more aware of others in the group. Put simply then, the intended function of the group is to assist people who have previous experiences of painful, untrustworthy and damaging relationships, to build proper and sustaining connections to others. The central elements of the psychodynamic approach have largely remained constant: the importance of earlier developmental experiences; the transference/countertransference relationship, defences and unconscious drives and motives (Wilson, 1991). The core tenet was that making early and/or unspeakable experiences and emotions conscious would allow for the working through of these experiences. However, the way in which these constructs are put into practice in the group have developed and changed over time as clinicians have grappled with the complex and diverse demands of facilitating groups for adolescents.

Changes and challenges in the psychodynamic approach   As group therapists began to experiment with facilitating adolescent groups, critical challenges began to emerge. The most important of these was posed by the fact that almost every adolescent individual brought with her- or himself a plethora of separation-related phenomena or experiences, such as regression, pseudo-maturity, and authority challenges (Blos, 1963) that would require the therapist to fulfil several different roles in the group. Whilst the adult group member required of the therapist to remain relatively true to his or her role as facilitator, this was not the case in the adolescent group! With these groups the need to be 'used' by the members in a variety of ways arose – as object of derision, as wise uncle, as playmate, etc. Obviously, new questions were going to be asked of the therapist in terms of theory and technique. For example, how to be a container, an authority and a teacher.

Didato (1974, in Dwivedi, 1993b: 9) suggests four therapeutic goals that the therapist should attempt to keep in mind:

> *(1) to increase capacity to experience powerful affects … without acting them out, (2) to increase capacity for empathy, (3) to strengthen identification with the therapist, (4) to encourage new behavioural patterns in helping the group resolve … conflict through non-physical verbal means.*

The rationale behind these goals lies in the almost critical need of the adolescent to integrate diverse and at times quite opposing parts of him- or herself. The dilemma is how to reconcile parts of the self that hold separation-individuation aspects and the parts loaded with regressive energies. In the group context these 'parts' are acted out in relation to the others in the group and the facilitator in an attempt to find resolution (Ackerman, 1955). At times flexibility from the facilitator is required while at times a resoluteness to withstand the attack on certain boundaries is needed. The results of this acting-out can often be distressing for all present, and often can threaten the very existence of the group as several prominent theorists have attested (Scheidlinger, 1985; Dwivedi, 1993b; Evans, 1998). Powerful feelings of being overwhelmed, being attacked or of not understanding is experienced while, occasionally, the therapist watches helplessly as the group disintegrates.

The traditional approach of a non-directive and passive attitude to the unfolding interaction in the group has, over time, begun to absorb elements and techniques from the cognitive, gestalt and psychodrama approaches in order to effectively initiate and facilitate the therapeutic action between the group members and the therapist. Core elements of the psychodynamic tradition have remained, such as an acceptance of adolescents' role experimentation inside the group, and the significance of transference/countertransference reactions that are aroused in the therapist and group participants. Whilst theorists have appeared to find it possible to retrospectively understand these aspects outside the group, identifying them and managing them effectively inside the adolescent group continues to pose challenges for the adolescent group therapist (Dwivedi, 1993a; Evans, 1998; Rachman, 1979; Scheidlinger, 1985).

Perhaps it would be useful to understand why, firstly, difficulties that are particular to the adolescent stage of development arise in the psychotherapy group, and then to consider some theorists' views on facilitating adolescent groups. In this way, some clarity as to the impact of psychodynamic theory and practice on the adolescent group can be gained.

Adolescence and the group

But what is it specifically about this stage of development that makes it such a challenge to create and manage a therapeutic group? Adolescents, by nature, have been described as 'exploitative, antagonistic and antisocial' (Dwivedi, 1993a: 29). Although the author was perhaps referring to those that present at mental health facilities, these words could be used to describe the already troubled adolescent who is now faced with the terrifying and possibly shameful and embarrassing prospect which the therapy group presents. Whilst adults may be more capable at containing the wide array of feelings evoked by the new set of circumstances of the group, adolescents are bound to express the feelings they feel through action; action that invariably may threaten the very integrity of the group (Evans, 1998; Goldberg, Evans & Hartman, 2001).

Violence, rule-breaking and other acts of aggression often will arise relatively early in the group, as group members struggle to 'be' in a very anxiety-provoking and at times threatening, environment. What is common to these behaviours is that they all are related to significant conflicts that are amplified in the adolescent stage of development: authority, affection, aggression, dependency and sexuality (Rachman, 1975).

Defensive mechanisms of adolescents   Importantly, it is through the act of 'relating' in the group that most teenagers will reveal the defensive mechanisms that they readily employ outside the group. Whilst the adolescent makes use of these defences in order to help him or her find shelter from the overwhelming threat posed by the group, they (the defensive mechanisms) have also been the most viable form of solution to real-life challenges and trauma (Rutan, Alonso & Groves, 1988). Very often, in the situation of the group, the adolescent is faced with over-riding feelings of inadequacy and shame, both in relation to his or her peers, but also the group leader. The fear of intimacy with another can be so overwhelming that the child's only avenue of self-defence is projection or denial (Rosenthal, 1971). Psychodynamic theorists have long conceptualised these defences as resistance, however, attempts to manage these in the case of the adolescent have overwhelmingly served only to increase their usage (Evans, 1998; Halton, 1994; Rosenthal, 1971).

   This concept of resistance, although theoretically significant, decries the fact that these defences employed by the adolescent make the major task of the group, the achievement of intimacy, exceptionally difficult and subject to almost constant attack. In this way the very reason for the group is avoided, and often the existence of the group can become somewhat tenuous. Examples of this defensive behaviour include 'silences, moving about the room, engaging in horseplay, scapegoating, talking about irrelevant subjects, acting out ...' (Scheidlinger, 1985: 107).

The abused adolescent   These defensive behaviours become more complex with the more troubled adolescent. Children and teens who have experienced physical, sexual and emotional abuse, a broken family home or community and familial trauma, will bring to the group exceptional levels of anger and aggression, very poor impulse control and very little hope in attaining a trusting connection to another (Dwivedi, 1993b; Raubolt, 1983). Often the demands placed on the group by these teens may be too excessive, and the group may cease to be of therapeutic value (Barrat & Segal, 1996).

Impact of adolescent behaviour on the group process

On the basis of extensive work with adolescents in psychotherapy groups, Behr (1988) provides a useful synopsis of the impact of this developmental stage on the group's process:

> *The whole of adolescence may be characterised as a boundary state which demarcates childhood from young adulthood. Consequently all the phenomena associated with boundary formation and dissolution can be*

*expected to replicate themselves in adolescent groups: projection ... split-
ting; denial; testing of limits; anxiety over loss of identity; confusion;
and bewildering changes in presentation of the self ... When adolescents
gather in groups the group boundary comes under immediate scrutiny
and assault ...*

(Behr, 1988: 120)

The same author synthesises much of the work done in exploring group
psychotherapy done with adolescents when he notes that what is particular to
the adolescent group is that the defences employed by the adolescent will
invariably be in the form of action around the very boundaries and rules of the
group. These could include teasing, indiscriminately leaving and re-entering
the room, both bringing and taking objects from the room, testing the therapist
continually and out and out aggression and abuse towards other group members and the therapist.

Impact of the psychodynamic model on the adolescent group

So what then will be the impact of a psychodynamic way of the thinking on the
group members? Taking a broader perspective of the group, an atmosphere of
permissiveness may only serve to lead to increase acting-out behaviours and
boundary 'incidents' (Dwivedi, 1993b). The tendency of the troubled adolescent to transform feelings into action can render warm, empathic and interpre-
tative responsiveness on the part of the therapist obsolete (Rosenthal, 1971;
Dwivedi, 1993b), and may increase the anxiety of the individual.

Adolescent vulnerability to interpretation

The experiences of many psychodynamic therapists who work with adolescents suggest that adolescents are highly vulnerable to interpretations made,
and may act out the relationships described in the interpretation, rather than
integrate these into the self (Evans, 1988; Goldberg, Evans & Hartman, 2001).
When an interpretation is made regarding an adolescent's earlier experiences,
these may only increase the confusion and anxiety felt by the adolescent. As the
adolescent is struggling to integrate vastly different experiences of him- or herself in relation to others, an interpretation regarding earlier experiences of the
adolescent (particularly one that is accurate!) may be experienced as an attack
that must be fended off immediately (Evans, 1998). The effect of the interpretation that is made may often be to evoke a state of paranoia in the adolescent,
or a sense of impending persecution that must be avoided at all cost. Thus the
anxiety that has remained latent in the individual may, as a result of being
recognised, begin to run rampant. In this regressive state, the adolescent
attempts to defend a very fragile sense of self in any way necessary, and the
unstructured environment of group will be sorely challenged to halt this flight
into a condition of primitive defensiveness (Hobbs, 1991).

The use of traditional psychodynamics in the adolescent group has nevertheless continued all over the world and most, if not all, literature regarding this type of therapeutic group originates from North America and Europe. It is useful to briefly look at some authors' experiences of conducting adolescent groups in order to form a practical picture of what has been described here.

Experiences of psychodynamic therapists

Writing in 1972, Geller considers what he terms a group of 'troubled adolescents'. He made use of what he described as a rather technical psychodynamic approach, with a minimum of group structure and little direction given on the part of the therapist. Little detail is given but he tells how the consequences of this approach were immediate and rather difficult to manage: 'Anxieties were evoked … Difficulties relating to closeness, intimacy and communication arose …' (Geller, 1972: 51). Nagliero's (1996) work with a group of adolescents with learning and behavioural difficulties reveals how the flexibility of the group's rules and the action in the room were immensely difficult for the group to come to terms with. He emphasised how the already latent fear of failure and non-acceptance amongst the group's members was intensified, and many members began to attack the boundaries of the group and the group therapist as a result of their fear slowly growing from session to session. He reiterates the call for a psychotherapeutic group for this particular group of adolescents, which is founded on a stable, unchanging setting with set rules that are consistently and emphatically enforced – a difficult task for the psychodynamic therapist perhaps?

Somewhat different insights are provided by a group run for boys between the ages of 13 and 16, referred for exhibiting angry and aggressive behaviour: Sharry and Owens (2000) describe how an ignorance of the 'cultural' world of the group members, combined with a directly confrontational manner (in terms of observances and interpretations made) resulted in the group members intensifying their resistance to the task of the group. In simpler terms, behaviours which were directed at breaking down the group itself, intensified, and rules of the group were flagrantly violated. Only through beginning to 'connect' with the boys on their terms, yet in a stable and consistent way, were the authors able to begin to bring the group to a state where it could begin to prove therapeutic.

Evans (1998) gives us the benefit of looking more closely at the experiences of one 14-year-old boy in a psychotherapy group. He was referred to the group for a whole collection of severe learning difficulties and behavioural problems. In the group he presented with a whole array of defensive behaviours: 'marked impulsiveness, projection, avoidance, flight, manic activity and aggression … The effect of these resistances was to place the boundaries of the group under duress.' Through beginning to set firm and non-negotiable limits, the effects of the boy's behaviour on the rest of the group became manageable, and the therapist was able to reduce the pressure felt by 'William' to a level at which he could begin to think about his own actions, and their impact on both himself and others around him.

When the group is made up of several adolescents who all have serious difficulties with behaviour the effect can often be what Canham (2000) calls **'ganging'**. In simple terms this entails a group atmosphere where there is a consistent and almost exclusive use of behaviours that are destructive and very difficult to manage. Canham set out in his group to create conditions where internal and external differences could eventually be tolerated by the group members, however, as he himself notes, that is an ideal situation, and it seldom occurs. In a similar vein to other group psychotherapists, he advocates the use of firm limits and a clear structure to the group process, to avert the dissolution of the group's therapeutic function. Importantly, a significant facet of the troubled adolescent's functioning is that she or he is almost always incapable of both tolerating and integrating exceedingly painful, shameful and traumatic feelings, a necessary principle which is central to the work in a psychodynamic group. Other therapists, such as Ghiradelli (2001) have given more focus in their psychotherapy group to being able to tolerate this acting-out that occurs in the group. Through using interpretations, he believed that he could recognise the boy's attempts at resisting intimacy in a manner that could instill some sense of hopefulness about forming a relationship to another. Although this could very well have been the experience of some of the group members, the amount of serious boundary activity in the group was considerable. It is difficult then to assess how the adolescents' experience of feeling safe in the group were affected, and how this would have impacted on their ability to form relationships in the group is subject to conjecture.

Limitations of the psychodynamic approach   What does seem clear is that the defensive behaviours that young adolescents bring to the group will significantly affect the usefulness and therapeutic function of the group. The threats posed to the boundaries of the group place a great responsibility on the group therapist to be able to manage what occurs in the group. What has become increasingly important to consider is that a traditional psychodynamic 'means' of management not only heightens the boundary action in the group, but has proved somewhat questionable in the context of traumatised and severely troubled adolescents. Theorists have, over time, questioned significant aspects of the psychodynamic approach to facilitating the adolescent group, but how much this has affected the use of a traditional model of facilitation in the group is not clear. Available literature reflects that it is still this model that is predominant in most group psychotherapeutic interventions with children and adolescents.

Perhaps it would be helpful to look at how theorists have begun to re-think the traditional approach to the young adolescent group. It could prove useful in beginning to formulate a model for working effectively with severely troubled adolescents in our context.

Adolescent groups: Reappraising the psychodynamic approach

In perhaps two of the most comprehensive reviews of adolescent group psychotherapy, Scheidlinger (1985) and Evans (1998) both take stock of current ways of managing the group and argue that the psychodynamic approach must be structured, when working with adolescents. The premise for their argument is that psychodynamic techniques have only been found to be effective when they occur in the context of more structured, planned and active techniques such as education. The non-directive, permissive and unstructured group psychotherapeutic style has proved problematic in that it falters in the face of the particular resistances brought by the troubled teen to the group.

Management of adolescent responses

The importance of what these two authors suggest is that whilst psychotherapists working with adolescents have traditionally concerned themselves with conceptualization (in terms of techniques), the emphasis should rather fall on management. Put simply, they argue that therapists' accounts of traditional adolescent groups reveal that the greatest stumbling block to those groups proving helpful has been that the destructive, painful and damaging behaviours and feelings evinced in the group have gone unmanaged, and ultimately have affected the group members themselves. In fact, Sheidlinger notes that the paucity of available literature on the adolescent group is directly due to the wide array of incredibly damaging behaviours brought by teens to the group that appear unmanageable (1985). The central challenge then is how to best develop the group and manage what occurs in there, so that the group can 'work'.

In 1989, Rachman, one of the foremost theorists in the field of group therapy with adolescents, stressed that '[a]dolescents need direction, organisation, consistency and clarity in their attempts at identity crisis resolution' (p 21). He went even further, calling for the group therapist to be demonstrative, active and compassionate in the group, an attitude that is directly in opposition to the non-directive and passive poise of the traditional group psychotherapist. Other theorists have developed the practical implications of this call, arguing that structured, planned and contained activities should be utilised in order to allow enactment rather than acting-out. In this way the demoralizing effects of unpredictable and anxiety-producing interpretations can be minimised, and the adolescent is enabled rather to experience their internal confusion in a context that is predictable, stable and perhaps even slightly dependable.

Active stance of the therapist So where to for the psychotherapy group? Increasingly, prominent theorists have begun to call for a highly structured setting in which there is an emphasis on containment, providing some support and positive regard at the expense of interpretation (Behr, 1988). Attention to punctuality, order, firmness, energy, enthusiasm, sensitivity and a degree of tolerance of uncertainty may be some of the qualities needed. Accordingly, this will mean the therapist must be more active right from the inception of the group, and clear decisions regarding management will need to be made and clearly yet compassionately communicated to the group. In theoretical terms, the common thread of these proposals is that it is not appropriate to transfer the unstructured, non-directive, passive and detached therapist from the adult psychodynamic group to the adolescent group (Behr, 1988; Dwivedi, 1993a, 1993b; Evans, 1988; Niebergall, 2001; Rachman, 1989; Scheidlinger, 1985).

What is significant here is that the particular difficulties faced by the individual in the adolescent stage of development make it very hard for him or her to build an even mildly trustworthy relationship in the context of the group. As noted by one of the authors previously, 'Much of this defensive behaviour will present as resistances which occur around the boundaries of the group, or as transference and countertransference interactions between group and therapist, respectively, which threaten the group's existence. The difficulties in using a traditional analytic approach in the adolescent group are to a large extent due to these defensive behaviours ...' (Truter, 2003: 28).

In working with adolescents in the South African context, we could even think a little bit more specifically about factors influencing defensive behaviours in this context.

Re-evaluating group psychotherapy in South Africa

Effect of deprivation on South African adolescents

The impact of deprivation of all kinds, whether it be material, psycho-social or emotional, cannot be excluded when thinking about an individual's prognosis in the therapy group. Canham (2000) argues that deprivation further complicates the child's experience in the group in that such a child exhibits both external and internal defensive behaviours. Furthermore, such a child's difficulties become even more complex in the presence of abuse. He explains:

> There are certain conditions which put to the test the relationship of individuals to their internal objects and the representations of these internal figures ... Foremost among these conditions are the impact of anxiety and the consequences of deprivation. Anxiety is often experienced as a threat and the need to identify someone to blame for this feeling can be extremely powerful. Deprivation often means a deficit in opportunities for the introjection of helpful and benign internal figures. When deprivation is coupled with abuse it often leads ... to a defensive internal manoeuvre designed to distance the ego from the pain ...
>
> (Canham, 2000: 125)

Alongside factors such as HIV/AIDS, poverty, violence and unemployment, many teenagers in South Africa grow up without a conscientious, thoughtful and present caregiver and authority. An aspect of this can be seen in Pamela Reynolds' (1997) contention that many children in South Africa have never experienced a stable and/or secure family environment. Furthermore, in conditions of poverty and overcrowding, the child's chances of developing a secure attachment to its primary caregiver are often greatly reduced. In this way many adolescents have never experienced a trustworthy, consistent and meaningful connection to an adult who is always present and dependable. Often, the adolescent may be pushed into gang-like relationships within the therapy group, as opposed to becoming part of the group (Canham, 2000). When this happens, the individual is far more likely to make use of aggressive and destructive means to defend him- or herself. What we do know is how emphatically this type of behaviour, albeit violence, aggressive outbursts, sullenness or oppositional posturing, alienates the individual from potentially helpful and protective adults such as parents, teachers and indeed, therapists.

Several authors have written about South Africa as a 'traumatised community' (for example Bloom, 1996; Stein, 1996). In such a society a child is bound to experience some form of failure, whether it be societal, familial or parental. In these conditions adults can come to be experienced as 'omnipotent and cruel' (Coid, 1993, in Stein, 1996: 45), unreliable, or even dangerous. Any child that perceives themselves under threat or facing impending abandonment will retaliate in an aggressive and even desperate attempt to avert the disaster that is being left alone. In psychodynamic terms, the work of Stein (1996) gives some useful insights into the emotional 'conditions' of many South African children and adolescents:

> Children who grew up within this adverse external environment often failed to achieve an appropriate level of psychological and emotional development, and were left with an unstructured, chaotic and destructive inner world ... Only by acting out this internal chaos in external reality ... will the individual feel confident to contain his own inner turmoil. This need to act out, combined with an absence of appropriate object-relationships, leads to forms of behaviour which are clearly antisocial and psychopathic.
> (Stein, 1996: 50–51)

In simple terms, many of our children have not experienced conditions in which they have been able to develop healthy, dependable and fulfilling relationships that are crucial to developing a trustworthy inner world of self-experience and autonomy. If we acknowledge that many of the teens who present for psychological help have never had sufficient care or nurturance, then we gain some insight into why

> [They] ... respond to early deprivations with continuing expectations which are unmodified from infancy. In extreme cases they are repeatedly demanding, frustrated, angry or depressed. They relate persistently in a need-satisfying manner. Such youngsters are difficult to help [sic] achieve their early potential.
> (Evans, 1998: 98)

In a synopsis of what constitutes appropriate treatment for such adolescents, Mattejat (2001) warns (just as other theorists have insinuated, hinted and proposed) that no form of insight-orientated group therapy should be attempted, and rather, that management of behaviour and effective coping skills should be the focus of the intervention. While the present authors do not share the categorical sentiment embedded in this assertion, it is seen as highlighting the limitations of a primary reliance on insight in psychodynamic groupwork with adolescents. This limitation is illustrated in the following case example.

Learning Problems Project

In 2002, one of the present authors facilitated a psychodynamically oriented group for eight young adolescent boys at the Child Guidance Clinic of the University of Cape Town. All of the boys originated from the Cape Flats area of the Western Cape and all had experienced some form of familial or community trauma prior to presentation at the clinic. The group was conceptualised as part of the Learning Problems Project (LPP) run at the clinic, and ran for approximately eleven months.

The role of interpretation in psychodynamic group psychotherapy

A fundamental principle in traditional psychodynamic group psychotherapy is that material provided by group members, either through behaviour, direct verbal communication or projective identification, should be returned to the individual or group through interpretation. In the case vignette the facilitator made use of direct verbal interpretations and in the analysis will illustrate how boundary activity steadily escalated, at times directly in relation to interpretations that were made.

Case material

Seven boys arrive for the first session. They have run up the stairs to the room and are all talking loudly to each other in Afrikaans. There are pillows on the floor for them to sit on, and each boy grabs one. Ganief, Andile and Clayton lie down on their pillows in the circle and Madoda sits in the corner with his pillow on his lap. I explain to the group that we will talk more about the purpose of being here but that first we need to all introduce ourselves to one another. Mohamed-Amien introduces himself first, and whilst he's doing so, Ganief begins to snigger. The group continues around the circle, until its Ganief's turn, when he introduces himself as 'Ben'. I immediately felt quite irritated at this, and offered that perhaps Ganief was feeling nervous at the beginning of the group, and that he therefore wanted to be seen as like me, in control. He seemed nonplussed by this for a moment and responded by saying, 'Naai, jy maak nie sin nie, pillows [No, you aren't making any sense, pillows]'. At this the rest of the group, except for Madoda, began to laugh and repeat this name he had called me. I was put off by this, and said nothing for a couple of moments, after which Ganief asked me if that 'other' woman [the facilitator of another group] was my 'tjerrie' [girlfriend]. Clayton, Andile and Stanley were egging him on as he asked this, and even though I felt that we were heading in the 'wrong' direction, I responded by saying that Ganief wanted to know more about me so that he could feel more comfortable. He laughed and threw the pillow he was sitting on over my head and asked me if we were having sex together. I was so taken aback for a couple of moments that I said nothing. He carried on, and asked me if she was 'lekker' [nice]. I wasn't really sure what to do then as I was irritated and very angry.

Trauma and the adolescent self

The above excerpt illustrates the difficulty in establishing and maintaining the therapeutic frame in the context of severely traumatised adolescent boys with limited empathic and affective abilities.

Ganief's question could be indicative of the lack of an experience of self in an 'emotional space' (Bloom, 1996: 61) stemming from his upbringing in the adverse environment of Lavender Hill. Several authors (Pretorius & Le Roux, 1998; Maiello, 2001) have proposed that male adolescents in contexts of deprivation, trauma and violence experience severe handicaps in language and relational style. Specifically, the affective and empathic abilities that the adolescent needs to be able to cope with a statement of an emotional nature (Jackson, Bijstra, Oostra & Bosma, 1998) are often severely impaired, or not developed at all. The implication of this is that Ganief felt threatened by the emotive nature of the interpretation that the therapist offered him, and responded in an impulsive manner that was experienced as hostile.

This is perhaps illustrative of Rosenthal's (1971) view that the troubled male adolescent's feelings of inadequacy and shame are heightened by feeling-related statements (such as the one the therapist made to Ganief), and results in resistant behaviour that serves to protect the traumatised adolescent from the pain of connection to a helpful and benign other (Canham, 2000). In line with the view of Canham (2000), this may be why Ganief's response to the interpretation felt destructive and hostile. In retrospect, the therapist experienced his actions as an attempt to damage the establishment of a frame to support what this therapeutic group was supposed to facilitate.

The sexually traumatised adolescent self   In this excerpt, Ganief's question regarding sexual activity between the facilitator and the female facilitator of another group may in part be attributable to anxiety in the adolescent related to the expression of feeling. It also reflects the adolescent's preoccupation with sexual material. However, Ganief's response is inappropriate, given the context: the first session of a group with an unknown authority figure in the room. His questions are also part of the discourse of the severely sexually abused child. Ganief's instantaneous sexualised behaviour in the first session of this group might have been identified immediately as such by a more experienced therapist.

Central to the psychoanalytic group approach is the view that an individual will bring his or her historical past to the group (Corey, 2000; Rutan & Stone, 2001), and that this individual's reactions to other group members and the therapist will be shaped by internalisations of earlier relationships to significant others and siblings. Accordingly, it is argued that traumatic experiences are suppressed, and then 'acted-out' when an opportunity arises. The dynamic group is posited as a context within which this process can be facilitated and then appropriately managed. Importantly, in the remedial part of the LPP programme, there were no incidences of Ganief's sexualised and violent behaviour. This may be attributable to the fact that the adolescents were constantly kept busy in the remedial group, and behaviour deemed disrespectful or inappropriate was not tolerated. Rauwald (2002) suggests that in contexts such as these (the teaching environment), it is not that difficult and painful emotions are not present, rather, they are suppressed, and simply are not given the opportunity to surface. The difficulty presented by the material brought by Ganief to the group was how to work with Ganief's experiences so that they could be returned to him in a way that he could manage. The interpretation would thus facilitate the development of more adaptive defensive strategies.

For the majority of the rest of the year, this conundrum would remain. How to maintain a balance between providing a context for the working-through of painful material, whilst at the same time managing acting-out behaviour that is both damaging and dangerous for the group? After termination the following conclusions were reached:

- Violations of rules on the part of group members invariably constituted sexual or aggressive 'acting-out'.
- Group members' boundary activity often stimulated or resulted in ambivalence on the part of the therapist.
- Interpretation on the part of the therapist was a precursor to most, if not all boundary violations by group members.
- Providing a therapeutic setting for adolescent boys to work through painful feelings and experiences must include an appropriate means for the management of 'acting-out' behaviour that is damaging to both members of the group and possibly, the therapist.

Conclusion

The inner world of the young adolescent very often closely approximates that which is meant by the term 'a borderline state'.

In the face of such powerful and often 'raw' states, the therapist using a psychodynamic approach has to adapt their way of being in the group. Therapeutic 'passivity' has to be replaced by a responsiveness (even a willingness to play), to the drama of the moment. Clearly this does not imply reactivity. Facilitation of a therapy group with such individuals will ask of the therapist to be creative, flexible, playful, authentic and empathic; but also invested in protecting the group's boundary, limit and moderate the use of interpretations and to focus the work in an active (often using activities or themes) manner. A mindfulness of the South African context and the resultant tensions carried by our youth means that the continuous titration of the anxiety level of these groups will always remain the primary task of the therapist.

Discussion questions

1 What is the relevance of the psychodynamic model of group facilitation in treating a South African group of adolescents?

2 Based on a developmental awareness, which activities could be used to facilitate the process of a young adolescent group?

3 What are the dilemmas surrounding the concepts of power and authority when working with South African adolescents?

8 Group therapy for single mothers

Monica Spiro

Learning objectives

By the end of the chapter you should be able to:

- Explain why group psychotherapy is a modality of choice with single mothers.
- Describe how feminist theories challenge traditional models of self-development.
- Utilise relational theory to formulate an approach to working with single mothers in a group setting.

Introduction

The most recent South African statistics indicated that 42% of children in our country are living with their mothers in a single-parent household.[1] This chapter examines how group psychotherapy can provide a transformative experience for women who face the challenges of being single parents. The chapter begins by examining the common trends in current research with single mothers and offers a comment, from a feminist perspective, on the limitations of the prevailing perceptions that emerge from the research. Then relational theory is introduced, along with the clinical implications that this theory holds when constructing psychotherapy for women. Thereafter, group therapy is presented as a modality that can enhance women's growth and development from a relational/cultural perspective, and the value of groupwork for self-empowerment is considered. The chapter closes with a case example from a slow, open group intervention provided for single mothers, and a comment on the therapeutic aspects of the group.

Current research on single mothers

The growth in the number of unmarried mothers, the impact of HIV/AIDS, and the increasing number of separation and divorces have resulted in a steady incline in the percentage of single parenting, particularly those households headed by women.[2] Locally and internationally, female-headed households have been identified as economically disadvantaged[3] and a higher incidence of maladjustment and psychopathology is documented among their family members.[4] Although a small body of research has attempted to counter these findings by highlighting the positive attributes of one-parent families,[5] most of the literature focuses on the deficits inherent in a single-mother family situation.[6] Much attention is given to the unfavourable statistics and results are most commonly interpreted as a 'consequence' of the shortcomings inherent in this family structure. Single mothers are often personally under attack for the perceived deficit.[7] Some attempt has been made to relate the deficiencies of the single-mother family to the lack of support provided by wider social structures. This outlook shifts the blame onto the authorities for not providing adequate family, childcare and economic aid which would compensate for the 'inadequacy' of the mother-headed household; yet, it still locates the deficit within the single mother family.

A feminist perspective

As an alternative viewpoint, the feminist standpoint and the larger perspective of female gender issues offer a different interpretation of the emerging literature on single mothers. Conventional (or mainstream) views of the lone mother oppress her by holding her responsible for the difficulties in her life, including the intergenerational transmission of poverty, and by blaming her for the increased pathology in her family. These views may also be criticised for portraying single mothers as victims of their circumstances.

The **social constructionist** approach is an epistemological approach that attempts to account for ways in which phenomena are socially constructed. Regarded as part of the postmodern movement, it is grounded in the relativist tradition and challenges essentialist notions that underlie scientific discourse. This approach positioned within a feminist perspective argues that mainstream epistemology (dominant, naturalised ways of constructing meaning) is the dominant discourse in society because it is supported by people in powerful positions and systems.[7] Recognising that mainstream knowledge is something that has been constructed by society challenges the belief that this body of knowledge, or rather set of assumptions, about single mothers is real or objective.[8] That single mothers have accepted the dominant social view of them is documented by family therapists who have noted how single mothers approach therapy as a means to heal the deficiencies they perceive in their family structure.[9] Another issue that may be taken up from a social constructionist perspective is that the prevailing debate of adequacy versus inadequacy of the single parent family runs the risk of creating a fixed identity for single mothers. Seccombe, James and Battle Walters (1998) expose commonly held perceptions that reduce the single mother to a stereotype of inherent incompetence. It may be argued that this fixed identity of the single mother separates the woman's experience from the context in which it is embedded. Furthermore, as Schnitzer (1998) comments, these narrow perceptions fail to recognise the actual diversity (in terms of individual strengths and weaknesses, social class, financial situation, cultural group, etc.) that exists among single mothers.

Therapeutic interventions documented in the literature

Women's accounts of the stresses of single parenting in the form of the economic, practical and emotional demands that their children make on them confirm the necessity of a therapeutic intervention with these women (Spiro, 2002). However, the trend of contemporary single-parent research has had consequences for the way in which psychotherapy has been constructed for single mothers and their families. A considerable number of studies examine the use of **family systems theory** as an approach to working with one-parent families.[10] Family systems theory treats the family as a system, and regards family therapy as a method of working within the system to effect change.

Advantages of the group approach

The prevailing experience of isolation and the common lament of a lack of adult company provide strong motivation for the advantages of a group therapy intervention. Furthermore, the noted commonality of experience and the very real financial constraints of these women are also factors that favour a group approach (Spiro, 2002). The majority of studies documenting group work with single mothers report on short-term life-skills and support groups offered to single mothers with a focus on bolstering a population (group of individuals/segment of society) perceived as vulnerable.[11] All these studies report on the effectiveness of the therapeutic interventions, highlighting improved self-esteem, parenting skills, life-skills, and relationships with others. These studies note decreased stress for the mothers and enhanced family functioning. As the evaluations were completed on termination, or soon thereafter, the long-term benefits of these groups have not been ascertained.

Three longer term therapeutic support groups[12] have also documented positive results. However, once again the interpretation of the outcome attributes the positive results to be due to the support and input that the women receive, which are seen as 'making up for' the deficits inherent in the single-parent situation. A notable exception to this type of interpretation is the study reported on by Bienstock and Videcka-Sherman (1989) where the value of the normalising function of the group is recognised and identified as an opportunity to counter the extensive pejorative societal view of single parenthood. More recently, Spiro (2002) has extended this theme by distinguishing the **relational aspect** as a **transformative function** in a long-term group for single mothers. Spiro suggests that the mutually affirming relationships fostered between the participants translate into the capacity to challenge the projections they receive as a marginalised group and provide an alternative vision for the individuals concerned. The following section will look more closely at relational theory as the backdrop to working with single mothers in a therapeutic group.

Relational theory

Over the last two decades, scholarship within feminist psychology research has resulted in an increasing understanding of the importance of the relational context in women's lives. The relational context refers to the myriad of relationships that are central to the psychological life of the individual. In the case of single mothers, it offers new insights into the construction of disconnection and isolation so commonly experienced by them. Single mothers commonly find themselves on the periphery of society, not fully welcome in a world that sanctions couples and two-parent families. They are further isolated by the absence of a partner in their home, and in many circumstances they carry the hurt and loss of a failed relationship. Within the relational context therapeutic interventions act as relational opportunities to repair and heal their experiences of chronic disconnection. In so doing, it serves to depathologise single mothers by recognising the constricting relational contexts in which they might live.

This section locates this feminist theory within the broader movement of relational theory and examines the basic tenets of the theory.

Difference from traditional self-development theory Traditionally, Western psychological theory has posited the notion of a developing self that emerges through a process of ever-increasing separation to become an autonomous, self-sufficient, and contained entity. The journey towards maturation has been measured in terms of advancing individuation and disconnection from early dependencies. The process is depicted as an uncovering of the individual self in a coherent and predetermined direction, which can become distorted by interactions with others.

In contrast, both relational psychoanalysis and infancy research make general claims to an inextricable link between self and other. They acknowledge that, as humans, we are born into and develop through a relational process. The human psyche is understood to evolve in relationships with others where the posited goal is one of self-differentiation. They propose that a full understanding of the individual thus necessitates an appreciation of the multiplicity of relational contexts in which the person is embedded. Psychotherapy is viewed as a relational opportunity to repair past damage. The healing of psychotherapy is then believed to occur in the interactive space provided by the therapeutic relationship.

Feminist theories of self-development Feminist theories of girls' development and women's psychology have provided another angle to relational theory. Gilligan (1982), adopting a **developmental perspective** in her study of adolescent girls, and Miller (1976), utilising clinical experience with female clients, have challenged the presiding view of development as a process of increasing separation and autonomy. In a political analysis of psychological theory, they contend that existing theories of separation are a construction of Western patriarchal society that values independence and autonomy. Their studies of women have confirmed the centrality of relationships in women's psychological development. In traditional psychological theory the centrality of relationships in women's lives would be seen as a deviation from the accepted model of self-development through self-differentiation and this deviation would serve to position women as pathological at worst and as less mature than men at best. Gilligan and her colleagues at Harvard, and Miller and her fellow clinicians at the Stone Center, have proposed **relational models** as alternative ways of conceptualising psychological growth. Over the past two decades their original works have been augmented by an extensive base of research and this has resulted in the establishment of a notable body of feminist psychology literature.

In summary, the two feminist models offered above, the Harvard developmental perspective and the Stone Center relational/cultural theory, differ from other relational theories in that relationships with others are not viewed as a vehicle for reaching the developmental goal of an autonomous and independent self. Rather relationships are viewed as a basic human motive and as the locus for ongoing development, with the end objective being relational competence, in other words, the ability to participate in mature, fulfilling and healthy relationships. Their non-traditional view of psychological development offers a different definition of psychopathology, which ultimately necessitates an alternative strategy for psychotherapy. Furthermore, by presenting a cultural analysis, the theory also addresses social injustices perpetuated by patriarchal systems. The focus on girls' and women's voices, and more recently on issues of race, ethnicity, social class and sexual orientation, gives expression to women's psychological experience and addresses how dimensions of power operate to suppress marginalised voices and safeguard positions of power and dominance.

Harvard developmental research

Gilligan listens to the voices of girls and women to offer support and validation to perceptions and outlooks that, she motivates, were previously dismissed or misunderstood in the context of Western patriarchy. Her research, and that of her colleagues, adds a body of knowledge on women's maturational processes. A theory of women's emotional development that emerges from this research highlights the centrality of relationships in women's psychological reality. Authentic relationships, defined as those that offer individuals the opportunity for a full range of expression of feelings and experiences, are presented as a prerequisite for women's healthy psychological development.[13]

Gilligan (1982) identifies variant experiences in the mother–child bond as the location of different identity formation between girls and boys and the origin of gender differences in relational patterns. In short, she states that daughters, whom mothers experience as more similar to themselves, are generally not forced to separate in the way boys are, and are encouraged and coached into relationships of mutual empathic interdependence. Mothers with sons, on the other hand, experience their sons as different to themselves and with cultural backing and reinforcement by the father, they tend to encourage their sons to separate and develop competitive behaviours. Thus, she concludes, sons usually have less practice and experience in participating in authentic relationships that offer mutual caretaking. From this developmental perspective, Gilligan suggests that we understand theories of autonomy and separation as representative of the male psyche and calls for a revision of theory to include an understanding of women's psychological development that encompasses a movement towards more mature interpersonal relating.

Understanding development as a process that occurs and is shaped by a particular relational context, Gilligan identifies the voice as the instrument of the psyche that reflects the individual embedded in this context. Authentic relationships are seen to provide resonance and encouragement for the development of an unrestricted voice. However, when the individual's needs, desires and knowledge conflict with the dominant voice, the desire to preserve relationships is believed to result in the practice of self-sacrifice and self-silencing (Gilligan, Lyons & Hanmer, 1990). Although this might begin as a conscious process, Gilligan suggests that the continuing absence of resonant relationships results in a dissociation or masking of the girl's own voice, which she then takes on as her own failure rather than a problem with the culture. Gilligan understands psychological distress as the product of this 'resistance'. She views symptoms as markers of 'relational crises' which she understands as 'losing touch with one's thoughts and feelings, being isolated from others, cut off from reality' (1991: 23).

Stone Center relational/cultural approach

The **Stone Center relational/cultural model** gives further weight to a feminist critique of established theories that conceive of development as advancement towards an individuated self. In their work with adult women clients, the Stone Center endorses a view of psychological growth as one that takes place in and through connection with others.[14] Their theory of women reinforces Gilligan's developmental model by hypothesising that rather than moving away from mothers and significant others, 'women add on relationships as they redefine primary relationships in age-appropriate ways' (Turner, 1997: 75).

According to their **'self-in-relation'** model, the goal of psychological development becomes the active participation in growth-fostering relationships where maturation is viewed as 'increasing levels of complexity, choice, fluidity, and articulation within the context of human relationship' (Surrey, 1985). Thus, the evolution of the self is viewed as commensurate with the growth of relational capacities. Rather than viewing self-sufficiency and personal gratification as the principal motivating factors for connection, this model recognises that the relationship itself, as a fulfilling and enhancing experience, is an incentive for establishing connections.

Miller and her colleagues do not view growth-enhancing relationships and what follows from them as static or even constant. Rather, connections, disconnections, and reconnections are placed at the centre of developmental processes, where movement from connection, into disconnection, and once again into reconnection is regarded as the normative flow of relationships.[15] They propose that it is in the process of reconnection that psychological development takes place. Conversely, circumstances of chronic disconnection are understood to result in constriction of the individual and psychological distress. Miller and Stiver have identified the central relational paradox as the situation that occurs when there is repeated disconnection without reconnection.[16] In this situation of continuing disconnection it is posited that the individual, in a desperate attempt to accommodate the relationship, removes aspects of herself out of the relationship. Paradoxically, this removal precludes the possibility of fulfilment in the relationship. They propose that the energy is then redirected towards altering the self or restricting emotional responses.

Surrey (1990) identifies mothers as particularly susceptible to the relational paradox. She posits that perceptions of motherhood, emerging from clinical and developmental psychology theories of this century require mothers to deny their subjective experience while they focus on their children. Although they are expected to be deeply engaged with their children, the removal of their voices and own interests results in their disconnection and disempowerment, with the consequence that they experience isolation in their internal and relational worlds.

The theory further articulates how the act of shaming women serves to silence their realities. From this perspective it is viewed as a socio-political force that sustains disempowerment. Miller (1988) indicates that women lose the ability to represent their perspective and, ultimately, to even know their reality. Jordan writes, 'By creating silence, doubt, isolation, and hence immobilisation, i.e., shame, the dominant social group (in this case white, middle class, heterosexual males) assures that its reality becomes *the reality*.' (1997a: 150).

More recently, writings from the Stone Center have focused on the experience of minority groups of women, hence the use of the term 'cultural' in the 'relational/cultural model' (Jordan, 1997c). The appreciation of diversity within women's experiences has on one level broadened the model, and on another level reconfirmed the socio-political comment that emerged from previous writings: that in a culture where hierarchies of power are entrenched, the possibility of embracing diversity is curtailed. From this perspective, it is hypothesised that differences between people, rather than providing opportunities for growth and expansion, become a cause for withdrawal and chronic disconnection. In a climate of persistent disconnection, minority experience is subdued and dismissed by the dominant voice, and isolation, accompanied by feelings of self-doubt and worthlessness, is endured. In this way, the power-over structure of patriarchal society remains unchallenged and positions of dominance are not disputed.

Much attention has been given to implications of the theory for psychological healing, particularly as it occurs in psychotherapeutic endeavours. Miller and Stiver draw attention to their concept of relational paradox where they view disconnections in relationships as inevitable and emphasise repairing the disruption in the active co-construction of a relationship. The therapeutic setting thus provides a relational opportunity for repairing disconnection by bringing the individual into a relationship where a climate of mutual empathy is fostered.[17] They propose that when the person experiences empathic responsiveness from the other, she is encouraged to allow more of herself into the relationship. The person is thus brought back into connection where pain can be shared rather than dealt with in isolation, and where learning and growth can take place in order to build relational competence. In other words, the active and authentic participation in the therapy relationship itself is posited as the goal of therapy (Miller & Stiver, 1994).

Relational theory and group psychotherapy

In her paper on 'Relationships in Group: Connection, Resonance and Paradox' (1994), Fedele brings attention to the differences between traditional psycho-analytic group theory and the model of group work promoted by relational/cultural theory. Traditional theory, resting on the ultimate goal of the development of an independent self, views the group process as a means of achieving this end. While their writings incorporate a relational under-standing of group dynamics and an appreciation of the relational task of the facilitator (e.g., Pines & Hutchinson, 1993), the theory differs from the relation-al/cultural model which gives primacy to **relational movement** and **connection** as the task of group therapy.

As Fedele (1994) notes, group therapy provides an exceptional forum in which to expand relational opportunities and address relational restructuring, as advocated by the Stone Center approach. She suggests that in the context of safety, where the therapist facilitates an empathic relational space, members experience new opportunities for connection, work with inevitable disconnec-tion, and are able to strive for reconnection and relational fulfilment. Thus, the real relationships fostered in the group provide the opportunity to challenge inhibiting transferential relationships from the past. New relationships can then replace these earlier constricting relationships with growth-enhancing connections that allow for relational movement outside of the group.

Phases in female self-development Schiller (1995, 1997) utilises the research emerging from the feminist inquiry into women's growth and devel-opment to propose that women's groups follow a different developmental course to the standard stages of development described in the group therapy literature. She draws on the relational/cultural model to suggest that the nor-mative development of women's groups is influenced by the centrality of con-nection and relationship in women's lives, and the difference in the dynamic of power for women to that of men. In the same vein as Bernadez (1996b), Hartung Hagen (1983) and Home (1991), Schiller identifies the major difference in women's groups as being a sense of connectedness and intimacy which usu-ally precedes the surfacing of conflict or the challenge of authority. Thus, whereas groups that include men may jockey for status and power immedi-ately following pre-affiliation, women need to establish a relational base, which includes approval from and connection to other group members and the facilitator, before entering the more challenging activities of power-wrestling and conflict. Once a relational base has been established, Schiller suggests that women move through a stage of **mutuality**, where trust and disclosure coexist with recognition and respect for differences. Thus, the framework of affiliation and connection is seen to provide the containment in which members can appreciate each other's differences. She views this stage as roughly corresponding with Shulman's (1992) and Schwartz's (1971) **working stage** and what Germain and Gitterman (1980) refer to as the **ongoing phase**. Schiller views the later stage of **challenge and change** as the core of growth for women. She notes that while the growth occurs for most men in the area of intimacy and empathic connection, and hence comes later for them in the group process, the work for women is in the area of learning to negotiate conflict without threatening the bonds of connection and empathy. Schiller draws on Miller's (1991) theory that traces the fear of conflict and confrontation to cultural constructions of its destructiveness to explain the precariousness experienced by women when asserting themselves and the difficulty encountered with allowing conflict to emerge.

Negotiating the power differential   The value of group therapy for self and group empowerment is well recognised by feminist advocates. Group-work has been firmly established within the feminist movement as a method for consciousness-raising and mobilising women's strengths to affect social change.[18] The collective experience of the group, where women can share and compare their range of experiences, is viewed as the tool that can provide them with the strength to re-evaluate conventional images of themselves, recognise the socio-political roots of their identity, and reconstruct personally significant realities for themselves. By discovering commonalities and recognising that personal problems are embedded in social structure, women can begin to address the social basis of their oppression through the collectivity provided by the group.

The relational/cultural model promotes the group as an ideal setting for women to redefine themselves by utilising a 'mutual power' model where non-hierarchical relationships replace the traditionally masculine 'power over' framework. In this model the feminine capacity to engage in a mutually empathic relational process creates the momentum for individual growth. Thus, the shared attentiveness and responsiveness in a group setting is identified as the catalyst for self-transformation. Surrey's collaborative work with Coll and Cook-Nobles (1997) leads her to the conclusion that 'working at a group level is more possible and powerful than between the individuals (194).' Stiver (1997) discusses the value of groupwork with disempowered people and promotes the view that a network of support can be most effective where there is suppression of authentic voice. She maintains that 'when faced with that power differential, the more we can find others who are also in subordinate positions, who are able to join together to validate our experiences, the stronger our voices become. In the face of power imbalances, we do feel in some degree of isolation, but it can be countered by a relationship to a network of support. That's how empowerment happens, which makes for the possibility of bringing about some changes in that imbalance' (47).

Facilitating a single-mother group utilising the relational/cultural model

The importance of the theoretical framework adopted lies in the implications it holds for guiding therapeutic interventions. In the case of the single-mother groups, the relational/cultural model's call for an approach based on the authentic engagement of the therapist, who is willing to acknowledge the mutuality of the therapeutic endeavour, results in the movement away from a need to remain neutral, towards an approach based on the communication of genuine concern and caring.

Despite the informal nature of the interaction between members and facilitators during this time, facilitators must refrain from bringing personal aspects of their own lives into conversation. Jordan (1991) clarifies that although both people are affected in the therapeutic relationship, the contract of therapy positions the client's subjective experience as the focus of the therapy and the therapist's subjective experience is attended to only insofar as it may be useful to the client. Thus mutuality refers to the dialogical nature of the relationship, where each person is emotionally available, attentive, and responsive to the other, rather than referring to a relationship of equal disclosure.

As Stiver argues (1997), the genuine relational context, where the therapist conveys her authentic engagement, provides the safety for the transference to emerge and be worked through. By working through the misunderstandings that may occur in the light of the transference projections, and by offering a corrective relational experience, the individual can begin to reorganize her experience and transform her relational expectations.

Instilling a sense of safety In addition, in keeping with the relational/cultural model, the anxiety of initially attending the group should not only be interpreted, as might be in traditional psychoanalytic practice, but attempts must also be made to allay the anxiety. This is done by normalising the experience and inviting older members to talk about their experience of first joining the group. New members can also be reassured that they are free to share as much or as little as they felt comfortable to do, thus reducing the concern associated with the initial outpouring or inhibition experienced in their first sessions. Furthermore, facilitators are free to share information that they deem would be useful to a member, for example, effective styles of parenting. From a traditional psychoanalytic perspective the facilitators might be criticised for playing out an idealised transference and assuming a parental role that, might be argued, does not allow for the issues to be addressed and worked through in the group. However, it could be argued that need gratification, particularly in the early stages, does not stifle their development, but rather encourages a process where members are able to move towards greater maturity and are more equipped to embrace the demands of their life circumstances. This approach is in keeping with Schiller's model, which encourages facilitators to nurture a sense of safety in the group prior to engaging in risk-taking. Once the group has negotiated the earlier stages of connecting and holding difference within the connection, the facilitator can assist the group in meeting conflict as a potential for growth – a phase that often requires the facilitators to be more active.

This developmental model, where the facilitators are attending to the needs of the members, also seems appropriate from the point of view that the group is not purely therapeutic, but also encompasses primary aspects of support. The group needs to respond to the paucity of resources and support available to single mothers in the light of their commonly communicated experience of constantly attending to the needs of others without receiving much support or nurturance for themselves.

Single mothers

This case example is the account provided by a single mother who attended a slow, open, unstructured single-mother group at the Child Guidance Clinic, University of Cape Town, South Africa. The group was initiated 11 years ago in response to the large number of single mothers who were presenting with their families at the clinic. In clinical interviews the women were consistently communicating the stress of their busy and over-committed schedules as they attempted to meet the financial and emotional needs of their families, leaving them little room to attend to themselves. Moreover, these parents were repeatedly voicing the uncertainties and self-doubts that arose in lone childrearing, further reinforced by the critical attitude of a society perceived as favouring two-parent families.

The group of six members was set up to meet on a weekly basis for the duration of one-and-a-half hours with the aim of identifying and working through the wider issues related to the women's identities as single mothers. The model evolved and grew in accordance with the expressed needs and observed requirements of the women who committed themselves to the agenda. The evolution has seen the group intervention develop from predominantly a support structure to a therapeutic enterprise where members undergo a process of personal transformation involving an alteration in how they feel about

themselves and the way in which they perceive their social world and their circumstances. Over time the model has been replicated to accommodate the growing number of single mothers who wish to join the groups.

Terri's account

Terri is a 40-year-old medical receptionist, who lives with her two sons, aged 4 years and 16 years, in a two-bedroomed apartment in Claremont, Cape Town. She has been a member of the group for two years.

Terri, the only daughter, is the middle child of five children born to working class parents. Her home life in childhood was characterised by intense parental conflict. Terri personally suffered verbal and physical abuse from her parents and brothers. She left school at the age of 16 and fell pregnant with her first son at the age of 22 years, and with her second son nine years later. She has had no contact with the father of her elder son, who denied paternity, but maintains a civil relationship with her younger son's father, who continues to be involved in his son's life by way of maintenance and visitation on weekends and school holidays.

Terri was at a particularly low point when she read a notice about the single-parent group in a community newspaper. She had stayed away from work that day, as she could not face going in to the office. She was struggling financially, had used a prepaid phone to call to inquire about the group. When the therapist on the other end of the line perceived her desperation and arranged an assessment interview for that same day she was both relieved and terrified – she felt that this was a possible lifeline and was terrified that she would be rejected and excluded. She wept through the interview as she shared the events of the past few years and her current circumstances and then cried with relief when she was offered a place in the group and transport was arranged for her.

I felt I was completely alone, and then you were there. It was like a lifeline thrown to me when just [my] nostrils were sticking out of the water, that's how deep I was. Ja, you sat there and you held out a lifeline to me. And I was always so scared that you were going to take it away from me again. You were explaining about the group and the concept and I was thinking, this is what I need, this is what I feel I need to be in. It's like a job interview, thinking am I going to pass the test? So it was very nerve-racking, very scary. I felt extremely vulnerable.

Her anxiety about being rejected extended to the first session when she was concerned that the other women in the group would not accept her.

First of all I was terrified, thinking what is expected of me? And if I go in there, what if I make a fool of myself? And what if they don't like me?

However, she began to relax as soon as she heard other members expressing similar concerns and struggling with similar situations to hers. She began to share some details of her present life and felt contained by the caring response of group members and the facilitators. As other members spoke about the issues in their

lives, so it triggered further feelings and thoughts for Terri, which resulted in an initial verbal outpouring.

I remember you saying to me [in the assessment interview], you don't have to talk; you don't have to say anything. Well, I never shut up … (laughs) … because it was like you're sitting in the dark and your light bulbs have gone out. You haven't got the money to buy new ones and you're waiting and you're hoping that this torch is just going to shine that little light a bit more so that you can see the door. And all of a sudden somebody comes and, whoosh, that light is on and you say, 'Hey, look, we're all here! You're not alone' – Whaaat!!! And this person was talking about something and I thought, I can relate to that; I know what you're talking about! I got so excited and then, okay, shut up, now shut up, you're talking too much, you know. And then somebody else, and I said, 'I know what you're saying!' It was like – wow, you know, I wasn't alone after all. These people are feeling what I'm feeling, most of them have experienced what I have experienced and I can talk to them. And I just wanted to talk, I mean I had verbal diarrhoea – I just wanted to go blah, blah, blah!

At first she expected that the facilitators would give her advice and guidance, but after a while she realised that the process involved her confronting and dealing with her personal issues.

In the beginning I thought, well when are you going to tell us what to do? When are we going to get given this advice? And then afterwards I thought to myself, but I'm doing it. I am doing it because of the way that you facilitate the group, by having that silent but very important presence that gives me that stability … One gets given the space to air or to take in and take away whatever you wish to take away.

A turning point came a year into the group when another member spoke about an abusive relationship she had had with her mother, and Terri, for the first time, began to confront the abuse of her past.

> When Louise spoke about her mother – that hit me. She was the catalyst that got me going when she came in and spoke about her mom. It hit me like a bomb and that is when I started.

Terri recognises a number of reasons that allowed her to do this. Firstly, her own trauma began to surface when she heard someone else dealing with a similar issue. The other member had stopped blaming herself and was firmly locating the dysfunction of the family with her parents, and mother in particular. Secondly, she felt valued by the group and this encouraged her to reconsider the family myth that she was the cause of her own indignity. Thirdly, the support and containment of the group gave her the courage to delve into and confront the painful issues of the past.

> We carry each other. There is enough trust and confidence in that group for me to come in, who is normally very positive and who is Miss Fixit, to say, 'I need you now'. And to be able to talk and say what is on my mind and what is bothering me – that I normally wouldn't do because I wouldn't feel that it was justified for me to do it because who cares about what I think.

Finally, she believes that she was aided by her need to challenge another group member's cynical attitude towards relationships and this member's self-sacrificial attitude when dealing with her children. Terri recognised that on some level she shared these women's feelings and therefore needed to challenge them.

> When Mary started talking I found her extremely cynical in the beginning, but because of her being so cynical, I became more positive. For every negative she gave, I gave a positive. I'd look at her side and I'd think, yes, I can agree with you, [men] are bastards; I know exactly what you're saying. Yes, and I've experienced it, but do you remember that love you were given, that feeling that you felt when it was good? So her voicing the negative allowed me to look at the positive. But I took away with me the positive and tried to leave the negative behind.

Terri believes that she could not have achieved the same movement and growth in an individual therapy. She admits that she had attended a couple of sessions with a psychiatrist a few years prior and had not returned for further treatment as she had felt that the psychiatrist was not particularly interested in her. This had only exacerbated her sense of isolation and feelings of worthlessness. She reports that the prompt response of the group facilitator, her seeming concern at the initial interview, and the transport and fee concessions that were arranged for her already allowed her to feel differently. However, she feels that the major advantage of the group is that she could not have trusted the lone therapist to accept, understand and care for her in the way that the group has.

> I don't think I could have spoken to anyone else about a lot of things like I have in the group. I don't think that I could have cried and laughed at times about things that would be totally alien to outside people.

> It's illogical to me [to go for individual therapy] because what is happening to me is happening as a human being around people, like these people within the group. One moment I did not want to talk about anything and I couldn't talk

about it. The next moment I felt I could because I trusted them enough to open up. And what I felt in the group is that I'm not getting advice, I'm getting acceptance, I'm getting understanding, I'm getting respect. And they're listening to me and they're telling me, 'Hey, listen, it was not your fault.' Whereas the [psychiatrist] sat there, even if I didn't speak about the abuse or whatever, whatever I did speak about, they never turned around and said to me, 'Listen, you're okay.'

It's more powerful because it's not only one person. You see, you and I could sit in this room and I could come here every day for six months and you can tell me, 'Terri, you're okay. You're a wonderful person, you're doing well, you can do it.' I couldn't walk out there and do it alone. Here there are seven people sitting there and they're saying, 'We hear you and you're still okay. You are still quite fine'. And somewhere along the line it's going to hit you that you've got to start believing that because it's not just one person who is telling [you]. It's not just your perception; it's everybody's perception. And nobody beforehand has turned around and said, 'Oh, but listen, before Terri comes in, let's make her feel good. You know, let's accept her'. Each person – you know they're being genuine. They're not trying to pretty you up and tell you, 'Oh, shame, she feels bad, let's just make her feel better'.

Another advantage that Terri identifies is the fact that the women in the group share common experiences.

I'd be sitting in a group and I've got nothing to say. I don't have a problem; I don't have an issue, nothing. And someone will say something, and all of a sudden my experience is here and I'm talking about it. And I'm relating to something that I've felt. And it's because of

what's been said and I want to share my way of looking at it.

Furthermore, Terri's trust in the group has been strengthened by the culture of honesty that pervades the group.

… it boils down to [honesty]. And that's where the trust comes from – that I trust these people enough to share my deepest fears with them. Because for me to turn around and admit that I had a mother that hated me, it's not a nice thing, it's not a fun thing. And I looked up – the day that I was talking – and there Louise was sitting, and the tears were hanging on her eyes, and I just wanted to go up and give her a hug because I thought she's feeling this with me because she knows what I'm talking about. Mary says she was spoilt as a child, but she empathised with me even though she never experienced what I experienced, but she would empathise. And this is the thing that you're getting from each of these people – honest feeling. Honesty, honesty. I feel it here. My heart's beating, your heart's beating. Guess what, you're okay. And that's it, you know.

Furthermore, she identifies that the two-way flow of give and take in the group and her contribution to others has allowed her to feel valued. Her ability to support others and help them through their pain has boosted her sense of self-worth.

Terri identifies that she has achieved fundamental shifts as a result of participating in the group. She suggests that her critical transformation has been the way in which she views herself. Her improved sense of self has allowed her to begin to think differently about relationships. For the first time she is valuing what she has to offer to others. In terms of sexual relationships, she is realising that she can make choices and take what feels good for her rather than simply responding because someone is willing to pay her attention. Suddenly the world feels full of possibilities and for the first time she feels confident, nervous and excited at the possibility of pursuing her goals with a growing belief in her own worthiness and a knowledge that she is deserving of all that is good.

> Right at this moment in time I'm sore right here, in my chest, where I'm sitting now thinking, what gave you the right to take that away from me? And then I sit and think: how can I take it back? I'm taking it back, I'm taking the power back – I know that. But I know that I'm not even quarter way to where I want to be emotionally. But I don't know how to do it, because I'm too scared somebody is going to stop listening, or that they're going to say, 'Please, she's a hopeless case, let's just forget about her', or 'Look at her, she's just talking and talking and talking and waffling, but she's not making any sense', or 'It's just all about her, her, her, her, her.' But I'm also saying, you deserve to go and have a life. You deserve to be loved, you deserve to be respected, you deserve to be given what you were not given.

> From the day that I walked into your place for the meeting, I didn't feel on my own anymore. Working through things here has forced me to look outside of what I've been running away from, what I've been running to, who I've been pulling into my life, who has been bad for me, and why I've been doing it. It has changed me radically. Because for the first time in my life, I'm starting to be honest with myself, really honest. I have to grow, and in order to grow I've not only got to take in good things, I've got to let go of bad things. So, it's like me stopping smoking five years ago. It's me stopping putting myself down because

> of what I was told all my life. I'm taking baby steps to be able to get to the stage – which I'm still trying to get to – to believe that I can be loved for who I really am. That I'm doing a good enough job for my children, that there is light at the end of my tunnel. My choice of friends and my perception on life is completely turned. If I had stayed thinking and doing what I was doing outside then I would not have taken on that job because I wouldn't have felt that I was good enough and that I needed to prove something.

Terri views her group membership as a long-term commitment. She believes that the group can serve a therapeutic and supportive function for her as she continues to face the daily challenges of single motherhood.

> It's not a case of needing [the group], I want it. I want it because of what I'm getting from it. I want it because I walk in and I see a change in people. I see a growth, I see a positiveness, and I think, wow, a year ago that wasn't there.

> The group allows me, as a single parent, to be able to go home and look at my kids and realise that we're not alone and that somebody has listened to me instead of me getting to the stage where I would be so frustrated that I would want to either bash my head or their head against the wall. This group brings people together that need a little space, and the space is given to them however long or however they need it. And they can be true to themselves.

> You have to take seriously and realise and respect that each person is different and they're going to grow differently to the next one. It's like a clan. It becomes like an extension of my family. It gives me the strength to go out and say, 'Hey, listen, I'm not alone'. And I can go look at my kids and say, 'I can love you just a

little bit more now because I've let it out, or I've listened, or I've taken from what Mary has said, what she has done and

I'm going to put it into practice here because I feel that it can work here.' You know, that's what it is for me.

Evaluation/analysis

Terri's account confirms the centrality of relationships in her experience of the group and the healing power of an interactive space. Her story indicates how she has been able to utilise her connections with others for the benefit of her own development and healing. Her narrative emphasises the importance of mutually affirming relationships, which offer her opportunity for validity and acceptance of herself and her circumstances. The mutually empathic relationships fostered in the group have had to repair and restore self-perceptions that have been damaged by early and prior relational experiences.

As in Terri's case, other women interviewed have spoken of the group as a life-transforming experience that sustained and challenged them during times of adversity. Most interestingly, they highlighted the interpersonal opportunities created by the group experience and identified this relational aspect as the unique site of their emotional growth. In-depth interviews with 10 participants, including Terri, elicited the following interpersonal factors as central to the group process:

Non-judgemental acceptance Non-judgemental acceptance from others allows them to confront and shift internally held negative perceptions of themselves that often date back to childhood and have been reinforced in relationships in adulthood. The women identified that the norms of honesty and genuineness in the group, in conjunction with the sheer number of people in the group, combine in a powerful way to challenge entrenched perceptions they hold of themselves.

Support The support emanating from the intimate relationships forged in the group has helped them cope with their circumstances. They indicate that they draw strength from each other and from the group energy that emanates from the confluence of members. They also spoke of the encouragement received from an awareness of other women who had successfully endured similar circumstances.

Commonality of experience Their shared life situation and the commonality of experiences were presented as a powerful aspect of the group experience. They identified the normalising benefit of hearing other women struggling with similar concerns, which then allowed them to challenge their assumptions of their own inadequacy. For some, hearing other people's struggles also placed perspective on their own concerns. The women further emphasised the value of being understood by people who can relate personally to their experience, and some reflected on the trigger effect of hearing other women speaking about issues that mirrored their own. Perhaps most significantly, the women articulated the transformative power of accepting others who were a reflection of themselves and thereby altering their perceptions of themselves.

Reciprocity   The women highlighted the reciprocity of emotional support as an important transformative factor. They explained that they found it more possible to accept support when the act was reciprocal and, furthermore, benefited by connecting with their own strengths and capacities when assisting others.

Challenge and confrontation between group members   While all members identified challenge and confrontation as a reality among members in the group, there were mixed feelings expressed as to its usefulness. On the one hand, some members felt strongly that confrontation was necessary to challenge entrenched self-defeating patterns of behaviour, while other members were more invested in maintaining the primary supportive aspect of the group. The ambivalence expressed by members seems to reflect the tension between the supportive and therapeutic aspects of the group, the need to hold and contain versus the need to probe and challenge. The anxiety associated with challenge and confrontation in the group may also be related to women's difficulty with conflict and discord, as reflected in Schiller's developmental model of women's groups.

Conclusion

Group therapy, with its myriad of relational opportunities and with the influence that emanates from a collectivity, can offer an appropriate forum in which to undertake relational restructuring. The case example provided indicates how group members and therapists have collaborated to create a secure relational space that tolerates painful experiences in an atmosphere of resonance and empathy. The opportunity for these women to move out of isolation is provided through the possibilities presented by the group membership and the larger relational unit. Through a process of active and mutual engagement, the group provides a healing space that fosters movement back into connection. The chance to bring experiences of diversity and disconnection into connection has resulted in a reintegration both personally and interpersonally.

Through the group process, the women are able to make a connection between their own experience and that of other women in similar circumstances. This is valuable in validating and depathologising their experiences and in the process rebuilding self-worth that has been bruised by negative attitudes emanating from a culture that invests in the notion of a nuclear family. The power that emerges from the network of support translates into the capacity to challenge the projections that they receive as a marginalised group. Thus, coming together, recognising and naming the experience of the group as a whole effectively releases the individual members from isolation and shame. The experience of personal self-doubt and disempowerment is replaced by an experience that fosters self-confidence and relational power and, in so doing, provides an alternative vision for the individual women concerned.

It seems that equally as important is the confirmation of each woman's relational capacities. In stark contrast to the isolation and loneliness associated with the experience of being on the fringe of society, and carrying the burden of failed relationships, the group experience can provide the women with assurance of their own relational capacities. The possibility of connecting intimately with others in a mutually beneficial manner serves to reaffirm the women's capacity for being a 'person-in-relationship,' to use Kaplan's (1997) term. It restores their sense of self-worth by confirming their confidence in their relational worth. Thus, the process of participating in the creation of this relational experience is in itself transformative.

Discussion questions

1 What are the differences between a relational/cultural model of group therapy and a traditional psychoanalytic approach?

2 Is it possible to incorporate both therapeutic and support aspects in the single-mother group? What are the tensions?

3 Would it be possible to include single fathers in the group therapy intervention? What implications would it have for group dynamics and process?

Endnotes
1 Kane-Berman, Henderson & de Souza, 2001.
2 Schlemmer & Smith, 2001.
3 Schlemmer & Smith, 2001; Sidel, 1996.
4 McLanahan & Sandefur, 1994.
5 E.g. Olson & Haynes, 1993.
6 Mclanahan & Sandefur, 1994.
7 Schnitzer, 1998; Seccombe, James & Battle Walters, 1998; Sidel, 1996.
8 Danziger, 1997; Gergen, 1999; Harding, 1996; Olesen, 2000.
9 Sheinberg & Penn, 1991.
10 Atwood, 1995; Korittko, 1991; Westcot & Dries, 1990.
11 Butcher & Gaffney, 1995; Lipman, Secord & Boyle, 2001; Shulman, 1994; Soehner, Zastowny, Hammond & Taylor, 1988.
12 Bienstock & Videcka-Sherman, 1989; McLeod & Vonk, 1992; Mulroy, 1995.
13 Brown, 1998; Brown & Gilligan, 1992; Gilligan, 1982; 1990 ; 1996; Gilligan, Rogers & Tolman, 1991.
14 Jordan, 1997c; Jordan, Kaplan, Miller, Stiver & Surrey, 1991.
15 Miller, 1988; Miller & Stiver, 1994, 1995.
16 Miller, 1988; Miller & Stiver, 1994.
17 Miller & Stiver, 1991; Miller & Stiver, 1994.
18 Favor, 1994; Home, 1991.

Groupwork and mental health

Shona Sturgeon, Nelleke Keet

Learning objectives

By the end of this chapter you will be able to:

- Identify the particular characteristics of groups for people with mental disabilities.
- Describe how just becoming part of a group challenges a person with a mental disability.
- Argue that successfully managing the process provides a gateway to reintegration into mainstream society.

Introduction

Mental health challenge   In the field of mental health South Africa has followed the worldwide move towards community care for people with mental disabilities.[1] Throughout this chapter the term **'consumer'** will be used when referring to a person with a mental disability.[2] Psychiatric hospitals now only care for people who are acutely ill. The resources to create and sustain community-based mental health services should have followed the consumers into the community but that seems not to have been the case.

As the World Health Organization points out, one in every four people develop one or more mental disorders at some stage in life, and mental health problems represent five of the 10 leading causes of disability worldwide, amounting to nearly one third of the disability in the world.[3] The implication of these statistics is clearly that the task of assisting the integration of people with mental disability into the community must be assumed by a wide range of professionals, appropriate people from the community, such as religious leaders, and peer support from consumers themselves. It is inappropriate, not only in terms of numbers, but also in terms of the principles involved, for only mental health professionals to be involved. In keeping with the concept of **'mainstreaming'**, the community in general and practitioners in particular will have to make a fundamental shift in their attitude towards people with mental disabilities.[4] 'Mainstreaming', in the context of mental health, requires that consumers no longer only receive attention from mental health practitioners. They should be seen and treated as part of society in general.

Groupwork as a solution This chapter advocates for, and describes the use of, community-based groupwork as a tool in improving the quality of life of consumers. In so far as groups constitute a microcosm of society, they are ideally suited as a medium to empower people with mental disabilities with the knowledge, attitudes, and skills needed for a life of quality in the community. The assumption is made that the reader is familiar with the fundamental principles and skills of groupwork, including the work of Northen and Kurland (2001).

Perhaps practitioners think that special sophisticated psychiatric knowledge is required to work in this field, or maybe there is a fear of, and stigma associated with, the idea of 'madness'. Alternatively, maybe there is an irritation with those people who are thought to avoid responsibilities on account of their 'nerves'. This chapter aims to change these ideas.

For this to happen, however, practitioners need, firstly, to recognise that groupwork is an appropriate medium for such work; secondly, to feel confident in practising groupwork in this community and thirdly, to feel excited by the opportunities offered in this field.

This chapter aims to demonstrate both the applicability of groupwork in promoting the well-being of people with mental disability, and to identify and discuss central concepts and techniques in such work. The well-known template provided by Northen (1988) and Northen and Kurland (2001) provides the structure for the discussion.

It is hoped that, no matter in what context the reader is presently working, he/she will become empowered and enthusiastic about working in the mental health field.

Mental health

The current intervention trend in the mental health field encourages consumers to attain as fulfilling a life as possible in the community and to curtail or limit periods of hospitalisation.

Positive mental health has been described as including:
- a positive sense of well-being;
- individual resources including self-esteem, optimism, and sense of mastery and coherence;
- the ability to initiate, develop and sustain mutually satisfying personal relationships; and
- the ability to cope with adversities (resilience).[5]

It is considered that these qualities 'will enhance the person's capacity to contribute to family and other social networks, local community and society' (Lavikainen et al, 2000: 16).

If one compares the symptoms of mental illnesses as defined in the DSM IV (APA, 1994) with these descriptions of positive mental health, one can appreciate the extent of the challenges faced by these people. For example, the diagnostic criteria for a major depressive episode includes markedly diminished interest in pleasure in all, or almost all, activities most of the day, and feelings of worthlessness. One of the diagnostic criteria for schizophrenia describes social or occupational dysfunction for a considerable duration. These symptoms not only cause distress to the individual, but also impair their ability to access the resources they need to function in, and contribute to, community life.

Focus on dealing with life

Although people with severe or chronic mental disabilities may need hospitalisation from time to time, the suggestion is that only 10% of concern and effort should be expended on the mental illness aspect of an individual's life, and the balance of 90% on strengthening the individual's capacity to deal with life in the community, in other words, their mental health. The Psychosocial Rehabilitation Consensus Statement for South Africa (2000: 3) highlights this point when it states that psycho-pharmacology alone is insufficient and that services should be provided which enable consumers to 'gain lost skills or never learnt skills' in order to '… normalise relationships with the environment, people and situations …'

The severe mental illnesses of particular concern in terms of their chronic nature would be schizophrenia and bi-polar mood disorder, but experiencing other conditions, such as post-traumatic stress disorder, depression and anxiety states can impact severely on the person's ability to function comfortably in the community.

People experiencing a wide range of mental health problems can benefit from participating in a group. Some disorders are more chronic in nature, while other disorders present once only as an acute condition. A common experience, however, is loss of sense of direction and self-confidence. Relationships are often stressed, leading to isolation, and life roles, such as work, family and community are threatened. While the use of groups in the acute hospital-based period is well documented (Yalom, 1983), and its value recognised by the authors, this chapter focuses on the less recognised use of groups in the community.

Challenges beyond the mental disability itself

The difficulties faced by consumers go beyond the symptoms caused by the condition itself. Ignorance and prejudice cause them to lose jobs, to struggle to find accommodation, or to become isolated and unsupported. The knowledge of mental disorders in the general community is very poor, and assumptions are made about the functioning of people with mental disabilities, including their danger to the community (Fellin, 1996). In addition, community-based resources such as job sharing and supported accommodation are not available.

Mental health care during apartheid   The apartheid system in the South African context created diametrically opposite, but equally problematic conditions for black people as opposed to white people with mental disabilities. Black people with mental disabilities, coming from disadvantaged communities, with general high levels of poverty and unemployment, were often doubly disadvantaged. They were generally discriminated against and deprived by the system, in that medical and mental health services were lacking or inaccessible. Consequently, they generally did not receive adequate in- or out-patient treatment.

However, although in black communities many who should have received medication went untreated, they remained linked with their communities. Perhaps because there was no alternative care available, or because of a different perception of the cause and handling of their condition, many consumers remained in their communities. Some sort of accommodation was made to contain and care for them, sometimes helpful and sometimes not.

In contrast, for the white population, professional facilities were reasonably adequate, often leading to overuse of in-patient services. This often resulted in institutionalisation of consumers and lack of community involvement. After hospitalisation acceptance and reintegration into their communities and its occupational, social, and recreational life, was generally more difficult.

Mental health care currently   Currently, in the new dispensation, while the goal of community-based care is the same for both population groups, the challenges to be faced are very different. The challenge in the black community is that consumers need to be educated and empowered to claim the right to services that are accessible, relevant and affordable. While these communities are often more tolerant, abuse can occur as a result of ignorance, cultural beliefs, and financial constraints. Black consumers need to be empowered to claim their basic human rights.

In the white community, the challenge is for consumers to become reintegrated into communities that often have little tolerance for functional disability. Reintegration is not a passive condition, but refers to positive mental health in which not only would the individuals, within their own potential, experience a positive sense of well-being, they would be active participants in satisfying relationships and contribute to their community. Sadly, service providers, who are constantly under pressure from high work loads, also are unable to tolerate the different pace that consumers require. Consumers need to be educated and empowered to deal with these entrenched attitudes (Petersen et al, 1997).

The philosophy and process of empowering people to be successful in the community is the basis of psycho-social rehabilitation as described in the World Health Organization's Consensus Statement (WHO/MNH/MND/96.2).

Use of groupwork

To discuss the process of using groups to address the needs of consumers, Northen's and Kurland's structure has been loosely applied (2001). Three stages in the life cycle of a group of consumers are examined: the orientation stage, work stage, and termination stage. In addition the role of the group facilitator and the planning and intake process involved in forming a group are also discussed.

The role of the group facilitator

It is the opinion of the authors that since as a practice principle, a group is owned by its members, the facilitator need not be a mental health professional.[6] The focus of the group should rather be on 'non-patient' roles of the members, such as their adjustment to the community. It is more important that the facilitator should be well versed in group process through either good training or experience.[7]

As in the case when individual therapy or counselling is indicated, the person requiring psychiatric intervention should be referred to the appropriate resources outside the group. Therefore, it is crucial that facilitators develop networks of mental health professionals to whom consumers can be referred.[8]

The understanding that the facilitator role could be taken on by a non-mental health professional, would allow a wider range of group facilitators to see themselves as potentially equipped to run groups with people with mental disorders. Primary health care policy has as its foundation the principle of mainstreaming, and this will necessitate a larger number of professionals to feel comfortable engaging in mental health care work.[9]

The group content should not be a set programme. Because of the complex nature of mental health problems, facilitators should gain the knowledge necessary to enable the group to move from being purely supportive to being developmental, that is, educative and empowering. If not confident in facilitating the group members themselves to set and manage the agenda, facilitators may resort to 'directing' the group according to a pre-set agenda. However, even if facilitators have limited experience, just meeting regularly with facilitators who really care will, in itself, provide a meaningful experience for the members. The facilitators' ability to create warmth and introduce 'fun' is empowering in itself.[10]

Planning and intake processes

Group purpose   Improvement in quality of life is the overall purpose of groups for consumers.[11] The particular focus of each group will vary depending on the particular needs and decisions of the members, which in turn, are influenced by a variety of factors. Fundamental in every aspect of group planning and facilitating is empowerment and education while taking into consideration the constraints of the disabilities of the group members (Meagher, 2002).

Membership determination and group composition   Experience has shown that groups in the mental health field may be heterogeneous regarding age, race, culture or mental disabilities. In fact the heterogeneity can afford potentially empowering experiences for members as they discover or develop new skills and take on new roles in relation to each other, for example as carers or group leaders themselves (Corey & Corey, 2002). Some commonality of goals must be present. Facilitators need to be aware of the impact of different disabilities on the group as a whole, for example, people with bi-polar disorder tend to be more vociferous than consumers with schizophrenia and the facilitator needs to ensure that all members are given the space to participate if they want to.

Groups can be located within institutions or in the community, the location to some extent affecting the overall focus of the group and the relations members have with each other outside the group. In relation to community-based groups, bearing in mind the isolation of many consumers, there are distinct advantages in the possibility of members meeting outside of the group experience. The size of the groups can vary and fluctuate, and generally, groups are better contained if they do not exceed 12 members.

Organizational structure   The organizational structure will vary depending on the purpose and location of the group. It is suggested that community-based groups should be open groups, with changing membership. In a sense they reflect society, allowing people to move at their own tempo. Some members may want to stay for many years, others move on and new people join the group (Fellin, 1996).

As part of the contracting it is very supportive for members to know that the group is open-ended, for example, meets weekly on a specific day and time indefinitely. This encourages members to remain linked to the group even when they start wanting to engage elsewhere, for example, take up temporary employment, or have a relapse and are admitted to hospital (Corey & Corey, 2002).

A debatable function of the group on a long-term basis is the socialising opportunity it provides (Patel, 2003). Some would argue that a group should not perform this function, while others would recognise that for consumers whose confidence and skills required for social engagement are severely challenged by their mental illness, the group provides the only opportunity for socialising.

Facilitators, however, encourage attendance and will continue to model appropriate social behaviour, thereby empowering consumers. While the consumers' interests in experiences outside the group are supported, pressure is never applied to make them feel they have to 'perform' and that staying in the group means they have 'failed'.

Some consumers may move on and leave the group, some may become involved in other activities, but remain in the group and perhaps return intermittently, and some may prefer to remain only in the group. Sadly, for those who would like to move on, the community provides few opportunities for gradual progression.

Groups are generally geographically based so people can get to meetings on their own, possibly even walk to meetings. Some members are accompanied by a friend or family member, and provided it is acceptable to the group, they can join the group.

Time management skills may be a challenge to some members, and the functional skills of attending on time may require much attention. The timing of groups is important in that groups may need to start fairly late in the morning as consumers may struggle early in the morning because of medication issues. Likewise, if on monthly injections, as the level of medication drops just prior to the next injection, consumers will find their behaviour changing, and facilitators need to accommodate this.

In order to function optimally, as with physical illnesses, the consumers have to learn to share or ask others to make accommodations for them because of their mental illness. However, doing so is a calculated risk, often leading to further rejection or resulting in people making decisions for them, even with the best of intentions. Even service providers fall into this trap.

Application and intake For continuity of service it is essential that community-based services, such as community groups, are developed and that they are made known to potential members as part of mental health discharge procedures at all levels of service (Orley & Sartorius, 1986). In addition, groups need to be publicised widely through the media, by non-governmental organizations, religious groups or health services. Word of mouth between consumers has also proved to be very effective.

In keeping with the empowerment philosophy advocated for such groups, it is suggested that facilitators do not select group members or set criteria for membership (Ross & Deverell, 2004). Instead, prospective members are encouraged to attend group meetings for a trial period. During this period both the prospective member and the group will reach a decision as to whether they can reach an acceptable accommodation to each other.

In addition to the usual groupwork skills required to assist entry of a new member,[12] facilitators require particular expertise to facilitate this process in groups of people with mental disabilities. Facilitators need to model support and unconditional acceptance of prospective members, while also normalising the anxiety accompanying freedom of choice, as either the group or a member may decide that membership is not appropriate.

In many ways, this period can be equated with the 'exploring and testing' phase (Northen, 1988; Northen & Kurland, 2001). As the power and responsibility is located within the group rather than in the facilitators, the 'testing out' is dealt with in relation to the group. The facilitators, from the start, set the tone that the group must take responsibility for the group process. The importance of this dynamic cannot be over emphasised, bearing in mind the context of disempowerment and stigmatism that both the groups' current members and the prospective group member have probably experienced.

The orientation stage

Initiation and early development of relationships When working with consumers in a group, the orientation stage is both crucial and protracted. People with a mental disability may find it extremely hard to interact with others (Tilbury, 1994). They find themselves trapped within a cycle of isolation, low self-esteem, and emptiness. This can block out their wish and ability to connect with others. The longer the person remains in this cycle, the more it becomes a comfort zone and thus the more unattractive and impossible it seems to engage with others. In many ways, successfully negotiating the orientation stage of group membership is the single most important task of the group process.

Trust issues have particular relevance in relation to the orientation of consumers to becoming members of a group (Northen & Kurland, 2001). By definition, many of the members will have real difficulties with establishing relationships, and will find the initial stage of group membership very stressful. Their mental disabilities and the side-effects of the medication may result in members having an unusual appearance and/or demonstrating strange behaviour. The only guidance that can be given in relation to these factors is that the deviation from the norm depends on what the group can tolerate (Tilbury, 1994).

Norms   It is essential that ground rules should be contracted on. For example that:
- Members must not be verbally or physically abusive to other group members.
- Members must be free from any substance such as alcohol or recreational drugs when attending the group.
- Their personal hygiene must be acceptable to the group.
- Their conduct in the group must be such that it can be accommodated by others.
- Confidentiality will be respected.[13]

Purpose of the group   A major challenge facing group facilitators is that often for consumers, the disability has taken precedence over all other aspects of their being. This concurs with Mechanic's statement (in Fellin, 1996: 34) that '... mental illness is usually thought of ... as characterising the whole person rather than just one aspect of his functioning'. The person has begun to see themselves in terms of their disability, for example, as 'a schiz' and it is quite frightening initially not to have this 'identification'. Consumers will need to be taught to firstly identify themselves by their name and only then possibly that they 'have schizophrenia'. While the same may not be true for a person with a disability such as post-traumatic stress syndrome or an anxiety state, the condition can, nevertheless, assume a central position in their lives. This means that the facilitator may need to start where the group is, in other words, preoccupied with the '10%' of their life concerned with medication and illness issues, with the facilitator seen as the expert.

The purpose, however, is to move the power away from the facilitator to the group members, to move the medication topic out of the group and to shift the focus to the '90%' of the members' lives concerned with strengthening their capacity to function well in the community (Northen & Kurland, 2001; Corey & Corey, 2002). It is imperative that facilitators remain focused on this process. The orientation stage only concludes when the focus has moved from the illness to the quality of life issues.

The work stage

In most groups the process of members becoming part of the group is limited to the orientation stage. In contrast, for consumers engaging with others will continue to be a central task during the work stage. In recognising this, the facilitator should intentionally and creatively ensure that all processes and activities contribute to this goal. Only once this is in place will consumers be 'freed up' to engage in other issues impacting on the quality of their lives, for example, job opportunities (Corey & Corey, 2002).

The 'meet and greet' phase of each group session remains crucial and will need to be skilfully facilitated. On one level, the members are encouraged to develop appropriate social skills and move beyond their preoccupation with self. On another level, it affords facilitators the opportunity to assess the mental state of individual members. Planning for, and facilitating the session can be adapted accordingly. If there are concerns about a member's mental state, facilitators will not address the psychiatric problem in the session, but will ensure that the member gains access to a mental health professional in as empowering a manner as possible (Tilbury, 1994).

The content of the work phase should address individual as well as group needs. As such, the work phase of consumer groups does not differ substantially from the norm. However, goal attainment may follow a circular pattern in the case of some conditions, as consumers' abilities to function and participate may vary in accordance with fluctuations in their mental state.

Common issues to be addressed

Loss and mourning of life goals   As in all work with people with health problems, loss, mourning and redefining life roles and goals is a major focus in work in the mental health field (Ross & Deverell, 2004). While this is understood in the health context, it is often overlooked in mental health work. Working on these issues is time-consuming, cannot be hurried, and forms a major task of the work phase of groups (Corey & Corey, 2002).

Significance of goal-setting   Facilitating consumers to identify their individual goals presents a particular challenge. The process of identifying the goals constitutes a major task for consumers and facilitators as the mental disability has often wreaked havoc with consumers' life goals (Corey, 1995). The sense of direction in life may well be lost because of loss of confidence and 'functionality' (relationship ability, socialisation, concentration, cognitive skills). In addition, facilitators have to empower consumers to set their own goals because through stigma others have often usurped their right to make decisions. All too often, consumers have become accustomed to others taking responsibility for them, which, while very disempowering, also offers a 'safe' alternative to the anxiety of taking responsibility themselves. The philosophy and process of empowerment is specifically addressed in literature concerned with the strengths-based approach.[14]

Expectations of others   Consumers need to have the freedom to be proud of and satisfied with their own decisions, rather than always feeling guilty that they did not meet others' expectations. If not really comfortable with their own goals, they are frequently left feeling they have to pretend that 'one day' they will meet their own previous expectations and those of others close to them. This state of mind gets in the way of consumers developing new 'valid' life goals as the goals they make tend to be experienced as 'interim'. The goals they set for themselves need to meet their own understanding of quality of life, while also being realistic and attainable. This includes taking cognisance of the context in which they live, as the group experience generally does not aim to make macro changes to the living context of members.

Stigma   Although there are similarities in the challenges faced by people with physical and mental health issues, those with mental health issues have to contend with far greater levels of stigma in every aspect of their living (Fellin, 1996). When identifying their individual goals, this reality impacts both on the image people with mental disability will have of themselves and the challenges they will face from the community. Despite struggling with the effects of stigma, ironically when living in deprived communities, consumers run the risk of censure from the community if they are seen to have more opportunities than others from their community.

Complication of fluctuating goals   Many mental disorders may be chronic in nature and manifest as alternating periods of stability and disability. Consequently, the needs and goals of consumers might fluctuate, creating a sense of uncertainty about the future which is, in itself, unsettling. Goals may thus need to be revisited and adjusted frequently (Tilbury, 1994). Facilitators should normalise this process by encouraging consumers to recognise and react to early signs of a relapse.

The termination stage

In accordance with the goal of attaining positive mental health, some consumers in open groups will reach the stage when they feel ready to leave the group (Corey, 1995). This need for termination might be prompted by a desire to explore other options (e.g. temporary employment) or because consumers find that group programmes no longer address their individual goals adequately. Ideally facilitators should regard this need to 'move on' as an indication of consumers' growth and an expression of their readiness to test their independence.

Facilitators should, as a matter of course, enable consumers to venture outside the group (Meagher, 2002). This could be attained by the group regularly reflecting on skills that were mastered, problems that were negotiated and support systems that were developed outside the group. Universalising the movement of people in and out of groups will:
- strengthen the self-confidence of consumers who plan to leave;
- create opportunities for dealing constructively with feelings of hope, anxiety and guilt which accompany termination; and[15]

- re-enforce consumers' knowledge that they could re-join the group at any time.

Facilitators must also be prepared to assist consumers who, because they might be experiencing a relapse, decide to leave the group. Ensuring that the consumer is linked with the appropriate mental health care resources would be the first priority. Thereafter, the facilitator should debrief consumers who remain in the group by normalising the event, and by reminding them that they have the power to invite the person back into the group as soon as his/her mental state has stabilised. The facilitator should further empower consumers by sharing and/or delegating the responsibility to visit the person if he/she is hospitalised.

Termination should also apply to facilitators. They should, from the outset, foster partnerships with consumers '… through the process of learning about one another's skills, knowledge, strengths, and abilities in mutual growth' (Meagher, 2002). As consumers master skills to contribute, participate, and engage with others, they will 'grow' into new roles (e.g. leadership roles) within the group. The challenge to facilitators is to decide when to step back and let the group become a self-help group, whether or not to take back the leadership role should the consumers request that, and when to assume the role of a co-facilitator supporting the consumer who leads the group. As with termination of consumers, this process should be normalised and done in partnership with the group.

Consumer group

Throughout the text case examples have been given, but the following short case study illustrates how difficult it may be for a consumer to become part of a group and yet how it provides a gateway into reintegration into mainstream society.

Ella, an auxiliary worker at a community based NGO, has been facilitating a weekly open group for the past three years. Currently nine members, of whom five have a mental disability, attend the group which lasts for two hours. A couple of weeks ago Jim (27), who was recently diagnosed with schizophrenia, visited the group for the first time. The primary health care nurse introduced him to Ella after he complained that he was feeling lonely and frustrated about staying with his parents.

At the venue (the local library) Jim was welcomed by all, and members started the session by introducing themselves and sharing their experiences since the last meeting. Although he chose not to participate, Jim then signed the attendance register along with the other members, which created a sense of belonging in the group.

One of the other members volunteered to tell Jim about the routine the group follows and added that Jim could also suggest topics for discussion or activities he would like the group to engage in. Ella suggested that the group's rules were revisited, so that everyone was reminded that participation is voluntary, that members will respect others' contribution, and that confidentiality will be upheld because members care for one another.

A member added that the group has just raised enough money to visit Robben Island, and that the outing will take place in two weeks' time. Ella led the group to discuss whether Jim could join the outing. Members decided that Jim should join, as they would want him to share in the excitement. One member recalled that she was invited to join a group outing shortly after joining the group, and that that episode convinced her that people really accepted her. It was concluded that Jim did not have to contribute towards this outing, and that he could participate in the next fundraising effort if he decided to become a member. Ella asked the member who acts as bookkeeper to review the group's finances, and the group confirmed their decision.

The group proceeded with the programme for the day, which included doing a few exercises and having a discussion around a member's current conflict with his sister who accused him of avoiding his chores at home. Ella ensured that every member had the opportunity to participate, and encouraged members to make suggestions about appropriate ways of dealing with the conflict.

During the refreshment break Ella assisted the member who acts as minute keeper to jot down the main discussion points, so that members could revisit them at a later stage. She asked Jim to add his contact details to the group file, and used the opportunity to alleviate his anxiety about not participating by referring to other members who also choose not to participate.

The group session was concluded after members planned for the next session during which Ella was not going to be present. They nominated a member to facilitate the session, and finalised the programme. Jim confirmed that he would be present and he departed alone after declining an offer of a lift home from a member.

Jim has since accepted the group's offer to become a member. Recently he reflected on his first few visits to the group.

Jim recalled that knowing that the group might reject him had made him anxious. He, however, also had become aware that he would not be accepted or rejected because of his illness, as he saw that members who had to deal with side-effects of the illness and the medication (e.g. poor social skills, muscle spasms and speech disturbances) participated and were accepted. Ella empowered Jim by replying that the group was there to ensure that members' needs were addressed, and that members held the power. Because all the members were confronted by problems, they treated one another with tolerance and did not stigmatise.

Jim added that initially he became frustrated by the group's unwillingness to deal with problems related to his illness. He noticed that they would listen to his concerns about his illness, advise him to speak to the clinic sister, and then change the topic. He nonetheless felt that his contributions were valued, as the facilitator and other members often asked whether he had had his concerns seen to.

Jim recalled the following highlights:

- the relaxed, welcoming atmosphere and making new friends (suitable venue, resources and socialising);
- the multi-faceted programme, which stimulated participation in both activities and discussions (right to choose and educative component);
- the fun created by the games, singing and refreshments (normalising and addressing loneliness); and
- the signing of the register, participating in planning, looking at other living arrangements (being empowered, learning new skills, reclaiming control and getting hope).

The members validated his observations and said that they noticed that he has started sharing his frustrations about living at home with them. Two members who currently live in a half-way house said that Jim was planning to visit them, and together they are considering other accommodation options.

Ella disclosed that although she is now the facilitator of the group, when she first joined the group as a member she had no friends, no job and no-where to stay.

Conclusion

Groupwork with consumers is challenging and rewarding. In this chapter it is argued that groupwork, facilitated by a wide range of providers, is a logical way of facilitating the integration of people with mental disability into the community. This is in keeping with the South African primary health care policy and is necessitated by the projected increase in numbers of consumers in the community and by the scarcity of mental health resources. Groupwork in this field, however, requires a particular mindset and specific skills, which this chapter has identified and described. It is hoped that, empowered with these insights, the reader will feel equipped, comfortable and excited about working in this field.

Q Discussion questions

1 What special insights and skills would enable a group facilitator to work in an empowering way with consumers?

2 How challenging is it to reflect on your own conceptions and attitudes towards consumers?

3 How would you use the insights you have gained from this chapter in your work place?

4 What would need to change in order for you to work in this way?

Endnotes
1 Freeman and Pillay, 1997; Fellin, 1996.
2 Meagher, 2002. This term and others like it, for example "service user", are the outcome of self advocacy and empowerment movements of people with mental disabilities. These terms demonstrate a move away from the passive, stigmatised patient role towards an active, participatory partnership.
3 WHO, 1984; Freeman & Pillay, 1997.
4 Desjarlais et al, 1995.
5 Lavikainen et al, 2000.
6 Orley & Sartorius, 1986.
7 Ross & Deverell, 2004; Gingerich, 2002.
8 Ross & Deverell, 2004; Tilbury, 1994.
8 Freeman & Pillay, 1997.
10 Corey, 1995; Corey & Corey, 2002.
11 Tilbury, 1994; Fellin, 1996.
12 Northen & Kurland, 2001; Corey, 1995.
13 Northen & Kurland, 2001; Corey, 1995.
14 Saleeby, 1996; Cowger & Snively, 2002; Rapp, 2002.
15 Northen & Kurland, 2001.

10 Substance dependence and groups

Peter Powis

Learning objectives

By the end of this chapter you should be able to:

- Identify the essential aspects of substance dependence which anyone involved in group treatment ought to know.
- Discuss relevant issues pertaining to clients who present with this problem.
- Present the model of 'stages of readiness to change' and its relevance to the groupwork context.
- Present a structure for a treatment programme within which group therapy can effectively function.
- Describe two types of group processes which together constitute essential ingredients for a comprehensive group treatment programme.
- Illustrate the facilitation skills required to work effectively with substance dependence.

Introduction

Substance dependence is one of the most common and invasive health problems affecting all communities in South African society. However, helping professionals frequently report that their experiences of working with substance dependence have been frustrating and unrewarding, and that they therefore choose not to work with people with such problems. Some of this frustration and avoidance is a result of negative and narrow stereotypes of addicts and alcoholics such as that they are manipulative, dishonest and resistant to change. While it is true that substance dependent clients present many challenges to group therapists, many of the difficulties experienced in the field are a consequence of firstly, a lack of adequate training in the field, and secondly of a basic misunderstanding of the nature of substance dependence. For example, failure to understand substance dependence as a **primary condition** leads many untrained counsellors into fruitless attempts to help clients address 'underlying issues' considered to be causative of the substance dependence.

Numerous problems can present with a substance dependence, including psychiatric problems such as mood disorders and psychoses, medical problems such as gastritis, and social problems such as poverty and dysfunctional relationships. As a primary condition, substance dependence is more often the cause of such problems, not the consequence as is so often assumed. Even when problems such as a psychosis or depression appear to exist autonomously and precede the onset of substance dependence, it is fruitless to address them while the client is actively abusing substances. Frustration is therefore inevitable as substance dependent clients are unable to respond to any form of therapy (social, psychological or pharmacological), until the primary condition of substance dependence has been addressed as a priority problem in its own right.

This chapter starts by presenting the reader with a basic understanding of substance dependence in the section which outlines standard processes within treatment and therapy. Next, the nature of substance dependence and substance dependent clients is discussed, as well as implications of these characteristics for group treatment. It is hoped that this will allow the reader to develop a more realistic yet optimistic attitude to substance dependence as well as more effective group facilitation skills.

Evidence suggests that substance dependent clients respond differently to treatment depending on their **readiness to change**.[1] Prochaska and Declemente's model of change and its implications[2] is presented in order to further assist the reader in designing effective group interventions for clients at differing stages of readiness to change. These stages are described in the section describing the psychological and spiritual aspects of substance dependence.

This chapter presents a structure for a comprehensive treatment programme which can be built around the two types of group intervention strategies presented:
- Damage awareness and motivation (DAM) groups.
- Relapse prevention groups.

The theoretical rationale underpinning these groups as well as a discussion of the requisite facilitation skills for running them are presented. Specific case examples are given to illustrate these group processes and the facilitator skills involved.

Processes in substance dependence therapy

The group processes discussed in this chapter may be utilised in a specialist residential substance dependence treatment centre, where people with a fairly serious substance dependence stay 'in-house' for a number of weeks or months, or a specialist out-patient treatment centre, where clients attend sessions a few times per week. In South Africa such treatment centres tend to exist in or close to urban areas. In addition there are certain generalist settings in both urban and rural areas, such as community-based centres, advice offices or clinics, and day hospitals, where substance dependent clients present with a variety of medical, psychological, family or social problems. Very often these problems (for example gastritis, abuse of women and children, tuberculosis) are directly or indirectly related to substance dependence. This connection may only emerge as the practitioner becomes better acquainted with the details of the client's life. In South Africa where very few specialist substance dependence treatment centres exist, especially in rural areas, it is often unrealistic to refer such clients to a specialist treatment centre for substance dependence. It is hoped that some of the guidelines presented in this chapter are of value to practitioners working in such settings, or students who may one day work there, and who wish to develop treatment programmes or adequate referral strategies for substance dependence.

Group therapy is well-suited to addressing many specific problems experienced by substance dependent clients. In particular, since groups are a microcosm of society, it helps members of substance dependence therapy groups to work on their relationship skills. Substance dependent clients show an inability to establish or maintain healthy relationships with themselves and others and this inability contributes to their substance dependence and to their difficulty sustaining an abstinent lifestyle (Flores, 1997). Groupwork recognises and works with this inability, particularly focusing on how members can communicate authentically with others. [This is illustrated in the case studies on relapse prevention groups later in the chapter.] However, if a group treatment programme is to be optimally effective, it needs to be complemented by additional services which ideally are all provided within the same context. The services described below should be regarded as essential, although the list is by no means exhaustive.

Assessment

As substance dependence manifests itself on all levels of being (physiological, psychological, and spiritual), the assessment should include all these areas. A thorough history should be taken of the duration, frequency, and quantities of substances used. In addition, a history of any past or present medical, psychiatric, psychological or spiritual conditions or treatment should be noted. Indicators of a 'dual diagnosis', where substance dependence is accompanied by another significant, equally important physical or mental condition, may call for special management.

The client's personal, educational and family history should be integrated into the overall picture, including any history of physical, emotional or sexual abuse. This may also require information from collateral sources. In addition the client's readiness to change should be assessed. [See the section below, on Psychological and spiritual considerations – Stages in clients' readiness to change.][3]

Detoxification

Many clients, most commonly but not exclusively those dependent on alcohol, benzodiazepine (sleeping tablets and tranquillisers) and opiate (heroin, codeine, wellconal, etc.) will need a carefully monitored detoxification process.

This may be done within the treatment setting or in another in-patient setting elsewhere prior to the client entering the programme. All group members should be sufficiently detoxified to be able to participate meaningfully in the group programme.

Involvement of significant others

The significant others of all group members should be involved in the overall treatment programme. Family members, friends, work colleagues and/or employers usually have direct experience of much of the destructive behaviour which accompanies substance dependence. The client usually screens out memories of much of this behaviour through denial, minimisation and shame, as well as through alcoholic blackouts or drug induced memory blanks. Gathering this collateral information and tactfully presenting it to the client is a crucial part of dismantling the denial system. In the process the family and other significant others, who may themselves be minimising the effects of the problem, can be given support to start with their own healing. They will also need guidance on how to support the substance dependent person's recovery while protecting themselves from further traumatic experiences should he or she not stay in recovery. Usually they have been enabling the substance dependent person in some way – i.e. unwittingly making it easier for them to continue with the manipulation, abuse, and deception which frequently accompany substance dependence. This enabling behaviour often arises out of a misunderstanding of substance dependence as something which is a consequence of something that happened in a person's life, rather than seeing it as a primary condition. Instead of setting boundaries on unacceptable behaviour, significant others end up excusing and tolerating it. Accordingly, it is suggested that the contract with new group members clarify that family involvement is an essential part of treatment, and that the information derived from this involvement may be introduced into the group context. Every effort should be made to ensure that this collateral information is accurate, and it should never be introduced into the group without asking the client's prior consent.

The substance dependent client in early treatment may resist the involvement of family and significant others. However, this resistance needs to be worked through so that the client can (i) face the real consequences of his/her substance dependence, (ii) develop more honest and open communication with significant others, and (iii) release the shame that lies trapped in unexposed and avoided secrets. It is suggested that significant others be seen in large groups of multiple families and significant others, as well as separately with the client.

Individual counselling

Individual counselling as an adjunct to group therapy should be focused on issues relating to substance dependence. These may include:
• Exploring the consequences of client behaviour and supporting clients to face and take responsibility for these consequences.

- Exploring issues which may affect the client's recovery such as shame, low self-esteem, fear of honesty and rejection, past emotional, physical or sexual abuse which may have been perpetrated on the client, and unresolved losses.
- Helping the client identify high risk situations. [See section on Relapse prevention groups.]
- Supporting the client in making lifestyle changes to stay clean and sober.

As substance dependent clients typically present at a time when things in their lives are chaotic, such counselling can be containing and support the client's optimal use of the group. There are however certain cautions which should be noted. Firstly, the helper should be alert to the tendency on the part of clients to get into **victim-thinking**, whereby they blame their own destructive behaviour on other people or traumatic life events. Secondly, for the first 6 to 12 months after leaving the supportive structure of a treatment programme, clients should not be encouraged to explore very deep issues which could distract them from the primary focus of their programme – that of changing their attitudes and lifestyle in order to stay clean and sober.

Special focus groups

In addition to the groups mentioned in this chapter, a 'complete programme' should incorporate groups which focus on some of the specific issues mentioned in the section on individual counselling. These may include **grief groups** to allow group members to start the process of mourning the many losses commonly experienced by substance dependent clients. In the process group members start to develop the ability to tolerate uncomfortable emotions – a life skill which they have usually not allowed themselves to acquire.

Gender groups, where men and women working in separate groups allow a safe space for group members to start working with abusive experiences, anger, and some issues to do with relationships and sexuality. Finally, every treatment programme should have a discharge plan, which may include **after-care groups** (usually once per week) which provide support to clients grappling with making and sustaining lifestyle changes in the real world.

Opportunities to listen to substance dependent people

It is crucial that people in treatment develop some hope and optimism that change is possible, and that they gain an understanding of how this change is achieved. There are few more effective ways of achieving this than to provide opportunities for group members to listen to other substance dependent people who have a track record of living clean and sober lives. It is important that such speakers have real credibility and are **living**, not just talking about the principles of a changed lifestyle. In this writer's experience speakers from the fellowships of Alcoholics Anonymous and Narcotics Anonymous who are living the principles of the '12-step programme' play an invaluable role in building hope and modelling recovery principles.[4] It is recommended that people in treatment make connections with these fellowships as part of the programme. Another valuable component is to provide lecture-discussion groups on important topics such as the nature of substance dependence, denial, the grief process, and dealing with shame. This helps clients to develop a conceptual understanding of their problems which complements the experiential aspects of the programme.

Spirituality

Substance dependent clients represent a diversity of spiritual backgrounds, ranging from those who want to follow a particular religious path, to those who are agnostic, to those who are atheistic. As spiritual emptiness is such an important aspect of substance dependence, a comprehensive programme should provide some form of spirituality which addresses this in a way that is meaningful and acceptable to all its clients.

The nature of substance dependence

Substance dependence is a complex but well defined condition or illness which operates and manifests itself on all levels of being. In order to understand the rationale behind the group therapy processes described in this chapter, it is necessary to understand the nature of substance dependence.

Physiological and neurochemical considerations

On the physical level there are numerous physiological and neurochemical manifestations and consequences which vary widely depending on the substances ingested, the amount, and duration of use. These consequences need to be assessed firstly so that unsuitable group members can be screened out of group therapy (e.g. alcoholic clients who have sustained reversible or irreversible brain damage resulting in cognitive impairment, which would compromise their ability to participate in a group).

For many clients there is a genetic component to their substance dependence. One inference may be that their formative experience was disrupted by substance dependent parents or significant others. Such clients ('adult children of alcoholics') may need special help to deal with issues arising from their upbringing as well as issues arising from their own substance dependence. Regardless of whether or not there appears to be a genetic component to the client's substance dependence, it has been clearly shown that substance dependence involves a neurobiological aspect whereby the functioning of the brain in affected individuals results in (i) a conditioned, self-reinforcing aspect to the repeated use of substances, and (ii) vulnerability to internal and external cues which may initially predispose certain individuals to substance dependence and, once a pattern of use is established, to craving for the substance of choice. In short it is helpful for clients to understand that once substance dependent, they have a condition which differentiates them from 'non-substance-dependent' people. This understanding helps explain their inability to control their use and can eliminate much of the confusion and shame which usually accompanies the condition.

Psychological and spiritual considerations

Denial   On the psychological level the symptom of primary importance is that of denial. It is this very powerful defence mechanism which allows a substance dependent person to repeatedly re-enact destructive behaviour – behaviour which has profound negative consequences for themselves and others. The fact that the substance dependent person thereafter denies the severity of these consequences, or blames them on something other than substance use, is quite baffling to the layperson. No group therapist can afford to underestimate the enormous power of denial in all its forms (such as justification, minimisation, blame and self-pity or victim-thinking). While the client is still in some denial, the chances of a sustained recovery are minimal. Dismantling denial is therefore the first and primary target of group therapy in the initial stages of treatment of substance dependence. The group process is structured so as to raise the clients' awareness of how substance dependence has affected their lives, thereby increasing motivation to change. Strategies for doing this are presented in the section on group intervention strategies. As discussed above, one strategy in this respect is the involvement of family and significant others. In sharing their experience of the clients' behaviour with the client and facilitator, significant others offer a more accurate perspective on the nature and consequences of substance related behaviour.

Ambivalent motivation and the wheel of change   Even as denial gradually makes way for awareness of the need to change, substance dependent clients manifest intense ambivalence about changing. On one hand they can see the need to change their substance use behaviour while on the other hand they feel fearful of living without substances and resentful of the lifestyle changes required to maintain recovery. They can indefinitely sustain an internal 'bargaining' process whereby a full commitment to change is avoided. If this ambivalence is not explored and resolved, relapse is inevitable, which for some substance dependent people could literally be fatal. [Strategies for dealing with ambivalence are mentioned below when discussing clients in the contemplation stage of change, as well as in the section on intervention strategies.]

How clients respond to groupwork will to some extent depend on how ready they are to change. The specific strategy adopted with a client or group of clients therefore needs to be adjusted to the individual's or group's readiness to change.[5]

Stages in clients' readiness to change   There are four stages in the process whereby clients become ready to change their substance dependence: the precontemplation, contemplation, preparation, and action stage. Clients in the **precontemplation stage**[6] are those who, usually because of their denial, see nothing problematic about their substance use and have no desire to change. In group therapy the facilitator's task is to create a climate of safety and trust where group members can be confronted with facts about their substance use.

If this is done firmly but supportively without eliciting defensiveness, group members can absorb new information. This should begin to raise their awareness of the effects of substance use and gradually increase motivation to change.

Those in the **contemplation stage** are more aware of the negative costs of their substance use but are ambivalent about changing. These clients benefit from similar strategies to those in the pre-contemplation stage. In addition there are specific strategies aimed at increasing motivation to take appropriate action. [See section on Group intervention strategies.] Most substance dependent clients will initially be extremely ambivalent about accepting the nature of their substance dependence and the changes required of them to stay clean and sober; the group facilitator should regard this as normal and something to be worked with.

Clients in the **preparation stage** have begun to accept that change is necessary but for various reasons are hesitant to take action. The task of the group facilitator is to continue to raise motivation to change, while also helping group members generate practical courses of action. Unless this is done clients can be paralysed by avoidance and procrastination and never reach the **action stage**. In this latter stage the group facilitator needs to support group members in carrying out their decisions to change and in removing real or imagined obstacles to changing their lifestyles. This should include encouragement to attend support groups such as Alcoholics Anonymous and/or Narcotics Anonymous. Attendance of these support groups also plays a crucial role during the next stage, **maintenance of change**, where group members are helped to develop new attitudes, values, life skills, and relapse prevention strategies which enable them to deal with life in new ways. They may also need help in dealing with 'unfinished business' such as unresolved losses and old resentments.

It is helpful to create a group consisting of members at different stages of readiness to change. The skilled facilitator then uses the group process in such a way that those in the early stages of pre-contemplation and contemplation are 'pulled' towards greater willingness to change by those in the more advanced stages. [See next section.]

Distorted self-worth and relationship difficulties It is important that the group facilitator be aware of the distortions of self commonly manifested by substance dependent people. In some individuals, these distortions may predate the onset of the substance dependence while in others they are more likely to be purely a consequence of the long-term excessive use of substances.

Many substance dependent people have a fragile sense of self, which may be revealed by extreme sensitivity to criticism, emotional dependence, and avoidance of real intimacy or connectedness. On the other hand they may display an inflated sense of self-importance revealed by attention-seeking behaviour, a sense of invincibility or grandiosity, and a sense of entitlement (exploitative relationships in which they expect to receive without giving). These symptoms of ego inflation are of course really a defence against a fragile sense of self. Whether they display low or inflated self-esteem, such group members have many features in common, including:

- Difficulty experiencing or expressing feelings moderately: They tend to either feel emotionally numb or to feel very intense emotions, especially when hurt or angry. Most substance dependent clients also express extreme emotions when things do not go their way, and have low tolerance of 'life on life's terms'. Related to this difficulty, a large proportion of chemically dependent people display extremism in many areas of their lives (an 'all or nothing' approach to life). For this reason a valuable by-product of group therapy is to help group members to develop the capacity to see themselves 'in process,' instead of reacting to situations and feelings impulsively and compulsively. This capacity to delay impulses and use feelings as 'signals' is often referred to as the **observing ego**.[7]

- Related to the above, many substance dependent clients have difficulty respecting the behavioural and emotional boundaries which people and society sets to deal with the flow of action and communication. They may also experience difficulty setting appropriate boundaries on their own emotional expression, allowing this to intrude into the emotional space of others in impulsive ways.
- Difficulty empathising with and listening to others.
- A sense of emptiness which is exacerbated by a growing sense of isolation from the world – especially the non-substance dependent world. This may be a product of the progressive nature of substance dependence; the condition progressively grips the dependent person to the point where their relationship with substances becomes dominant to the exclusion of all previously valued people and activities. (This is often referred to as a preoccupation or obsession with substances.) Indeed, many substance dependent people report that even prior to the development of their substance dependence they felt 'apart from' the mainstream of life.
- A deep sense of shame usually accompanies this sense of isolation. This shame may also precede the active substance dependence or simply be a consequence of it. The fact that the nature of substance as an illness is not well understood by helping professionals or the public at large perpetuates the stigma for the dependent person. They cannot understand why they are unable to control their use of substances like most other people can. [Refer to section on Distinguishing substance dependence from substance abuse.]
- Many of these characteristics manifest themselves in distorted thinking or distorted 'internal conversation'. This may include ruminating on the unfairness of life and other people (blame and self-pity), and 'catastrophising' (for example, considering themselves to be hopeless; interpreting a small disagreement as a sign of personal rejection).

As they have learned to use substances to deal with their feelings and the world around them, it is crucial that substance dependent clients learn new ways of relating to themselves and others. Group therapy provides a rich context within which to correct these maladaptive coping responses. The group context provides important opportunities for clients to learn new ways of relating to others and for identifying and expressing feelings in more appropriate ways.

For this to happen there needs to be a very clear contract with every group member. This contract should absolutely clarify the behavioural norms, boundaries, limits and expectations of group members. These would include what is acceptable and unacceptable behaviour, the expectation of listening and treating one another with respect, the times of the groups and the expectations of punctuality, and consequences of violating norms and boundaries. In addition, the contract should clarify confidentiality, and emotional and physical safety within the group. Releasing shame requires that group members reveal their shameful secrets and presupposes a deep level of trust. This cannot be achieved without clear norms and boundaries.

It is suggested that with substance dependence group members contract not to form exclusive relationships with one another. Because of their difficulty adhering to boundaries, the contracting process provides a very important opportunity for resocialisation of substance dependent people. It is therefore crucial that group facilitators apply the contract rigorously and enforce consequences when it is violated. Failure to do so results in loss of respect for the facilitators and the group process.

Distinguishing substance dependence from substance abuse

Not everyone who uses or even abuses substances is substance dependent. Substance abuse is a repetitively or intermittently planned activity practised with the intention of getting intoxicated (Parran, 1996). While substance abuse can cause considerable harm, most substance abusers eventually 'mature' to the point where they use substances in moderation.

On the other hand substance dependence is a primary, chronic and progressive illness (the intensity, and/or amount of use increases over time with increasingly damaging consequences). The illness is characterised by intermittent loss of control of use (Parran, 1996) and continued use despite repetitive harmful consequences in the user's life (Parran, 1996) and usually some form of preoccupation with substances and substance related activities. These characteristics will not be found with the non-dependent substance abuser.

Whereas the substance abuser may be able to use substances in moderation, the person who has become substance dependent should be helped to accept that they will never be able to use habit-forming substances again. For group members this acceptance only comes at the end of a process involving the stages of change mentioned above.

While this chapter focuses on group interventions for substance dependent people, some of the techniques and principles described may be applied to groups with substance abusers.

Group intervention strategies

The role and attitude of the facilitator

When working with substance dependence the group facilitator needs to take a more active role than in most other forms of group therapy. Substance dependent people tend to regard people outside of their substance using subculture as ineffectual, like many of the authority figures they have resisted in

the past (Flores, 1997). They have also been used to getting away with manipulation, dishonesty, and avoidance in the outside world. They will tend to form
negative transference distortions to therapists who allow them to repeat the
same patterns in the group (Flores, 1997). Facilitators therefore need to communicate an attitude of calm strength which is capable of supporting and challenging group members. This attitude provides an experience where the 'old
behaviour' which characterised their active 'using behaviour' is no longer reinforced. Developing the 'presence' in the group takes time and experience.

Whether the setting is an in-patient or out-patient one, most but not all group
members are likely to be in complete denial (pre-contemplation), or ambivalent
about change (contemplation). They may also be fearful (and therefore defensive), and partly or wholly hostile to the idea of being in group treatment. Group
members will not own most of these feelings and will therefore tend to project
them onto the therapist(s). It is therefore strongly recommended firstly that facilitators work in pairs rather than alone, and secondly that they be armed with an
acute awareness of themselves and the dynamics which arise in such a group. It
is especially important that they are aware of their feelings in the group. These
feelings are useful diagnostic information about the general attitude of the group
as a whole, and the feelings of individual members. For example, if the facilitator becomes aware of feeling incompetent and powerless, it is probably a reflection of the way the group members feel. As these feelings are uncomfortable for
group members they tend to unconsciously project them onto the facilitators.
Facilitators therefore also need to be aware of their vulnerabilities as people so
that they do not identify with or take personally the many feelings which are
projected onto them. A group facilitator who lacks confidence could interpret
feelings of helplessness and incompetence as indicators of a real lack of competence, and succumb to the group (unconscious) pressure to take on these feelings.
Similarly a facilitator who wants to be popular with group members would be
vulnerable to manipulation and would lose the respect of the group.

It is evident in the case study on a DAM group in progress that the therapeutic value of any group lies in it evoking an optimal amount of discomfort
in group members. Facilitators therefore need to be sufficiently mature and
'whole' to tolerate and contain these uncomfortable feelings.

Damage awareness and motivational (DAM) groups

DAM groups form the backbone of a group-based substance dependence treatment programme. They are especially helpful in dismantling the denial systems of clients in the pre-contemplation and contemplation stages, but also
help strengthen motivation in clients in more advanced stages of readiness to
change. The aims of DAM groups are the following:
- To create opportunities for sharing and identification which raise each
  group member's awareness of specific damaging consequences of substance use to self and others (i.e. specific incidents from client's lives which
  illustrate these damaging consequences).
- To raise awareness of distortions in self-image or misplaced beliefs about
  self. For example the misplaced belief that 'despite my substance use, I

have been a caring and responsible student/worker/parent/partner/son/ daughter'.
- In the course of this awareness-raising process to increase concerns in group members about their substance use which in turn serves to increase their motivation to change by developing the discrepancy between their goals and intentions, and their actual behaviour and real life situations.[8] [See case study below for an example.]
- To encourage honest, trusting and constructive communication within the group (this would include sharing feelings which are brought up by what-ever is being discussed in the group, and openly identifying with other group members).
- Open communication in turn allows group members to develop the capacity of the observing ego which Flores (1997: 594) defines as 'the capacity for insight, self-honesty and reflection'.

It may be helpful to facilitators and group members to structure DAM groups so that the effects of substance use on specific aspects of life are explored sep-arately and systematically. So groups may on different occasions focus on: damage to self (physical, mental and spiritual and moral); damage to family and friends; damage to finances; damage to work, career and/or studies; and damage to recreational activities and creativity.

Building motivation in DAM groups   As group members 'wake up' from their denial and start to see the damaging consequences of their substance use, motivation to change begins to develop naturally. However, Miller and Rollnick (1991) described 'motivational interviewing' techniques specifically for building and enhancing motivation to change in clients who have not fully committed themselves to active change. Many of these techniques are of value in both individual counselling and group therapy. The technique of **develop-ing discrepancy** is one such of the processes described by Miller and Rollnick (1991). In this technique the group facilitator helps the client to become aware of the discrepancy between what he or she intended for their lives, and what has in fact happened as a result of their substance abuse. [An example is given in the case study involving Erica, below.] In the course of DAM groups there are many opportunities to build and enhance motivation to change by eliciting and amplifying self-motivational statements.[9] Miller and Rollnick mention four categories of statements which group facilitators should aim to elicit and amplify. Any statement by the group member which:
- reflects recognition of problems relating to substance use;
- reflects concern or worry about substance related problems;
- indicates a real intention to change substance use behaviour; or
- suggests the development of an attitude of hope or optimism that change is possible.

The case example below illustrates the use of some of these techniques.

A DAM group in process

Joseph, a 37-year-old alcohol and mandrax dependent client has, with some difficulty, just shared a specific incident which illustrates his neglectful and abusive behaviour towards his wife and children. Erica, a 56-year-old alcohol and tranquilliser dependent woman, has been looking detached and irritated as though she cannot relate to what Joseph has shared. However, the facilitators remember that Erica's daughter, Beverly had told Erica that she was no longer prepared to leave her 16-month-old son with her because she regarded her as too unreliable. One of the facilitators comments on Erica's apparent detachment and irritation and asks whether she can identify with Joseph. Erica looks quite taken aback and says that she cannot identify in any way. (Thereby revealing her denial and implying that her problem is far less serious than Joseph's; that she is a good partner, parent and grandmother because she would never abuse or neglect the people she loves.) When pressed by the facilitator and other group members about whether she has ever been under the influence of substances while caring for her grandchild, Erica eventually admits that she has. With further pressing it finally emerges that Erica has carried her baby grandson around while under the influence of alcohol. This has threatened his safety in a way that contradicts her self-image as a caring and responsible grandmother.

The facilitators asked questions such as 'How does this incident affect the way you see your drinking and use of pills?', and 'Now that you can see this, what concerns do you have about your drinking and taking pills?' and 'Is this the kind of grandmother you would like to stay or would you like things to be different?' These questions are specifically aimed at increasing Erica's motivation to change by eliciting and amplifying:

- her recognition that she has a problem;
- her concern about this problem by developing discrepancy between her goals and intentions as a grandmother on one hand, and the reality of her putting her grandson's well-being at risk on the other; and
- her intention to do something about the problem.

The group facilitators then helped Erica to enter the world of her feelings of shame around this incident, and facilitate her expressing these feelings to the group. She has suppressed her feelings about her substance use and many other issues in her life for many years. Simply getting in touch with her feelings and expressing them is itself therapeutic.

Other group members were encouraged to identify with Erica's feelings, even though the specific incidents in their lives were different to hers. This process of revealing and exploring a source of shame has prevented Erica from disidentifying (making herself different from others in the group) from Joseph and the group. This would have perpetuated her social isolation which characterised her life prior to entering treatment. (A golden rule of group therapy is that group members' behaviour in the group will reflect their often longstanding patterns of behaviour outside the group.)

Apart from challenging Erica's denial system, the facilitator is using the technique of **bridging** (Flores, 1997). This involves linking members of the group who may share similar issues or types of damage, by leading group members to clarify these links. This is especially helpful in keeping would-be isolated group members connected to the group. Such would-be 'isolates' are often more open to fellow group members linking them to the group than to the facilitators doing so.

The issues emerging from the focus on Joseph and Erica triggered some strong emotions in some other group members. In identifying with Joseph and Erica, they were remembering similar incidents from their own experiences of using substances. This process was the beginning of their emergence from denial. As they identified with each other they started to see the common factor* in the behaviour of which they were most ashamed. This new awareness had at least two important consequences: firstly they started to internalise the motivation to change, and secondly the sharing allowed them to start letting go of the shame which had remained trapped by their denial and secrecy. By sharing their damaging behaviour they were also starting to own and take responsibility for their actions.

While the facilitators allowed the sharing of these experiences to unfold, they noticed that Shamiela, an 18-year-old dagga and heroin addict, was becoming increasingly angry. On inviting her to share what her anger was about, she reluctantly spoke of her experience of growing up with a father who abused substances and who often became abusive and neglectful when under the influence. This sharing not only provided a valuable opportunity for her to express repressed feelings, but also gave the older members of the group an opportunity to develop some empathy for how their family members had suffered from their substance use. This led to discussion of an issue which frequently emerges in treatment – that of sub-stance dependence patterns which reproduce themselves over generations within families. Shamiela was not the only group member who had grown up with a substance dependent parent. Many of these group members had promised themselves that they would grow up differently from the substance dependent parents who had caused them pain. They had however become ashamed of how they had become much like the very parents who had harmed them. Shamiela herself could see how she was well on her way towards repeating the patterns of her father which had caused her so much suffering. This further reinforced a personal understanding in group members of their powerlessness to use substances in moderation and of the genetic or inherited component of substance dependence for many people.

By evoking the expression of these feelings in a safe setting, the facilitators were able to help group members to develop the capacity of the **observing ego** (Flores, 1997). In this case they were helped to identify feelings of shame and observe themselves in the process of reacting to these feelings by avoidance, wanting to run from the group, and wanting to push people away through angry defiance. With repeated experiences this capacity can be generalised to the outside world where they will at times be called upon to tolerate uncomfortable feelings.

The common factor being that they could not predictably control their use of substances nor their related behaviour, despite intentions to the contrary, and that this had caused harm to themselves and others.

Relapse prevention groups

These groups are important for clients in the preparation, action, and maintenance stages of change. They may also help clients in the contemplation stage to realise that change is not as difficult as they had imagined. Relapse prevention groups are not appropriate for clients who are not considering making changes to their substance use (who have not reached the latter stages of the contemplation stage. These clients need to participate in DAM groups until they have started to move out of their denial.

Wanagaratne et al (1994) report that substance dependent people most often attribute relapse to three types of situations: uncomfortable internal feeling states (e.g. anger, sadness, anxiety), conflict situations, and situations involving peer pressure to drink or use drugs. Relapse prevention groups are therefore largely aimed at helping clients to learn the skills to cope with such situations without resorting to the use of substances. Specifically these groups aim to help clients to:

- Identify high risk situations which include external situations such as old drinking or drugging haunts and mixing with former fellow users and internal high risks such as old patterns of thinking or 'internal conversations' (what the AA and NA members call stinking thinking), as well as negative feeling states such as anger, anxiety, loneliness and depression. As group members habitually use substances to take away negative thoughts and feelings, negative emotions challenge their ability to sustain abstinence.
- Develop coping skills for dealing with these situations/thoughts/feelings where this is realistic and possible; this requires that clients be involved in an honest appraisal of their strengths and weaknesses.
- Develop the humility and the ability to avoid situations which are avoidable and with which they are unable to cope (e.g associating with substance dependent 'friends').
- Develop the skills to cope with cravings which inevitably arise from time to time in recovery.
- Develop strategies for dealing with 'slips' so that if they do occur they do not have to become full-blown relapses.

In relapse prevention there are many different possible areas of focus and many techniques which can be used. It is therefore impossible to give a comprehensive review of all relapse prevention techniques in a chapter of this nature, and the reader is encouraged to consult the references provided. However, a few examples of relapse prevention group activities are described in the case studies below.

It is the writer's experience that the group should provide the context where new behaviour can be enacted. Action is an essential ingredient of change. Maintenance of sobriety usually depends on taking action (even if that action is to avoid a situation). Knowledge of what to do is useless without the confidence to act. Such confidence is best developed by practising the action in a simulated situation. For this reason relapse prevention groups are often fun, lively and filled with action.

Case study 1: Relapse prevention group

Faizel, a 19-year-old dagga, mandrax and alcohol dependent man is leaving the in-patient treatment centre in four days' time. He is a tall, strong young man but without his drugs and alcohol he is quiet and shy. He has started to realise that after all that he has lost through his substance dependence, he cannot afford to use substances again. However, he lives in Mitchells Plain, and although not a fully fledged gangster, he was involved in some gang-related activities and some of his old using friends are gangsters. He is worried about what he is going to say to these people when he comes across them in the street. He expects them to tease him and to put pressure on him to use substances with them.

He first describes his home situation to the group in some detail. The facilitator then asks him to select four group members who could adequately play the roles of his former friends. Other members of the group are very familiar with the type of situation which Faizel faces. They are able to play the roles of these 'friends' very convincingly, welcoming him back into the community with invitations to share a 'slowboat' (dagga cigarette) or a 'button (mandrax) pipe'. When he tells them that he has stopped they start teasing him and putting more pressure onto him. At this point Faizel looks confused, unsure of himself and lost for words. The facilitator then stops the group and asks the observing group members and the four 'friends' to give him feedback. Faizel hears the group telling him that his lack of confidence gives them the impression that he is about to give in to the teasing, and is less than committed to staying clean. The group challenges him on his commitment and there is a brief explo-ration of some of his fears about being in recovery. Being a 'kwaai buttonkop' (heavy mandrax addict) was very much part of his previous identity. The group explores the payoff of having this counter-culture image which some people appear to admire. The facilitator helps reinforce his commitment to recovery by asking motivational questions which remind him of the mess his life was in when he came into treatment. (For example: 'Do you remember what you felt like when you spent those two nights in jail and your mother had to come and bail you out? Where were your friends then?', 'How would you like things to be different?')

The facilitator asks some of the group members to model more confident and effective ways of talking to his former 'friends' in a way which is appropriate to the Mitchells Plain street context. They speak clearly and confidently in the local slang and make eye contact without being overly aggressive. Both the verbal and the nonverbal behaviour is highlighted to Faizel who is then asked to repeat his role-play, modelling on what he has just observed. He has to do it a few more times before he conveys a convincing impres-sion of someone who is serious about refusing drugs. When he achieves this to the group's satisfaction they give him a round of applause and he breaks into a broad smile. All the active participants de-role from the role-play, and sit down.

The group also reminds Faizel to phone people from his Narcotics Anonymous group so that he can get sup-port as soon as he leaves this high risk sit-uation. In doing so he will prevent himself from ruminating on whatever feelings may come up from exposure to this situation (e.g. anger, cravings, self pity).

Case study 2: Relapse prevention group

A very common trigger for relapse is the negative inner voice which cunningly creates any justification to use substances. This is the voice of one side of the ambivalence; the part of the person which still wants to use substances, is afraid of change, or does not believe that lifestyle change is really necessary. This voice is so subtle yet powerful that every substance dependent person needs help to anticipate, recognise and neutralise it. It is helpful to give it a name so that group members can externalise this part of themselves and more easily take responsibility for controlling it. We could call 'him' or 'her' 'the Trickster' or 'the Inner Addict.'

Jeffrey is a 45-year-old cocaine and alcohol dependent married man with two young children. His wife has completely lost trust in him because of his womanising and other lies and deception while actively using. Although she has not divorced him, she has not yet decided whether she will accept him back into a relationship, preferring to wait and see how seriously he works at his recovery after he has completed treatment. Jeffrey will therefore not be returning to his wife and children when he leaves the Treatment Centre. Although he is ashamed of his actions while using and intellectually understands his wife's decision, he had hoped that she would forgive him and take him back immediately. He is therefore feeling disappointed, angry and sorry for himself. It is dangerous for anyone in early recovery to entertain such feelings on their own for any length of time.

He has identified that a major high risk situation for himself will be at the end of the working day when he faces going home to an empty and unfamiliar flat. As soon as he starts to feel angry and sorry for himself, the 'inner voice' of his 'Trickster' starts to 'talk' to him in the following vein:

'After all you've done to go for four weeks of tough in-patient treatment, she still won't trust you enough to take you back. After all that, you're sitting here all alone with no guarantee that she's going to change her mind. You could go to an AA or NA meeting, but what's the point, you might as well have a drink, or just one line of coke. That'll make you feel better and nobody has to know about it.' (The voice of the inner addict is whispered into his ear by a fellow group member sitting behind him; this person also knows the voice of self-pity very well). Jeffrey is already starting to look restless and uncomfortable, and the 'Trickster' goes on: 'You know how that one line or drink just settles you; maybe after doing that amazing rehab programme you can actually control it – you've been clean for two months now.' Jeffrey appears to become increasingly paralysed in his seat.

The facilitator stops the group and first asks Jeffrey how he is feeling. He says that he is feeling angry with his wife and tempted to go and use. The facilitator then asks the observing group members to give Jeffrey feedback. They tell him that the longer he allows himself to sit, giving attention to the sly inner voice, the more helpless he is becoming, and the more likely he is to give in. The facilitator asks Jeffrey what action he could take to deal with this inner voice before it gets the better of him. With the help of the group he comes up with a number of possible courses of action, starting with the most important one of telephoning another person in recovery – preferably his AA sponsor. (A sponsor is someone from one of the 12-step fellowships with considerable experience of recovery, who can support and guide another person in recovery to live according to their new lifestyle programme.)

He role-plays the same scenario again, this time getting out of his chair very early in the dialogue, phoning his sponsor, telling him how he feels, and arranging to meet him at an AA meeting in an hour's time. He is given feedback on his verbal and non- verbal behaviour and the group gives him a round of applause. Some of the remainder of his time in treatment is spent helping him to come to accept that his situation is a direct consequence of his drinking and drugging.

Conclusion

In this chapter on group therapy with substance dependence, an ideal multi-faceted treatment context has been described. The range of treatment services comprising this context is considered to be essential for a group therapy programme to be optimally effective.

The nature of substance dependence has been discussed. This understanding enables group facilitators to set appropriate group norms and avoid many of the common mistakes made by novice and experienced group therapists. Substance dependence has been described as a primary condition characterised by intermittent loss of control, preoccupation, and continuation of use despite harmful consequences. The latter characteristic can largely be explained by the power of the defence mechanism of denial. A primary focus of group therapy is therefore to challenge and penetrate this wall of denial.

Further common characteristics of substance dependent people have been described along with the implications for group therapy. These include: ambivalence about change; a distorted sense of self-worth and relationship difficulties; extremism; difficulty experiencing or expressing feelings moderately; and a sense of emptiness, shame, and distorted thinking. Many of these characteristics are indicators of the appropriateness of group therapy for substance dependent people. Group therapy provides an ideal relationship context in which group members gradually learn to replace 'old behaviour' with new, more constructive behaviour.

In order to create the kind of group climate where the desired change processes can occur, group facilitators need to display a delicate combination of qualities. These include a strict adherence to group norms and expectations, an ability to both challenge and support group members, and sensitivity to the emotional vulnerability which group members often conceal behind a mask of grandiosity and indifference.

In discussing the nature of substance dependence, Prochaska and Declemente's model of the stages of readiness to change (Miller & Rollnick, 1991) was discussed. One implication of this model is that group members require a flexible approach, depending on their readiness to change substance related behaviour. Along with the penetration of denial, a crucial aspect of group therapy with substance dependent people is to build motivation to change. Two specific types of group process are discussed in detail which constitute important focus areas for substance dependent clients. These are **damage awareness and motivational (DAM) groups**, and **relapse prevention groups**.

Practical case examples are presented which illustrate many of the principles and techniques discussed in the course of the chapter.

It is hoped that the reader will be motivated to move beyond the ambivalent attitude which many novice and experienced group therapists display towards working with substance dependence. Along with the challenge of managing HIV/AIDS, South Africa has few more pressing health challenges than that of managing the problem of substance dependence. Those who are willing to take up the challenge are strongly encouraged to experiment with the principles presented in this chapter, and to consult the references which follow.

Discussion questions

1 **a)** What is your understanding of the idea that substance dependence is a **primary** condition?

   b) What important implications does this have for a counsellor or group therapist?

2 Distinguish between substance abuse and substance dependence. Give at least five characteristics of substance dependence in your answer.

3 Give five process goals or aims of damage awareness and motivational (DAM) groups. What four kinds of group member statements should be elicited and amplified in these groups?

4 Give at least six examples of internal and external high risk situations which need to be addressed in relapse prevention groups (three examples of each).

Endnotes
1 Miller & Rollnick, 1991.
2 Ibid.
3 A useful description of the assessment is outlined by Jarvis, Tebbut and Mattick (1995).
4 'AA's 12 steps are a group of principles, spiritual in their nature, which, if practised as a way of life, can expel the obsession to drink [or drug], and enable the sufferer to become happily and usefully whole.' (Twelve Steps and Twelve Traditions; AA World Services Inc. New York 1953:15). The programme is ideally conducted under the guidance of a 'sponsor' (someone in recovery who is practising the principles in his/her own life and acts as a guide or mentor).
5 Prochaska & DiClemente, 1986.
6 Ibid.
7 Flores, 1997: 594.
8 Miller & Rollnick, 1991.
9 Ibid.

11 Groups for perspective transformation in health professional education

Madeleine Duncan

Learning objectives

By the end of this chapter you should be able to:

- Outline historical concerns in professional socialisation.
- Explain the need for health practitioners in contemporary society to become sensitised to issues of diversity.
- Propose principles for a transformation curriculum using six educational strategies.
- Explain the use of median groups to effect attitudinal change.
- Review resistances to a transformation curriculum.

Introduction

Graduate health professionals in South Africa play a significant role in promoting social justice and community development through the primary health care approach and compulsory community service (Department of Health, 2002). They collaborate with individuals and communities for the attainment of health objectives and, in doing so, require vigilant attitudes that affirm diversity, oppose discrimination, and promote inclusion. Goduka (1996: 30), writing on the moral imperatives of traditionally white universities in South Africa, states that:

> *Affirming diversity does not mean tolerance, acceptance, patronisation, benevolence or compassion, for these come from a place of implied superiority or favours granted individuals who are not part of the norm but who deserve some special treatment. The moral imperative grounded in the ethical and humanistic approach and devoted to the restoration and advancement of human dignity is at the core of affirming diversity.*

Given this benchmark for the affirmation of diversity, how may higher education programmes create space for students and educators to engage creatively with the challenges of advancing human dignity in the contexts of research, learning and service? Health professional training in particular needs to transform the perspectives of graduates about issues of power, difference, and interdependence as these pertain to the process of building healthy communities in a multicultural society. This chapter describes how groups are used to promote these curriculum outcomes in the four-year undergraduate occupational therapy programme at the University of Cape Town.

Historical context

The need to change the perspectives and attitudes of health professionals became evident during the South African Truth and Reconciliation Commission (TRC) special hearings on the health sector in June 1997 (Chapman & Rubenstein, 1998). The TRC revealed how the health system had been based on racism and how the culture of apartheid was perpetuated by complacency, ignorance and apathy on the part of many health professionals (Baldwin-Ragavin, De Gruchy & London, 1999). Despite codes of ethics and professional conduct stating the contrary, professional socialisation during the apartheid regime predisposed health professionals to collude in systematic violations of human rights in the grey zones of everyday practice. Perspectives about privilege, power, and race became submerged in the taken-for-granted ideology of so-called 'separate development' for Black people leading to segregated and disparately resourced health services.

Why perspective transformation?

Seedhouse (1991) suggests that practitioners may appear indifferent and insensitive to the politics of power because they have been socialised to follow ethical codes that have historically evolved within disease-based and patient-centred conceptualisations of health. Ethical codes that embrace concerns about social justice or the physical, psychological and social health consequences of human rights violations are more likely to sensitise practitioners to their role in promoting human dignity in the course of everyday practice.

Commenting on the TRC health sector hearings, Chapman and Rubenstein (1998: 127) argue that 'when health concerns are limited to the objective of curing disease and healing impairment, the likelihood increases that health professionals will not relate in a holistic manner to issues relating to the human worth and dignity of their patients. Such moral disengagement may be a critical factor in abusive behaviour'. They recommend that 'human rights education represents a long-term strategy for developing a civil society that respects and nurtures human dignity. Conversely, the protection and promotion of human rights is perhaps one of the most effective means of promoting health and human well-being' (ibid: 150).

The TRC challenge to educational institutions training health professionals was clear. Could curricula be developed that would promote **perspective transformation** and the moral engagement of staff and students within a rapidly changing social, health and education system so that a progressive realisation of a culture of human rights occurred?

First steps: Affirming diversity

There are no easy curriculum answers to address the complex educational issues raised by the TRC health sector hearings (Chapman & Rubenstein, 1998). Most clinicians, academics, and students are at heart morally sensitive but their personal power to effect change in systems or morally corrupt contexts is often limited. Personal power is strengthened through perspective transformation because it requires moral engagement: a stepping back from established ways of thinking about the world in order to ponder and if indicated, embrace alternative attitudes and behaviours.

Perspective transformation means freeing the self from the taken-for-granted ideology of social conventions, beliefs and modes of operation in order to view the world and its possibilities for affirming human dignity differently (Schubert, 1986). By learning to listen and understand deeply, alternative ways of looking at and behaving in our complex world may be developed (Mezirow, 1991).

By raising awareness about attitudes towards a range of diversity issues such as gender, age, race, class, and (dis)ability (Nieto, 1992), a first step towards resisting apathy and complacency may be taken. For example, client-centred health care may be approached from a pathologising perspective (disabled people are different from able-bodied people because they are impaired and therefore require care) rather than from a human rights and empowerment perspective (disabled people are fully human and therefore deserve equal opportunities to participate in society). The challenge at hand was to identify suitable curriculum strategies to promote these outcomes.

Responding to the challenge

Diversity is a fact of daily life and should therefore penetrate the inner core of the teaching and learning process if perspective transformation is desired. Slattery (1995: 56) suggests that curriculum is more than 'a tangible object or the implementation of planned lessons or course guides, it is a process of running the lifelong learning racecourse'. With this interpretation of curriculum in mind, the Division of Occupational Therapy at the University of Cape Town started developing a transformation curriculum in 1995 aimed at the affirmation of diversity. This would be a 'living curriculum'; one that immerses participants in critical examination, interpretation and understanding of oppressive and liberating attitudes within everyday academic and service learning contexts.

The traditional didactic approach of teaching ethics as a set of rules and principles was expanded to a phenomenological approach in which the attitudinal and moral-ethical dimensions of professional practice is progressively and iteratively examined throughout the four-year undergraduate programme. Occupational therapy students participate in service learning from their first year of training thereby creating a phenomenological platform for transformation initiatives. Attitudes and perspectives are particularly challenged in service learning contexts where the legacy of apartheid is most evident such as forced removal informal settlements or where human rights issues are most pertinent such as mental institutions and prisons.

Shaping a transformative educational environment

Adult education principles inform the development of human potential and are therefore foundational to the implementation of comprehensive health care programmes within the primary health care approach. Undergraduate health professionals who experience their own education as liberating are more likely to embrace attitudes that promote the development of human potential in the contexts of their work world. A transformative educational environment is one that practises what it preaches; it is a **'living curriculum'** that involves actively transforming knowledge and being transformed by it through the praxis (dynamic engagement) between educators, learners, and learning systems in a reciprocal process of exploration, action, and reflection (Freire, 1978).

The 'living curriculum' or what Shubert (1986: 33) and Slattery (1995: 56) call 'currere', is an iterative cycle of human inquiry; an inward–outward journey of communication and encounter; an ongoing interpretation and sense making of lived experience aimed at transforming 'being' in the world. Activities in a tertiary, living curriculum aim to foster:

- A sense of connectedness by creating a space for reflection and raising awareness of shared humanness and envisioning justice and compassion in an uncertain world. Transformative education, in other words, tells us not only what we are but also what we hope to become.
- The enactment of those values, beliefs and behaviours that give expression to the values of a particular discipline or profession. Currere may for example, find expression in **'class-as-community'** for it is through group reflection, dialogue, debate and discourse analysis that values may be shaped, attitudes revised and perspectives transformed. 'Class-as-community' in the occupational therapy undergraduate programme refers to a cohort of students who study together for four years. Students spend a significant amount of time learning together thereby creating opportunities for a sense of community to be fostered for the attainment of educational objectives.
- The inclusion of the wide range of knowledges and learning styles within different social groupings represented in a particular student group or class of learners. The outcome of this kind of curriculum can be independent, critical, and reflective thinkers who have a strong sense of personal power and who see themselves as proactive individuals engaged in the continuous re-creation of their work world (Brookfields, 1991).
- Moral engagement and **conscientisation**, which has been defined as 'learning to perceive social, political and economic contradictions and to take action against the oppressive elements of reality' (Freire, 1978: 15). These processes lead to a sense of personal power in acknowledging and (where possible and appropriate) opposing discrimination and oppression in its various forms whether internal (personal) or external (systemic).

Reflection: Shaping perspective change

Slattery (1995) suggests that curriculum or 'currere' is in essence the interpretation of lived experiences or a reconceiving of one's perspective on life. Reflection and critical thinking promote perspective transformation because they require 'thinking through' of the complex relation between the temporal and the conceptual; between the 'already am' and the 'hope to yet become'. Slattery (1995: 57), building on the work of Pinar and Grumet (1976) and Schubert (1986) highlights four, iterative stages or moments of reflection (regressive, progressive, analytical and synthetical) that should underpin curriculum development. The task of the living curriculum is to create learning opportunities for the moments to occur either individually or collectively. Examples of such opportunities are provided later in this chapter.

Regressive moment   During this moment reflections and dialogue return to the past. The past may, for example, be introduced through giving students prior readings about historical events that shaped the profession of occupational therapy. The readings may highlight assumptions about the universality of Western values and worldviews. Reflection is triggered by the educator (or individual students) raising questions about how the past, for example the legacy of apartheid education, impinges on the present. Students from historically advantaged and disadvantaged educational backgrounds may 'think through' (either privately or in dialogue) how the past manifests in who they are and what they do in the 'here and now' as co-learners and prospective practitioners of occupational therapy. During the regressive moment the self is observed functioning in the past but is enabled to return to the present by engaging with the next stage or moment, i.e. the progressive moment. This is a conscious step introduced by the educator or student as part of an explicitly structured reflective experience.

Progressive moment   This is when we envisage the 'what is not yet present' and discern where our jointly constructed futures may yet take us. This moment is both social (for example how may occupational therapy contribute to social redress and community development) and personal (for example how may I turn historical disadvantage into advantage?). During the progressive moment alternative ways of being in the world are imagined, leading to the next moment or stage. The progressive moment may be introduced through posing personal-professional scenarios for collective discussion or individual journaling.

Analytic moment   This is when one explores the dynamics and meanings of past, present, and future. By 'bracketing' what is, what was, and what can be, one is loosened from, and potentially more free, of the past, and hence one is more free to choose the present' (ibid, 1995: 57). The analytic moment involves attributing possible explanations for social and or personal events. An analytic moment may for example occur when students are able to recognise how power operates and are able to 'label' various forms of hegemony at play within the profession of occupational therapy. By implication, they are also able to extrapolate this understanding to their personal experiences of hegemony either as historically advantaged or disadvantaged learners. Choosing the 'present' may imply recognition of the potential within each individual practitioner to become an agent of change.

Synthetical moment   This moment puts the three preceding stages together to help inform the present. Students may for example gain a clearer idea of their current professional identity; their place in society or their personal-professional goals. By beginning with individual experience and making broader connections, the synthetical moment enables the interconnectedness, interdependence and common humanity within the group (or class-as-community) to emerge. Examples of such moments are shared later in this chapter.

These four moments offer a helpful frame for appreciating or precipitating shifts in perspectives that may occur through a range of education strategies for perspective transformation. Reflection and critical thinking about personal and professional values, beliefs, and attitudes must be highly valued within the training programme and explicitly elicited by a range of educational strategies. The next section briefly describes six education strategies used within the Division of Occupational Therapy to promote reflection, guide professional socialisation and trigger perspective transformation.

Education strategies: Perspective transformation

Strategy 1: Statement of Intent

The Division directs its business towards a strategic vision and purpose; both of which are aligned with the Faculty and University Mission Statements. A Statement of Intent sets the tone for normative behaviour in the Division. It was drawn up by staff and students following a series of anti-bias training workshops in 1996 and has been used to frame the contracting of norms and goals for median groups as well as other transformation initiatives, including curriculum design, within the Division since then.

> One of the cornerstones of our therapeutic approach is a value for human relationships. Occupational therapists meet many different people through their work. Past experiences influence the relationships we form. We believe that our attitude to any human condition that is different from what we ourselves are familiar with is usually based on assumptions, stereotypes, prejudice, and personal values. It is our personal and professional responsibility as staff and students to explore and deal with these biases on an individual and organizational level. Forms of discrimination that occupational therapists encounter relate to resistance against the diversity of disability, age, gender, class, sexual orientation and religion amongst others ... We are committed to raising awareness about diversity and trying to address all issues that lead to discrimination. The richness of shared experience and group process will be used in strategies to promote learning and develop skills to address discrimina-

tion in constructive and creative ways. Together we want to unlearn
prejudice, foster awareness of human rights and celebrate diversity.
(UCT Division of Occupational Therapy, 1999; Watson, 2002)

The Statement of Intent is supported by a set of **perspective triggers** or
questions aimed at raising awareness, critical thinking and reflection about
attitudes that promote the affirmation of diversity.

Strategy 2: Perspective triggers

The triggers are revisited intermittently at appropriate opportunities in the
curriculum. They form the subtext of educational decision-making processes,
for example guiding written feedback to students; informing the tone and content of handouts or ensuring that discussions remain vigilant about oppressive
practices. The triggers act as a rudimentary, reflective filter to facilitate the construction of inclusive knowledge, the deconstruction of unintentional prejudice
and the development of affirming attitudes. Service learning supervisors and
clinicians working with students are, for example, equipped with skills in giving written feedback based, amongst others, on vigilance about the perspective
triggers. Perspective triggers can take account of the following aspects:

Language   Do we use language in ways that perpetuate or oppose racism,
ageism, disabilism, sexism and other isms? Do we reinforce or challenge
stereotypes about gender, class, ability, religion or other dimensions of difference by our choice of words?

Culture   What prejudices do we hold towards people who are different from
us and how may these lead to the unintentional oppression of others?

Educational preparedness   What assumptions do we make about people
who have different educational histories to our own? How do these assumptions influence the reciprocity of knowledge sharing amongst us?

Status   What impact do our stereotypes about social status have on the balance of power in relationships between people? Do our attitudes affirm or
negate human dignity?

Knowledge   How may we affirm the indigenous knowledge of different
social groupings? In what ways do our biases marginalise the voices of other
perspectives?

Power   In what ways can the direction and force of influence be equalised?

Strategy 3: Class constitution

This is a working, one page document guiding the ethos of 'class-as-community'
and consists of a set of norms that guide collegiality during the knowledge con-

struction process within a particular cohort of students. It suggests ways in which the politics of identity in the group may be managed and aims to scaffold diversity, promote inclusion, and build cultural sensitivity. Each cohort of students develops a constitution soon after they enter the undergraduate programme and revisits it at strategic points, especially during median groups, throughout the ensuing four years of training.

Typically a constitution may consist of a purpose statement, an analysis of current strengths and challenges amongst the cohort of students, and a series of guidelines for class interaction and interdependence in the knowledge construction process. The process of developing the constitution is workshopped against the backdrop of relevant literature, anti-bias exercises, and group discussions about pertinent issues such as historical influences on professional values and ethics.

Strategy 4: Journaling

Journaling becomes a way of academic life for occupational therapy students throughout their four-year undergraduate programme. They are trained to value reflexivity; to 'think about their thinking' and to appreciate learning as the co-construction of knowledge between the self, the 'other' (for example fellow students, colleagues, clients or community members) and the environment. Students are encouraged to write 'learner's logs' on critical incidents or significant professional insights during service learning including ethical dilemmas, personal disjunctions due to perceived value clashes, concerns about human rights abuses and anxieties about working in a transforming society (Buchanan, Moore & Van Niekerk, 1998). Median group experiences (see below) are also journal-led, especially in the first year, adding depth to the learning that occurs from the group process through formative written feedback.

Substantial effort is put into giving written feedback in ways that affirm professional values and reinforce the transformation of perspectives. Use is made of the perspective triggers (listed under strategy 2) to guide the impact of the feedback. The longitudinal outcome of this approach to curriculum has yet to be investigated. Qualitative analysis of student service learning journals in community placements however reveals the development of vigilant attitudes and a growing sense of personal power in addressing moral and ethical disjunctions (Duncan, Buchanan & Lorenzo, 2004).

Strategy 5: Integrated assessment

Learning is substantially influenced by assessment practices. According to Biggs (1996: 5) 'transformative programmes are those that use assessment to drive institutional learning'. Assessment should therefore consist of multiple, complimentary formative and summative methods that collect quantitative and qualitative evidence of students' progress along the lifelong learning continuum. The moral dimensions of the student's thinking may be revealed and shaped by formative methods such as essays, journals, and portfolios. Summative methods such as orals, practical demonstrations, and written tests may likewise gauge levels of understanding and meaning-making about ethical and diversity issues, reasonable for each stage of professional development.

The Division makes use of six unifying criteria in all practice learning evaluation forms, namely 'integration of knowledge, understanding, technical skills, problem solving, attitudes and ethics/human rights' (Hager, Gonczi & Athanasou, 1994: 8). The importance of perspective transformation is emphasised by explicitly signalling the assessment of attitudes and awareness of ethics/human rights.

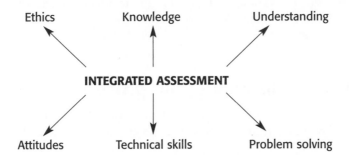

Figure 11.1 Unifying features of an integrated assessment
Adapted from Hager, Gonczi, Athanasou, 1994.

Strategy 6: Groups

According to Seedhouse (1991), 'determining how best to conduct one's life in the presence of other lives is the founding question of ethics' (281). Groups create opportunities for shared reflection about issues of critical personal-professional concern. Dominant social and professional discourses, ideologies and values may, for example, be thought through (Blackwell, 2000). The Division expanded the use of groups for educational purposes to include:

- **Large gatherings:** 'division-as-community', i.e. (all staff and students; approximately 80–120 people depending on voluntary attendance).
- **Median groups:** 'class-as-community', i.e. a cohort of approximately 30–40 students in a particular year of study who remain relatively constant for the four-year period of study.
- **Small groups:** 5–8 students working on problem-orientated tasks for example research projects and tutorials. These are not usually directly linked to transformation objectives but their group dynamics reinforce the large and median group processes.

Large and median groups are educationally useful strategies for creating collective reflection space about the ethical, moral and attitudinal dimensions of professional behaviour. An ethics, human rights and professionalism module that runs iteratively across all four years of the undergraduate programme provides the theoretical background to experiential learning in groups and in service learning contexts. Occupational therapy students do service learning from their first year and are expected to accrue a minimum of 1 000 hours of fieldwork during their four years of study.

Students work in all sectors of society including health (e.g. hospitals, mental institutions, mobile health clinics); industry (e.g. factories, mines); education (e.g. mainstream and special schools); and justice (e.g. prisons and places of safety) as well as non-governmental organizations (e.g. service organizations for special need populations such as street children and refugees); private practice (e.g. mental health, learning disabilities and medico-legal) and public enterprises (e.g. insurance industry, corporate business). Exposure to the world of work highlights for students the need for perspective transformation and for reflection about their emerging professional identities.

Educating through group process

Global trends in curriculum design favour the use of group-based learning. Group dynamics influence how and what people learn and who they may become. Groups open up the possibility for students to construct knowledge together whilst also learning how to work as members of a team and in so doing, to become sensitised to alternative visions of society (Wenger, 1998). Unfortunately, the pressure of getting through curriculum content often means that the tacit dimensions of the learning process in groups are either not addressed or deemed relevant to professional socialisation. Valuable opportunities for effecting attitudinal shifts about issues of diversity are therefore lost.

Optimising the educational benefits of groups requires academic staff to be:
- Skilled in identifying appropriate triggers for small-group learning.
- Informed about group theory, methods, and processes irrespective of their discipline-specific expertise.
- Skilled in group handling, i.e. enabling groups to reflect on group processes in order to learn about diversity and social discourses.

Not group psychotherapy

It is important to differentiate the training of health professional students in group work as a means for achieving therapeutic, social or development outcomes with clients from using groups as transformation strategy in their own professional education. The emphasis is on acquiring group work skills based on a range of theoretical models congruent with the domain of practice of a particular profession.

Occupational therapy students are, for example, trained to use group tasks, processes, and dynamics for development purposes in:
- Comprehensive health programmes, for example, psycho-education with mentally ill clients and life skills training with youth at risk.
- The attainment of occupational performance outcomes, for example, income generation projects with disabled persons; leisure enhancement

with retired individuals and play therapy with learning disabled or emotionally disturbed children.

The use of groups as transformation strategy in their own professional development extends the educational benefit of training in groupwork with clients. Students in the Division understand that large and median groups are not used to create a therapeutic or personal development space for themselves although there may be positive spin-offs such as increased self-confidence in sharing opinions. Rather, the emphasis in these groups is on:

- Contributing their perspectives about professional experiences so as to expand their own and their peer group's understanding of the surrounding socio-cultural context within which they practise occupational therapy.
- Appreciating the significance of informed, collective moral engagement, activism, and advocacy in effecting social change through personal-professional perspective transformation.

Large group gatherings

'Division-as-community' gatherings focus on promoting inclusive organizational behaviour amongst staff and students. These gatherings, held twice or three times a year, aim to establish an ethos of collegiality within the Division and awareness about the Statement of Intent (strategy 1). During these events, students take responsibility with staff for developing the Division's transformation agenda. Large group experiences act as intermittent reminders for the Division-as-community that transformation is an ongoing, lifelong learning agenda worthy of attention in the interest of nation building; professional development, and social relevance.

One gathering, for example, discussed the annual social event that is usually held in honour of the graduating class. Historically it took the form of a dance and meal at an upmarket venue. Group discussion focused on inclusion and exclusion; many students acknowledging that it had 'never entered our minds' that the venue, time, dress, food, alcohol, dancing, and late night transport excluded a number of students. Assumptions were unpacked against the backdrop of the Statement of Intent and the perspective transformation triggers and an alternative, more inclusive event was planned. At other gatherings, persons serving on human rights bodies or working at transformation training organizations are invited to workshop with participants on relevant topics emerging from within the life of the Division.

Defining median groups

Typically the median group consists of 15 to 35 people who meet formally for social learning through an exploration of the internal events of group behaviour and thought. The group and its socio-cultural context is the object of discussion, not the individual (Lyndon, 1995; Baworowska & Schick, 2000; Maxwell, 2000).

Parameters of median groups

The median group is not used to gain insight into how the unconscious mind of the individual operates; to assist with regression to earlier stages of infantile dependence for therapeutic purposes or to train group members in interpersonal skills. It is not a group psychotherapy session nor is it an opportunity for facilitators to 'psychoanalyse' the group. The emphasis is developmental and, for the purposes explained in this chapter, educational. It is on the '... the work of the group itself ... to humanize the group rather than to socialize the individual' (Lyndon, 1995: 40).

This is an important distinction as it pertains to the motivation of students to engage in the transformation curriculum without feeling personally threatened, 'therapeutised' or 'analysed'. It does not mean that median groups are not anxiety provoking or emotionally demanding. However, knowing that the focus is on the 'class-as-community' or on 'profession-as-community' rather than on the individual tends to motivate students to participate; especially since they also gain first-hand experience of groupwork. While theoretical substantiation for median groups is gleaned from group analytic literature, the essential educational purpose is for students to learn to listen deeply and reflectively and to understand the implications of adopting inclusive, affirming perspectives as novice health professionals.

Structure of median groups

The UCT Division of Occupational Therapy has incorporated median groups into the curriculum since 1995. Sessions are run four times a year with each cohort of undergraduate students. This translates into 16 sessions per class throughout the undergraduate programme. Two members of the academic staff act as constant facilitators throughout the 16 sessions. There are two teams of facilitators in the Division. They meet at designated intervals for in-service training and to review the educational benefits of the transformation curriculum without compromising group confidentiality.

Although large and median groups form part of an explicitly structured transformation curriculum, students attend on a voluntary basis. [See Dealing with resistance, below.] Attention is drawn to this learning opportunity during lectures on ethics, human rights and professional values as well as during service learning tutorials. Their peers who are attending extend invitations to students who aren't attending to join the median groups. They tell students about the anticipated learning outcomes and educational objectives (for example enhanced reflective practice, cultural competence, and professionalism). Irrespective of attendance, students are encouraged to engage with relevant literature in making theoretical sense of their group learning (Lyndon, 1995; Baworowska & Schick, 2000; Maxwell, 2000). Participants evaluate the group experiences by offering anonymous written feedback to group facilitators during the formal curriculum review process.

Cultural context: Promoting dialogue and reflection

The cultural context of the 'class-as-community' becomes the foreground of dialogue within the median group. 'Cultural context' in this instance refers to diversity amongst students within the class as well as the socio-cultural environments in which students do service learning. The shared experiences of the 'class-as-community' during service learning are explored with the aim of understanding socially constructed attitudes and assumptions that operate in their midst and beyond (Blackwell, 2000). Shared experiences determine the meaning and significance of events brought to the groups' attention through individual service learning stories.

The pervasive influence of the cultural context on the attitudes and behaviours of the individual (non-specific i.e. no particular student is singled out) as social being and health professional is explored through:

- Discerning the group matrix (the tacit web of communication and interrelationships that evolves in the group). Collective assumptions, attitudes, and ideologies may become identified when stories (for example discomfort in dealing with poverty or social injustice) are shared.
- Recognising social behaviours that are enacted in the microcosm of the 'class-as-community' (for example, the natural drift of racial or religious sub-groups towards each other). The impact of this behaviour on stereotyping, prejudice and bias is generalised through 'outsights' (Lyndon, 1995) to protect the integrity of specific sub-groups in the class. According to Madigan (1996: 49) outsights promote an understanding that 'what we know in our lived experience is shaped through the cultural weave of community discourse'. Outsights are facilitated through progressive and analytic reflective moments, for example seeking to understand the link between professional identity and social responsiveness by reflecting on how it may have been possible for clinicians during the apartheid era to become complacent or apathetic in the face of pervasive oppression.

Outsights as insights   Median group discussions, interspersed by reflections or interpretations from the facilitators, offer students a space in which to make sense of the world in which they practise their profession. They also begin to gain insight into their reactions, biases, attitudes, and stereotypes as these are evoked by the context and people with whom they interact. Their practice stories, especially those highlighting human rights and ethical issues, are often emotive, requiring deep listening and sensitive containment by the facilitators. Containment (i.e. the diffusion of unease by providing structure, support and direction) may be offered by listening for the unconscious group mind as it tells a social story. Facilitators are able to offer possible 'outsights' (reflections that may point to shared assumptions operating through attitudes, ideologies and group culture) at appropriate times and in affirming ways, always seeking to trust the groups' capacity for interdependence in the knowledge construction process (Lyndon, 1995).

Group process and personal progress   As time progresses, the 'class-as-community' starts to venture its own interpretations of 'group mind as culture'

(De Maré, 1991). Students learn from their first year how to dialogue in generative, supportive ways during the median group space and to use the time to consider their personal progression from 'individual' to 'social being' to 'health professional with social responsibilities'. The group is free to explore its own intra-group communication; the content of which changes over the years as students mature and are able to identify praxis between occupational therapy theory, experience and personal/professional development. Prejudgements about what can, or cannot, be said are curbed with reference to the class constitution and other group-specific norms that are re-negotiated over the years.

Different cohorts of students develop different styles of dialogue. Their conversations become mediated through the ideological structures they experience in day-to-day life as student professionals in South Africa. For example, the introduction of compulsory community service dominated the manifest content of median groups with the final-year class in 2002. Latent content focused on issues of patriotism, social redress and the power of the Department of Health to influence the lives of graduates. Third- and fourth-year groups, in particular, tend to engage more readily with a myriad of political, cultural, and psychological practices that they have come to realise they either believe in or endorse through their professional attitudes and behaviours.

Finding a voice As the conversational forum (Madigan, 1996) within the median group becomes familiar and safe territory for students, they begin to challenge dominant cultural ideas, for example the assumed superiority of White secondary education. Minorities in the group start finding their voice when there is evidence that the student cohort they find themselves in is committed to understanding and redressing prejudicial, biased or complacent attitudes. This is always an exceptionally humbling and enriching space to witness; a space where people from different worldviews, experiences and social histories find meaning in their common humanity or gain an understanding of the 'other' perspective. The synthetical moments in median groups are often powerful learning experiences that students later refer to as perspective transforming.

For example, during a discussion on the marginalisation of disabled people in the workplace, a student from a previously disadvantaged group in South Africa said she could empathise with disabled workers. She had faced many challenges under the Bantu (apartheid classification of race) secondary education system which was characterised by gross inequity in the distribution of resources relative to White schools. She alluded to the marginalisation she continued to experience both within the class-as-community and the tertiary education system. Few of the previously educationally advantaged students present in the group had any idea about conditions at Black schools during the apartheid era nor were they aware that their assumptions about educational preparedness could be experienced as prejudiced. The ensuing group discussion surfaced a range of perspectives about difference and social power enabling both sides of the racial divide within the class to recognise the potential for oppression in its various guises. This also led to a very meaningful discussion about the power imbalance in the professional helping relationship and ways in which practitioners may stay alert to human rights abuses in the grey zones of everyday practice.

Facilitating for critical consciousness In their role as adult educators, the facilitators aim to educate for critical consciousness in ways that students do not feel 'singled out', put on the spot, or that their experience of difference is minimised. This is made possible by encouraging engagement with the regressive, progressive, analytic and synthetical moments of reflection (see above) at both a group and an individual level.

Educators are also sensitised to their own prejudices by engaging in anti-bias training and regular curriculum discussions. According to Blackwell (1994) it becomes 'incumbent on the group conductor to demonstrate a readiness to address and validate Black people's experience and to challenge all members of the group to analyse together the sorts of attitudes and ideation they have internalised in relation to race and racism. If the conductor *(facilitator)* does not address the issue herself she cannot realistically assume that anyone else will' (ibid: 204, italics added). It is therefore advisable for facilitators to seek supervision, peer learning or anti-bias training for themselves in order to optimise their sensitivity within the group to issues of diversity.

Running a median group

Setting the scene

- Prior to the group, a circle of chairs is arranged in a room that affords privacy. Enough chairs for all students in the class and two facilitators are available signalling the importance of every individual; whether they choose to attend or not. We try (lecture schedules sometimes cause delays) to start and end the one-and-a-half-hour sessions on time. This creates a designated space in the stream of life on campus that is set aside for learning to listen deeply for perspective transformation.
- As seats are taken, students seek refuge in closeness to those whose ways of acting and reacting they are familiar with. Sub-groups within the class cluster together and some chairs remain empty, at times becoming the focus of discussion.

Getting started

- Facilitators position themselves within eye contact of each other and assume stillness and receptivity; an invitation to 'be present with those gathered'.
- Sometimes the facilitators may offer a reflective statement on the atmosphere of the group as it settles down; a summary of its educational purpose or they may simply invite people to presence (i.e. become aware and reflective) themselves in the listening space.
- Animated chattering slowly gives way to a tentative silence; a silence that students eventually come to tolerate, understand and work with in creative, perspective transforming ways. The starting silence may precipitate a monologue (one student speaking) about a significant service learning

event or anxiety about a forthcoming test. At other times a dialogue (two people talking) exposes a class issue such as perceived privilege in the allocation of service learning placements or share difficulties in dealing with the emotional impact of witnessing poverty.

- Newcomers to the median group, especially first-years, express frustration about 'wasting time when we could be doing something really worthwhile like going to the library'. Their discomfort is acknowledged and the group may be asked why listening and honouring the presence of others is considered a waste of time. Discussion about time and performance pressure may ensue, paving the way for a tentative interpretation about the way one unconsciously accepts cultural norms, such as those about time usage, and how these norms may initially create resistance to reflective moments.

Facilitating process

- Talk for talk's sake is curtailed by timeous comment. For example, during the first few sessions, a reflective statement about the core purposes of gathering or, during later sessions, a tentative hypothesis of the unfolding group discourse may be made, i.e. a summary of that which may be collective and socially defined.
- Facilitators remain non-directive, trusting the process to unfold in response to the group's collective experience. They listen deeply, respectful of every individual contribution as a valued glimpse of the unfolding group voice. With the group purpose in mind, they listen for transformation issues in the subtext (i.e. they tune into emerging group themes) and ponder what the metaphors that surface in the conversation might infer about the group mind.
- Their task is either 'open' or 'guided' facilitation rather than group analytic interpretation because this calls for advanced experience and training in translating unconscious dynamics into 'what has been expressed but also suppressed' (Pines, 1993: 102).
- According to Kennard, Roberts and Winter (1993: 109) 'open facilitation is, in effect, a lubricating activity, to facilitate movement in whatever direction the group chooses to go … Guided facilitation gives the group a nudge in a certain direction.' It usually suggests 'a hypothesis about what is going on beneath the surface of the group, the underlying theme or latent content' (ibid, 1993: 110). Facilitators say just enough for the group to pick the hypothesis up if they are ready to do so. If they choose not to, nothing is lost. Chances are that the group will return to the hypothesis at a later stage during synthesis moments.

Achieving constructive dialogue

- Groups initially struggle to achieve constructive dialogue. They may revert to informal chatting until a thoughtful reflection by the facilitator enables them to take cognisance of the perspectives of those around them or to appreciate the sub-text of the group discourse as indicative of the cultural context within which they practise occupational therapy.

- In due course, the group begins to rely less on the facilitator(s) to help it stay focused and is able to use its own thoughts, symbols, and analogies to explore current issues (usually emerging from practice learning experiences).
- Perspective transformation is the foremost educational purpose of median groups. This focus gives direction to the group goals, content, and norms.
- Termination of the median group and graduation issues usually coincide and are dealt with according to the groups' unfolding needs.

Case notes: Perspective triggers

Refer below for an example of how a facilitator uses perspective triggers in order to shape a group discussion into constructive dialogue and thereby also create an opportunity for perspective transformation within the group. The extract is taken form a facilitator's group notes.

> The issue of what to talk about was solved again with one student talking about the 'culture shock' of her practice learning placement. She had seen a man eating a sheep's head during a community meeting in an informal settlement and was 'disgusted when the eyes popped out'. This monologue was followed by other stories of 'culture shock' about informal traders selling sheep entrails and a 'joke' about chicken feet dipped in chocolate as a snack. I posed a question: could it be possible for the persons described in the stories to also experience 'culture shock' at any

> of the 'taken for granted' cultural behaviour of those represented in the group? Co-facilitator suggested that we come to internalise as 'normal' that which we are familiar with and as 'abnormal' that which is not part of our frames of reference. I then asked the group how this phenomenon might lead to pathologising or marginalisation of others who are different from us.

Discussion focused on prejudice and professional power. The group explored ways in which we have come to attribute professional theory and experience with status and that while knowledge is power, it can also be persecutory.

Here one can reflect on the latent meaning of the stories, the 'joke' and the metaphors. What would have happened if the facilitators had offered symbolic interpretation?

Dealing with resistance

Students who experience disjunction between their current knowledge and skills and the demands of service learning carry their anxieties into the median group. Anxiety may also be generated due to the work of the group or within the student's personal life. Some students have shared that once they started to reflect deeply and to engage with the realities of life as health professionals in the South African context, they were no longer as 'carefree' as students who follow, what appear to be, less personally demanding programmes. Others resist the notion of spending time in the median group, seeing it as superfluous to their development as health professionals. One student for example said, 'I want to learn about therapy not about prejudice. I'm not like my parents were during apartheid and I don't need to learn about difference because I do not notice it.'

Resistance as a defence against change has to be respected especially given that the average age of occupational therapy students is between 18 and 22. The essence of transformation is to continually change towards another more relevant form, substance or character in response to the demands of the context. As young adults some may not yet be developmentally ready to engage with the extent of introspection and reflection required by the transformation curriculum hence our insistence that participation in median groups is voluntary. No pressure, whether explicit or implicit, is placed on a student to attend and by keeping the number of sessions low throughout the year, the potential intensity of the group process is regulated.

A range of defence mechanisms such as isolation, projection or splitting may however be used to protect repressed feelings from rising during some median group sessions. Different defences surface depending on the time of year (e.g. prior to exams) and contextual circumstances at practice learning sites (e.g. political unrest in the townships). The group may for example, collectivise its defences by projecting distortions of perceived competence onto 'the other' ('they get better experience at service learning site X than at service learning site Y') or by splitting those in perceived positions of power into 'good' or 'bad'. For example, a monologue by one student about some perceived injustice towards a client may lead to dialogue about 'expert' and 'incompetent' clinicians or a comparison of the quality of supervision received by students during service learning being similar to siblings competing for parental attention.

The task of the facilitator is to recognise the defence and to honour its function in containing the group's (individual's) anxiety. Some interpretation of the defence may be indicated but only if it meets the educational purpose of the median group, i.e. perspective transformation. It should, in other words, not be aimed at 'therapeutising' or 'analysing' either an individual student or the group. Pines (1993: 100) suggests 'mostly I believe it correct to listen, to contain, to process and to digest. When to act? This is the most difficult question. The simple answer is – when you have something to contribute that is valuable and which has not yet been said.'

Future possibilities

Strategies, processes, and challenges in the use of groups for perspective transformation in tertiary health professional education have been described. The purpose of these initiatives is to make the classroom a democratic setting where everyone feels responsible and enabled to contribute to the co-construction of knowledge. Tertiary education is no longer only about getting a qualification; it is also about graduating individuals who are socially responsive. No education is politically neutral and it is therefore incumbent upon educators to offer learning experiences that respect and honour the social reality of all groups in our society as these are represented in a particular cohort of students.

Groups are 'living systems of dialogue' (De Maré, 1991). As such they offer numerous possibilities for the achievement of a range of educational purposes including the kind of perspective transformation that is needed to redress past injustices and to build the new South Africa.

Discussion questions

1 Suggested here is a curriculum that values the process of professional socialisation as much as the task of educating for competent practice. What are the implications of this approach to education in the context of resource constraints, pressured academic timetables, and ever increasing curriculum content demands?

2 It has been said that morality and attitudes cannot be imposed, yet professionalism requires allegiance to a professional oath and/or a code of conduct and ethics. What are the advantages and disadvantages of explicitly structuring educational experiences that challenge students to self-reflect and to participate in 'living systems of dialogue'? Does professional education have a mandate to shape morality and attitudes or should this be a voluntary, tacit process?

3 Academics are experts in a particular discipline and not necessarily experts in teaching or in promoting optimal learning through groupwork amongst their students. In what ways may the capacity of educators be enhanced through training in small and median groupwork skills?

Acknowledgements

To the many occupational therapy students who have given wholeheartedly of themselves in the pursuit of deeper understanding and self-awareness in order to serve others better ... thank you for sharing your perspectives.

To Lindsey Nicholls, visionary occupational therapist and valued colleague for introducing median groups to the UCT curriculum and for sharing her expertise in group analysis so generously.

Appreciation to Elelwani Ramugondo, Roshan Galvaan and Fadia Gamieldien for transformative median group facilitation and feedback on the first draft of this chapter

12 Supporting health care professionals at primary care level

Pat Mayers

Learning objectives

By the end of this chapter you should be able to:

- Identify the challenges for health professionals working in the primary health care system in the Western Cape, South Africa, with particular reference to the impact of HIV.
- Describe a support group intervention for health professionals.
- Identify constraints which inhibit the formation and sustainability of support groups for health care personnel in primary health care.

Introduction

Fundamental changes in the system of health care delivery have occurred in South Africa since the new political dispensation in 1994. The reforms are aimed at unifying fragmented health services into a comprehensive and integrated National Health System[1] and at reducing disparities and inequities in service delivery and health outcomes, ensuring equity and access to basic health services for all. The means of achieving these objectives is the comprehensive **primary health care approach**, which is described in detail in the next section.

The primary health care system in South Africa faces particular stresses relating to a lack of capacity and resources and the impact of HIV/AIDS. This chapter examines the challenges faced by health professionals in primary health care systems, focusing particularly on the Western Cape, South Africa. It describes a support group for medical doctors who work at the primary health level, and identifies some of the issues relating to HIV/AIDS which these professionals have to confront. The discussion which follows the case study discusses how support groups for these professionals can help alleviate some of the personal and professional challenges they struggle with.

The primary health care approach

The primary health care approach reflects a *philosophy* which emphasises this approach as an integral component of overall social and economic development. It has a *political* meaning, in that it depends on multisectoral action and community involvement, and it is a *strategy* which denotes the way in which health services are organized and delivered, aiming to make essential health care universally accessible.[2]

Primary care (also referred to as primary medical care or primary curative care) traditionally refers to first level contact between clients/patients and communities and organized health care, but has been expanded to include not only entry into the health care system, but ongoing care until the health problem is resolved, or the client/patient is referred to the next level of health care. Once treatment at a secondary level, for example, a district hospital, is completed, the person is referred back to the primary level centre for further care.[3] Policies which have been implemented in South Africa since 1994 have meant there has been a redistribution of health care delivery, with greater emphasis being placed on care and treatment at the primary care level. Between 1994 and 2002 there was a 5% increase in the number of fixed clinics, 9% increase in the number of community health centres, and the number of mobile clinics increased by 8%. (Van Rensburg, 2004: 433–434). This increase has made it possible for more people to have access to the primary level services. Treatment at primary care level in the public health sector is free for essential health care.

However, in many areas of South Africa, primary health care facilities may be the only available and or readily accessible health service for the majority of the population (Ijumba, 2002). This means that the primary health care services, providers and facilities in many respects shoulder the responsibility for the essential health needs of the majority of South Africans.

The next section goes on to discuss the impact of the primary health care system on health professionals in South Africa, particularly as regards the challenges they face, many of which relate to HIV/AIDS issues. Thereafter, HIV/AIDS is specifically discussed, with a focus on the unique, additional challenges that it brings to the health care professional.

Challenges at the primary health care level

Health care workers at the primary level have to offer a caring, competent and comprehensive service in a resource-constrained system, which is hampered by problems such as budgetary constraints, inefficiency, poor infrastructure, lack of appropriately trained personnel, loss of skilled personnel, in particular professional nurses, as well as the increase in patient numbers and in many instances, acuity of health problems. These challenges are discussed in greater detail below.

An overloaded and under-resourced system   The South African health system is under-resourced and financially constrained. The increasing numbers of sick people impact on this situation, which is aggravated by limited social services and poor economic support structures. Despite significant strides since 1994 in the provision of primary health care facilities, problems relating to inadequate resources are a continued source of stress for health workers and may compromise the quality of care. This lack of resources includes: inadequate, inefficient and unreliable transport (e.g. to deliver medicines); inadequate infrastructure and space; old, poorly planned buildings; shortage of equipment; and lack of communication access.

Daily, there are long waiting periods for patients who attend primary care clinics, and busy clinics may have to turn patients away. Insufficient or erratic delivery of pharmaceutical supplies further compromises the primary care service, as patients, once seen by the health professionals, may be sent home without essential medication. Health professional participants, in a research study conducted by Ijumba (2002), stated: 'we come to a point where we cannot work because there is no equipment' (196); 'I need an ambulance, but then there's no phone, because the phone lines are down …' (195).

The socio-economic level of many patients requiring treatment and care may make it difficult for the health care worker to respond appropriately. Poverty and unemployment have impacted on people's health and their ability to access affordable health care. A doctor may need to prescribe medication for a malnourished and impoverished patient, whose real need is adequate nutrition, but is unable to afford food. Lack of food may also increase the likelihood of the recurrence of the problem that initially brought the patient to the clinic.

The health worker–patient relationship is particularly important for persons with HIV/AIDS, as the health professional becomes a source of hope for the patient. An HIV+ patient, reluctant to go to the standard health service, may choose to wait for his/her regular follow-up appointment at the HIV clinic. This results in delay in treatment, until the trusted health professional can deal with a problem that should have been dealt with in the intervening period.

Training issues Appropriate training is crucial to the effective delivery of health care at any level, and in particular at the primary care level. Well-prepared, multi-skilled health workers who are able to regularly update their competencies, are critical to the quality of the service.

Although great strides have been made in the training of health professionals in primary care, most health professional education and training occurs within the urban centres, and until recently, has been largely hospital based. Health professional trainees have had limited exposure to the health needs of persons at the primary care services. According to Ijumba (2002), training does not address competences needed in a number of areas, including cultural diversity, data collection and analysis, and intersectoral collaboration. This may be a factor in the stresses experienced by health care workers on entering the primary level services, as they feel that their training has not equipped them to perform the tasks that their jobs entail.

Security and violence The South African health sector has experienced a high incidence of violence, concomitant with service delivery. Steinman (2003) reports that 61,9% of the health care workers in South Africa had experienced at least one incident of physical or psychological violence in the 12 months prior to the survey. This has resulted in a high level of anxiety, particularly among health care workers in the public sector. Health care workers may be verbally and physically threatened by patients they serve, and have reported incidents of physical attack, verbal abuse, bullying/mobbing, racial and sexual harassment. Furthermore, there is risk in travelling to the primary care facilities, and there is a lack of security when on duty, especially at night.

Negative stress has also been identified as a cause of violence, and extensive restructuring in the health sector further exacerbates the situation (Di Martino, 2003). Di Martino further states that 'privatisation, decentralisation and rationalisation, often accompanied by downsizing, heavier workloads, longer hours of effective work and more temporary work, may eventually lead to a climate of violence driven by uncertainty, growing exasperation and vulnerability' (ibid: vii).

Lack of support   Many health professionals experience a lack of support from superiors. Van Dyk (2001) reports that health workers feel they work in isolation, that creativity is discouraged because innovative ideas and suggestions are not implemented, and that the necessary supportive structures are not always in place. This may lead to resignation from the service, or ongoing dissatisfaction in the working environment, which could result in lack of motivation and burnout.

Poor or inappropriate referrals   An appropriate referral system is an essential component for an effective primary health care service, in order that patients are treated at the appropriate level of care – whether primary, secondary or tertiary. All patients, unless in an emergency, should be seen at the primary care level and referred appropriately. However, concomitant with restructuring of the secondary and tertiary level services, there has been an increased load on primary care facilities. The resultant delay in referral may create difficulties for the health worker and patient.

Inappropriate referral is a further problem. There appears to be a practice, anecdotally reported by health professionals, that HIV+ patients who attend a routine clinic are advised to go to the HIV clinic regardless of their complaint. A further concern relates to the resistance encountered in patients who need to be referred to a secondary level care hospital, in the belief that secondary level referral implies hopelessness or to an increased seriousness of the condition.

An additional challenge is that of caring for people with HIV/AIDS, which brings with it a unique set of personal and professional issues for the health care professional.

HIV/AIDS in primary care

HIV/AIDS is the condition which has probably brought the greatest challenge to health and social care in the last 50 years, with the greatest impact in Africa. It has become a major cause of the burden of disease in South Africa. The HIV prevalence rate for adults, based on antenatal survey data, rose from 12,91% in 1997 to 19,4% in 1999.[4] The Human Sciences Research Council (HSRC) (2002) national survey reported that the national prevalence rate of HIV was 11,4%. It is predicted that 6–10 million South Africans will die of AIDS in the next 10 to 15 years, and 6 million South Africans will be living with HIV/AIDS by 2010, unless major behavioural changes alter the epidemic's course.[5] The increased health care burden will fall mainly on the public sector, as 80% of the population make use of the public sector for their health needs.[6]

Up until 2004 antiretroviral therapy was not available for most patients, and drugs to treat opportunistic infections were in insufficient supply. Stephenson (2000) comments that as a result of the lack of antiretroviral therapy, patients continued to rotate through the health system, as increasing numbers of people became symptomatic and required care. In August 2003, in response to pressure from a number of sources, the South African government announced a national antiretroviral treatment roll-out programme, which has begun only in 2004. While this initiative will benefit clients/patients, it will, however, initially further strain an already under-resourced health service, as the effective management and care of persons receiving antiretroviral therapy will require training and ongoing support of the health professionals who offer treatment.

A further concern of the health services in South Africa is the increasing incidence of tuberculosis (TB), which is associated with the HIV epidemic, and the health services are increasingly treating persons who are HIV+ and have contracted TB. By the end of 2000, the WHO reports that there were about 11,5 million HIV-infected people worldwide who were co-infected with tuberculosis, of whom 70% were in sub-Saharan Africa (WHO, 2004: 36). HIV/TB patients are also more likely to experience other illnesses while on TB treatment, adding to the burden of complexity, for which many health professionals are inadequately prepared (Floyd & Wilkinson, 2000).

Burden on primary health care providers   HIV/AIDS has imposed a substantial and complex burden on primary health care services. Since the major source of HIV transmission is heterosexual, and from mother to child, it is especially doctors, nurses and midwives in the community clinics who bear the brunt of the care needs. According to Petersen and Swartz (2002: 1008), 'Primary care health providers are the first, and sometimes only, health personnel to come in contact with patients who are HIV positive.' In general, the role of the health professional has changed, both within the health system and in the wider society. Health professionals are expected to be more responsive not only to the disease or illness with which the patient presents, but to the person presenting with the disease or illness. In particular when health care professionals deal with HIV+ patients, the services they are called upon to provide exceed the bounds of conventional medical care and treatment: 'Each health care professional working in the field of HIV/AIDS needs to become a comprehensive caregiver, adviser, educator and counsellor in diverse cultural and social contexts' (Van Dyk, 2001: iii).

In order to fulfil these roles, health professionals need to deal with a range of issues including personal fears of HIV and risk of contagion, feelings of helplessness in the face of an unpredictable and, although treatable, currently incurable disease, dealing with large numbers of young patients, repeated exposure to death and dying, and legal and ethical dilemmas.

Gibson, Swartz and Sandenbergh (2002) have identified a number of external factors which present the health professional dealing with HIV+ positive patients with more difficulties. These include the difficulty in promoting behavioural change in patients, reluctance in discussing sexual habits, community denial, stigma and rejection from communities, working with loss, and increased overload of HIV/AIDS patients in the health system. The authors identified further negative effects of HIV/AIDS at primary health car level: staff illness and death owing to HIV/AIDS, loss of skills in the workforce, and impact on workforce dynamics.

An issue that affects both patients and health professionals is that of stigma. Persons living with HIV/AIDS experience various degrees of stigmatisation (Taylor, 2001). However, the experience of marginalisation and stigmatisation does not confine itself to those with HIV/AIDS alone. Health professionals may find themselves marginalised because they are willing to do the 'unpopular' patient care. Doctors and other health professionals, because of their willingness to care for and treat to the best of their ability those who are HIV+, find that they experience a secondary marginalisation. A doctor gives an example: 'I got told that I must find another room for my clinic as HIV does not belong there ... and they want to use the room as a tearoom.'

Burnout   The problems in the primary health care system as described above and in particular, the considerable stress caused by the overwhelming numbers of HIV+ patients in the system have accumulative emotional effects which are far reaching. Vicarious traumatisation and compassion fatigue occur as the result of accumulation of experiences in psychotherapists and other health care providers and are major influencing factors in the development of burnout.[7] Already in 1993 Grossman and Silverstein reported that social workers, nurses and other health care professionals who work with people with HIV/AIDS were experiencing burnout from the excessive demands on their energy, strength and resources. Silverman (1993) raised the possibility of HIV caregiver's stress syndrome, noting that there was a relative lack of attention paid to the stresses experienced by providers who care for persons with HIV/AIDS.

Burnout is often not perceived as a crisis, as its onset tends to be slow and insidious, manifesting only when people are so exhausted and overwhelmed by their environment that they take extraordinary means to alleviate their distress, such as leaving the job, developing serious psychosomatic illness, or abusing substances.[8]

Despite the lack of attention it has received, burnout is a central factor affecting the quality of work in health care, leading to symptoms such as emotional exhaustion, reduced personal accomplishment, loss of a positive attitude towards clients and the intention to leave the service.[9] One way of approaching the management of burnout is the provision of support groups. The case study below describes a support group for health professionals in the Western Cape. The discussion which follows builds the case for health professional support groups and considers some practical implications relating to their implementation.

A support structure for health professionals

Origin and purpose of the support group

A group of medical doctors in the Western Cape identified a need for supportive help in their roles as health professionals working at primary care level. They had become aware of their increasing levels of stress, frustration, difficulty in coping with the workload and the impact of the acuity and complicated nature of the patients' health conditions, which was exacerbated by the patients' difficult social conditions. The option of a support group was explored and began with three members in 2001, with the author as facilitator. Three years later with a regular membership of five to six persons, the group meets on a weekly basis. The purpose of the group is to reflect on and deal with the experiences of health professional practitioners working in the field of primary level HIV/AIDS care.

Group process and development

The structure of the support group is open and flexible. Topics which emerge in each session are relevant to the expressed needs. It is an enabling milieu for the ventilation of feelings, sharing of information and ideas about approaches to care, and for constructive engagement with issues pertinent to the profession.

Group members deal with professional and personal issues, which are often intertwined. Themes are varied, and include manifest and latent ones related to professional role, competence, integrity, responsibility, and the context of their role as health professionals.

The use of narrative forms an important aspect of the group process. The group has become acquainted with patients and their families through the sharing of stories about them. These stories facilitate the emotional 'unloading' by group members. The shared narratives enable members to bring their feelings about their work and the people they care for professionally to the group, which is a safe, accepting and non-judgemental environment (Morgan, 2000; White, 2002). As the individual stories are shared with the group, there is for example, understanding and acceptance of the loss expressed about 'Jane', the patient who seemed to be doing so well, only to die from acute meningitis at the new year, and encouragement in the story of 'Zelda', the patient turned activist who shares her knowledge with her community.

Frustrations expressed include those relating to treatment options available to the health professionals in their roles. Prior to the antiretroviral roll-out, it was difficult to source medications and doctors and patients went to enormous lengths to source medications (e.g. referral to a health centre offering a drug trial, or family contributions to enable one member to buy medication from a private pharmacy). Doctors could only prescribe treatment for opportunistic infections. Currently, frustrations revolve around the overloaded health system, inadequate referrals, training deficits and professional dilemmas, among others.

As group members share their stories of frustration, loss, courage and joy, they listen to each other, share ideas, give advice, problem solve together, network, support each other, and create a sense of meaning and fulfilment in spite of the frustrations and negative experiences encountered in the primary care work environment. Dilemmas about their roles as doctors are also discussed and, according to a group member: 'We were never trained to be more than medics – diagnosing and treating. Now I have to know about welfare grants, social services, where to find food parcels, because no one else will help if I don't.'

Benefits of the group

The benefits of the group experience include mutual support, self-understanding, guidance recognition, and feeling cared for by others. Yalom (1985) refers to curative/therapeutic factors that operate in therapeutic groups, including: instillation of hope, universality, imparting of information, and interpersonal learning, and group cohesion. These do not occur in isolation from each other and are also pertinent to a support group. Shulman's (1992) conceptualisation of the group as a 'mutual aid system' is also useful to consider. He refers to the group members' experience of the 'all-in-the-same-boat' phenomenon, the development of a universal perspective, having a support structure, assistance in individual problem solving, and strength in numbers experience in dealing with a communal challenge (1992: 275–281). Shulman (1992: 274) explains this as 'sharing data', a process in which each group member's life experience and current practice is brought to the group and shared, thereby helping others. These benefits were evident in the group process over time.

The role of the facilitator

The facilitator in a support group for health professionals has to take into account logistics such as group members' busy professional lives, extended clinic commitments, and emergency calls. Grossman and Silverstein (1993) recommend that facilitators of support groups for professionals working with people with HIV/AIDS should: have experience with people with HIV/AIDS; be knowledgeable about group processes; be open to others' feelings; be aware of nonverbal communication; and have experience in dealing with their own feelings regarding death, dying, sexuality, homophobia, substance abuse and minority issues. While all these qualities

and skills are important, the author's experience is that the facilitator should primarily be sensitive to the needs of health professionals and their work environment, be knowledgeable and skilled in group process, and be able to interpret the processes and dynamics of the group.

The facilitator has to be caring, interested in the personal lives of the members, yet not intrusive. A self-reflexive stance is important. Support of each member requires the creation of an environment which is structured enough to contain, yet open enough to deal with the difficulties of members who cannot always be regular in attendance, work in different environments, and arrive late due to clinic duties which have demanded their time.

Techniques of facilitation

A useful technique for starting the group session is the use of the 'agenda-go-round'. Each group member is given the opportunity to express feelings and describe the experiences of the previous week. The facilitator listens to the discussion and reflects on aspects that are linked, universal or need further explanation. The techniques used are reflection, process commentary, gentle confrontation and maintaining a balance of the discussion in the group. Facilitation could include encouraging technical expertise when required, ventilation of feelings and dilemmas, and promoting problem solving. The facilitator needs to be sensitive to the meta-communication in the group – that which is unsaid – but evident in the communication patterns of the members. The task is to reflect on this and facilitate discussion on painful issues. Being angry with 'the system' is acceptable, yet being angry with one's patients is often not, and the facilitator has to explore areas which may be difficult to discuss, in order to promote a healthy response to the diffi- culties of working in this field. The facili- tator's task is to create a culture of accept- ance, understanding and openness, and to be a container, encourager, and gentle confronter, while the members deal with professional issues and personal feelings arising from these.

Beyond the group – commitment to social action

Some group members have become very supportive of and/or actively involved with activist groups and activities, and have attempted to raise awareness of the issues and needs in HIV/AIDS care through engaging with the media and political structures as needed. Maslach and Ozer (1995), citing Cherniss and Krantz (1983), state that involvement in action-orientated groups or communities or even small victories in the political or social arena can counteract helplessness and pessimism that are commonly evoked by the absence of long-term solu- tions to the problem.

Discussion on value of support system

The mental health literature reflects the recognition given to the risk of burn- out, and the importance of support structures. These support structures include education programmes, group discussions, guidelines for staff sup- port, and psychosocial support groups. Yet, despite the impact of HIV/AIDS worldwide, and the acknowledgement of the stresses faced by health practi- tioners/caregivers, there appears to be no formal provision or budget for sup- port programmes. Service managers do not seem to see or understand the need for provision of supportive structures for their medical staff. By contrast, because there is no recognition of this need, health professionals have to find time after hours to seek the support that they need.

Impact on performance of health professionals The energy and resources that health professionals bring to their tasks will depend to a great extent on their ability to take care of themselves (Watkins, 2001). Involvement with people is one of the major causes of burnout, and it is not surprising that the supportive role of other individuals is central in dealing with it. Social sup- port, particularly from one's peers, is predictive of a lower risk of burnout.[10] Given the potential source of stress and burnout in the role of providing care to people with AIDS, it is important for professionals to make use of or to strengthen support systems within and outside of their work settings. The extent to which health professionals experience support and cooperation could be critical for their willingness and their ability to deal with the stresses of HIV/AIDS care (Maslach & Ozer, 1995). There is also recognition of 'bereave- ment overload' when health care workers deal with increasing numbers of per- sons who get sick and die, as well as the impact of living in communities where multiple deaths occur due to the epidemic. The difficulty is compounded as a result of the overloaded and pressured service, and the provision of care struc- tures (e.g. time during a working day to access support) for personnel may increase the demands on those who continue to render services.

Support in challenges of caring Doctors are being challenged to care for their patients, and themselves, in a manner for which they were not prepared. However, if adequate support is provided, health professionals are then able to develop positive and sustaining relationships with their patients and cope with the diverse intense emotions arising from the work. A containing space is required in which these relationships can be talked about and understood. The American Medical News (online, 1995) reports similar findings from a support group run for doctors treating persons with AIDS in Dallas, Texas. 'If I didn't have this group', one participant is quoted, 'I do think that I may not have been able to stay involved with treating AIDS patients as long as I have.'

Dealing with emotional stress The goal of support groups is to provide a safe place for the release of pent-up emotions related to the job, facilitate a sense of competence and coping in health workers and help them to feel that they can deal with the stresses encountered in the work environment. It is a 'safe space for workers to disagree with and challenge feelings of helplessness'.[11]

To do this effectively, James and Gilliland (2001) note that there are two important requirements: the support of the administration, and a facilitator who is sensitive to the issues involved, and can walk the tightrope 'between allowing the group to vent feelings and keeping the group in problem-solving mode'.[12] According to Grossman and Silverstein (1993), administrators believe they already provide in-service training for health care professionals, and they fail to understand the nature of support groups. They then deny formal 'release time' for the health care professionals in the personnel establishment to partic-ipate in a support group. Conversely, providing a structured support group which staff members are required to attend may cause some stress in the plan-ning and management restructuring stage. Miller (2000) citing Miller, Gillies and Elliot (1996), states that HIV/AIDS health workers require support that is accessible when needed, a facilitator whose expertise they could trust (usually an 'outsider'), a mixture of group and individual support, complete confiden-tiality, support unlinked to management, management endorsement of receiving support, and clear ground rules.

Structure of support groups Ideally, however, support should be built into the organizational structure.[13] Jacobs (2001) developed a draft protocol for the care and support of heath care workers in the Western Cape. The protocol recommends that support groups be formed with colleagues, and suggests that employers provide for fortnightly appropriate professional mentorship and support at clinic level for all health care workers (lay counsellors and profes-sional staff) who deal with the emotional and psychological consequences of HIV infection and its impact on their lives and work.

Support groups may not be the answer for all health professionals, as indi-viduals need to find the most appropriate form of support. Support for all health professionals is needed as evidenced, but further research is required to determine the best forms of support and the structures that need to be put in place to facilitate appropriate support. Informal support networks play a sig-nificant role, but may put added pressure on other social relationships.

Gueritault-Chalvin, Kalichman, Demi and Peterson (2000) recommend that burnout prevention interventions should take into account individual differences and tailor programmes to individual needs.

Role of mental health professionals   An important question is whether the mental health professionals can play a role in promoting the mental health of doctors, nurses and other health workers who interface with persons at primary level, and in particular those with HIV/AIDS. This is an urgent challenge for South Africa, and requires a creative response. There needs to be an attitude of care and empathy, in order to develop a system that not only cares for the patients, but also for those who treat them, so that the carers can continue to care. The challenge facing the health services is to provide a system of support, which enables health care workers in the front line to continue to do the work.

Conclusion

This chapter has provided a brief overview of the role of health professionals in the primary care system, with particular reference to the Western Cape, South Africa. It identifies some of the challenges encountered by health professionals, particularly in relation to an overloaded and under-resourced system, training requirements, security and violence, lack of support structures, and an inadequate referral system. It outlines the emotional impact of working in the system, particularly with reference to the high incidence of HIV/AIDS patients who present at the primary care level. The chapter has identified the need for a support system for primary care health professionals, and describes a support group for health professionals who work at this level. It outlines the benefits of such a support group, and discusses the role and techniques of the facilitator. It highlights the need for flexibility in the provision of support structures for health professionals, and recommends that support structures should be built into the organizational structure. The health care system needs to care for the patients, but also for those who treat them, especially health professionals who are in the front line, and who interface with and carry the major burden of patients at primary care level.

Discussion questions

1 With reference to your practice area, what are the issues and challenges that health professionals have to confront?

2 How could a support group assist health professionals to cope with their daily practice?

Endnotes

1   Van Rensburg & Pelser, 2004.
2   Van Rensburg, 2004; WHO, 1988.
3   Dennill, King & Swanepoel, 1995.
4   Pelser, Ngwena & Summerton, in Van Rensburg, 2004.
5   Dorrington, Bourne, Bradshaw, Laubscher & Timæus, 2001.
6   Steinberg, Kinghorn, Söderlund, Schierhout & Conway, 2000.
7   James & Gilliland, 2001.
8   Ibid
9   Bellani, Furlani, Gnecchi, Pezzotta, Trotti, & Bellotti, 1996.
10 Maslach, 1982 cited by Maslach & Ozer, 1995.
11 James & Gilliland, 2001: 626.
12 Ibid.
13 Gibson et al., 2002; James & Gilliland, 2001.

Conclusion: Groupwork – A unifying language

Lily Becker, Willem de Jager, Madeleine Duncan, Monica Spiro

The central thesis of this book is that groupwork has a major contribution to make in advancing the development of any society and particularly in a transforming country such as South Africa today. Previous chapters have presented a range of settings and tasks where current issues and challenges of our macro society are addressed and negotiated within the microcosm of the group. These writings have also focused on the value of groups for the individual on a personal and interpersonal level. This chapter draws together the themes emerging from the preceding chapters, and makes suggestions for reclaiming the potential of groups and groupwork to meet the needs of individuals, groups and communities.

It is interesting to note that the authors of the chapters of this book are drawn from various professions that embrace diverse knowledge bases and give emphasis to different aspects of mental, physical and social health. Yet, from points of diversity, they have been drawn together by the common thread of groupwork, which provides a unifying language to their work. Through this common interest they are able to begin a conversation, which encompasses the richness of the myriad of traditions that are present in their diverse professions. In so doing, the authors have participated in a creative group process where individual voices, each expressing something unique, have amalgamated to produce a new communication. This articulation may, at first glance, seem to be a sum of the individual parts, but on further examination it transcends the specific voices and offers a fresh collective response to the challenges that face practitioners in post-apartheid South Africa.

The process has been an enriching one; working collaboratively, the authors have reconciled approaches, biases and contradictions in the incorporation of difference and new ideas. We have had to shift and grow in the process through which an integrated response has emerged. This collaborative journey is another example of a group experience as explicated in the writings of this book.

Groups in action: A thematic analysis

By integrating the various perspectives from each of the chapters into a greater whole, an appreciation of how groups work in action to promote social cohesion, may unfold. A thematic analysis of the central principles and values of groupwork emerging from the text follows.

Connectedness

Connectedness refers to the association between people that binds them and allows for a reciprocal exchange of experiences and capacities. It promotes the attainment of shared interests, aspirations and goals. We share a common humanity and have a desire to belong. Groups are able to transcend socio-cultural boundaries by affirming human relatedness and shared goals.

The commonality of the human experience is validated in the relational space of the group. A sense of connectedness enables the commonality of experience to be validated. According to Teffo (1999: 162) 'the acceptance of the validity of each person within the community leads us to the acceptance of the concept of a circle – where all humans enjoy "absolute" human equality by virtue of their membership to the human society that lives within the circle of the human race'. The story of South Africa has been of 'us' and 'them' – where the individual and the group 'self' accentuated difference, and where one group was deemed superior to the other. In no other context does the 'self' encounter (i.e. meet face to face) the 'other' as much as in a group. In the group, the 'self' is reflected in and discovered in the 'other'. Connectedness brings to the fore shared dimensions of human experience.

Transformation

The theme of transformation echoes throughout this book. Transformation refers to the changes occurring in South Africa at a personal and communal level, towards a more inclusive and participatory society. For this to be realised intrapersonal and interpersonal growth is required. The groupwork method has the potential to socialise individuals and to humanise society (De Maré, 1991). Small, medium and large groups enable diversity in all its forms to be explored, appreciated, and understood. Respect for human dignity and social justice can be facilitated by transformative education within groups and through groupwork methods. Personal and communal empowerment can occur as people are mobilised through consciousness-raising to become aware of alternative options. The act of envisioning a better future, whether individually, or collectively, may be fostered by the inherent properties of the group process.

Restoration, restitution and social healing

Groups can also be resources for individuals and collectives who require emotional support, to become involved in helping and self-helping in a spirit of mutual aid. The group itself becomes the source of help. The potential exists in groups to promote interpersonal and inter-group restoration, restitution and social healing. Restoration is closely aligned with reparation and restitution, and refers to the processes of 'making good'. Social healing, i.e. the process of promoting a cohesive society, is dependent on the capacity of individuals, groups, organizations, and governance structures to effect restoration and restitution through reparative actions with emphasis on peace building and resolution of conflict. These actions may occur at an interpersonal level (for example, the restoration of a personal relationship), at an inter-group level (for example, restoration of peace between rival factions), or at a socio-political level (for example, the restoration of dignity of disenfranchised people). Given the recent oppressive history of South Africa and similar unfolding histories in other developing countries, it is vital that the principles of groups are used more actively to restore and to heal on a broad community level.

Collective reflection

A further theme relates to the reflective space that groups provide for accessing feelings, converting the unspeakable to language, and for thinking. Collective reflection allows for 'making meaning' of processes that are operative in the group itself, in communities, and in societies. In this group space, people are more likely to achieve creative solutions by re-thinking the lessons of history and re-examining traditions, symbols and narratives. The linking paradigm of groups, communities, and societies alerts us to the integrating processes underlying our common humanity. The group acts as a container for collective memory, a space for the witnessing of the difficulties and triumphs of life and reflection on issues of common concern. This notion of 'validating the presence of others' is commensurate with the African concept of 'witnessing' that receives, legitimises and confirms our individual experience in the eyes of others. This collective presence mirrors, affirms, and comforts.

Communality

Communality may be seen as the opposite of alienation. It infers relational belonging, having significance among fellow humans and is captured in the expression 'finding you in me'. The effects of capitalism, globalisation and the advance of technology can isolate individuals, thereby restricting relational experiences. In South Africa, a meeting of worldviews occurs: the incessant Western drive for self-actualisation can result in an isolated deified self. The individual, striving for self-realisation, becomes highly individualistic, autonomous, and egoistic. On the other hand, the African self is embedded in connectedness. In a group we experience the juncture of the human tension between different worldviews. The group makes us attend to and recognise the truth of different perspectives, i.e. the need to self-actualise while remaining connected and inter-dependent within a community of people.

While the individual is drawn toward autonomy and independence she/he can also experience isolation, alienation, and atomisation. Groups offer important relational opportunities for the promotion of a sense of belonging, of being 'rooted' in the human community.

Mutuality

Mutuality may be described as a process of give-and-take, of reciprocity and sharing. Groups, especially in the broad area of therapy and rehabilitation, create safe spaces for personal sharing and mutual learning. Individuals and collectives (i.e. a gathering of people such as refugees) that share a common agenda can become involved in helping and self-helping. Groups are venues where individuals in an atmosphere of empathy and therapeutic receptivity, can share and process emotions, conflicts and symptomatic concerns, while reaching out and supporting others who are doing the same. Mutuality also is relevant in building communities. The reciprocal exchange of strengths, resources, goods, ideas and neighbourliness enhances the quality of daily life through mutual aid.

Social action

Given that personal and political power is interrelated, groups may be used as effective springboards from which to direct action for social change. Group action may mobilise the political commitment to effect positive change in accordance with national social redress policies and constitutional rights. Advocacy groups can address social and health problems affecting communities more effectively than individuals can on their own. We have seen how a supportive network becomes created through commonality of needs and mutual aid and how interpersonal connectedness generates power. The culture of silence, oppression and apathy that marginalised people experience can be overcome using groups as forums for education and empowerment.

The way forward

We have seen how practitioners from different disciplines use groupwork in a variety of settings. The role and techniques of the leader changes according to the particular group, its needs, and purposes. Values such as justice, self-determination, humility, courage, goodwill, non-discrimination, and tolerance have been intrinsic to groupwork practice since its early beginnings. Based on these and other values, sound groupwork practice and effective leadership can create a humanising effect within the group, which can resonate into the broader context. In South Africa today, the essential activities of groups, which emphasize relationship, support, mutual aid, empowerment and democratisation, are vital components conducive to the social development and social healing of the society as a whole. In this way, we are operationalising the visions of De Maré (1991), in that the broadening horizons, the interrelationships and the mutuality inherent in the group perspective, can take us through small, median and large groups into societal connectedness and social cohesion.

References

Aall, P. 2001. What do NGOs bring to peacemaking? In Crocker, C. A., Hampson, F. O. & Aall, P. (Eds.). *Turbulent peace: The challenges of managing international conflict.* Washington, DC: United States Institute of Peace Press, (365–383).

Ackerman, N. 1955. Group psychotherapy with a mixed group of adolescents. *International Journal of Group Psychotherapy.* Vol. 5.

Adams, R. 1990. *Self-help, social work and empowerment.* London: Macmillan Press Ltd.

African National Congress (ANC). 1994. Reconstruction and Development Programme (RDP). Johannesburg: Umanyano Press.

Ahlin, G. 1985. On thinking about the group matrix. *Group Analysis.* 18, 111–119.

Alcoholics Anonymous. 2001. *The big book of Alcoholics Anonymous* (4th ed.). New York City: Alcoholics Anonymous World Services Inc.

Alonso, A. & Rutan, J. S. 1984. The impact of object relations theory on psychodynamic group therapy. *American Journal of Psychiatry.* 141 (11) 1376–1380.

American Medical News. 1995. Author unknown. Doctors who treat AIDS support each other. *American Medical News* (12/11/95). 38 (46), 28.

American Pyschiatric Association. 1994. *Diagnostic and statistical manual of mental disorders* (4th ed.). Washington: American Psychiatric Association.

Amoo, S. G. & Odendaal, A. 2002. The political management of ethnic conflict in Africa: A human needs-based approach, Track Two. *Occasional Paper,* September, 11(4), (5–37).

Andrews, J. 2001. Groupwork's place in social work: A historical analysis. *Journal of Sociology and Social Welfare.* Vol. 18 (4) 45–65.

Anthony, E. J. 1968. Reflections on twenty-five years of group psychotherapy. *International Journal of Group Psychotherapy.* 18, 277–301.

Anthony, E. J. 1991. The dilemma of therapeutic leadership: The leader who does not lead (Chap. 5) (S. Tuttman, Ed.). In Roth, B. E. (series consulting Ed.), *Psychoanalytic group theory and therapy: Essays in Honor of Saul Scheidlinger* (pp. 71–86). American Group Psychotherapy Association Monograph Series monograph no. 7. Madison: International Universities Press.

Atwood, J. D. 1995. A social constructionist approach to counseling the single parent family. *Journal of Family Psychotherapy.* 6, 1–32.

Azar, E. A. 1990. *The management of protracted social conflict: Theory and cases.* Hampshire: Dartmouth Publishing Company Limited.

Baldwin-Ragaven, L., de Gruchy, J. & London, L. 1999. *An ambulance of the wrong colour: Health professionals, human rights and ethics in South Africa.* Rondebosch: University of Cape Town Press.

Barker, R. L. 1999. *The social work dictionary* (4th ed.). Washington, DC: National Association of Social Workers.

Barnes, B., Ernst, S. & Hyde, K. 1999. *An introduction to groupwork: A group analytic perspective.* London: Palgrave.

Barnett, T. & Whiteside, A. 2002. *AIDS in the twenty-first century: Disease and globalization.* Basingstoke: Palgrave Macmillan.

Barratt, G. & Segal, B. 1996. Rivalry, competition and transference in a children's group. *Group Analysis.* 29, 23–35.

Baworowska, H. & Schick, H. 2000. Culture as group mind: A summary of the achievements of Patrick de Maré in understanding median groups. *Group Analysis.* Vol. 33, 21–27.

Becker, L. 1988. Brief dynamic psychotherapy. An exploration of attitudes and practice among a group of local clinicians – some implications for practice. Unpublished Masters Dissertation. University of Cape Town.

Behr, H. 1988. Group analysis with early adolescents: Some clinical issues. *Group Analysis.* 21, 119–133.

Behr, H. 1990. Block training: The influence of the modified setting on the group-analytic process. *Group Analysis.* 23, 347–352.

Bellani, M., Furlani, F., Gnecchi, M., Pezzotta, P., Trotti, E. & Bellotti, G. 1996. Burnout and related factors among HIV/AIDS health care workers. *AIDS Care.* 8 (2), 207–221.

Bernadez, T. 1996. Women's therapy groups as the treatment of choice. In De Chant, B. (Ed.), *Women and group psychotherapy,* pp. 242–262. New York: Guilford Press.

Bernard, H. S. & MacKenzie, K. R. (Eds.) 1994. *Basics of group psychotherapy.* London: Guilford Press.

Bienstock, C. R. & Videcka-Sherman, L. 1989. Process analysis of a therapeutic support group for single parent mothers: Implications for practice. *Social Work with Groups.* 12(2), 43–61.

Biggs, J. 1996. Assessing learning quality: Reconciling institutional, staff and educational demands. *Assessment and Education in Higher Education.* Vol. 21(1).

Bion, W. R. 1961. *Experiences in groups.* New York: Basic Books.

Bion, W. R. 1962. *Learning from experience.* London: Heinemann.

Blackwell, D. 2000. The politicisation of group analysis in the 21st century. *Group.* Vol 24 (1) 65–73.

Blackwell, D. 1998. Bounded instability, group analysis and the matrix: Organizations under stress. *Group Analysis.* Vol. 31 (4) 532–546.

Blackwell, D. 1994. The emergence of racism in group analysis. *Group Analysis.* Vol. 27, 197–210.

Blackwell, D. 2000. And everyone shall have a voice: The political vision of Pat de Maré. *Group Analysis.* Vol. 33, 151–162.

Bloch, S. & Crouch, E. 1985. *Therapeutic factors in group psychotherapy.* London: Oxford University Press.

Bloom, L. 1996. The emotional damage of apartheid: A psychoanalytic view. *Psychoanalytic Psychotherapy in South Africa*. 4 (2), 55–71.

Bloomfield, D. 1997. *Peacemaking strategies in northern Ireland: Building complementarity in conflict management theory*. Houndsmills, Basingstoke, Hampshire: Macmillan Press Ltd.

Blos, P. 1962. *On adolescence*. New York: The Free Press.

Boon, M. 1996. *The African way. The power of interactive leadership*. Johannesburg: Zebra Press.

Brookfield, S. 1991. *Developing critical thinkers: Challenging adults to explore alternative ways of thinking and acting*. San Francisco: Jossey-Bass.

Brown, A. 1992. *Groupwork* (3rd ed.). Aldershot: Arena.

Brown, D. & Zinkin, L. (Eds.). 2000. *The psyche and the social world: Developments in group-analytic theory*. London: Jessica Kingsley Publications.

Brown, D. 1998. Foulkes's basic law of group dynamics 50 years on: Abnormality, injustice and the renewal of ethics [22nd S. H. Foulkes Annual lecture]. *Group Analysis*. 31 (4), 391–419.

Brown, D. 1998a. Fair shares and mutual concern: The role of sibling relationships [Special section: papers from the sib-links workshops] (Brunori, L. & Wooster, G. E., Eds.). *Group Analysis*. 31 (3), 315–326. (Rigid equality; flexible fairness [323]).

Brown, D. 2000. Bion and Foulkes: Basic assumptions and beyond. Chapter 10 in Pines, M. (Ed.). *Bion and group psychotherapy*. London: Jessica Kingsley.

Brown, D. G. 1987. Context, content and process: Inter-relationships between small and large groups in a transcultural workshop. *Group Analysis*. 20, 237–248.

Brown, L. M. 1998. *Raising their voices: The politics of girls' anger*. Cambridge, MA: Harvard University Press.

Brown, L. M. & Gilligan, C. 1992. *Meeting at the crossroads: Women's psychology and girls' development*. Cambridge, MA: Harvard University Press.

Buchanan, H., Moore, R. & Van Niekerk, L. 1998. *Writing for Clinical Reasoning. American Journal of Occupational Therapy*. 52 (4), 291–295.

Buchholz, E. S. & Mishne, J. M. 1994. *Group interventions with children, adolescents and parents*. Northvale, New Jersey: Jason Aronson.

Burns, T. & Stalker, G. 1961. *The management of innovation*. London: Tavistock Publications.

Burton, J. (Ed.). 1990. *Conflict: Human needs theory*. Houndsmills, Basingstoke, Hampshire: Macmillan Press Ltd.

Burton, J. 1987. *Resolving deep-rooted conflict: A handbook*. Lanham, MD: University Press of America.

Butcher, L. A. & Gaffney, M. 1995. Building healthy families: A program for single mothers. *Clinical Nurse Specialist*. 9 (4), 221–225.

Canham, H. & Emmanuel, L. 2000. Tied together feelings. Group psychotherapy with latency children: The process of forming a cohesive group. *The Journal of Child Psychotherapy*. 26 (2), 281–302.

Canham, H. 2000. Group and gang states of mind. *Journal of Child Psychotherapy*. 28 (2), 113–127.

Carmen, R. 1996. *Autonomous development*. London, New Jersey: Zed Books.

Chandhoke, N. 1995. *State and civil society: Explorations in political theory*. New Delhi, London: Sage Publications.

Chapman, A. R. & Rubenstein, L. S. (Eds.). 1998. *Human rights and health. The legacy of apartheid*. Washington, DC: American Assoc. for the Advancement of Science and Physicians for Human Rights in conjunction with The American Nurses Assoc. and the Committee for Health in Southern Africa.

Coetzee, J. K. & Graaff, J. (Eds.). 1996. *Reconstruction, development and people*. Johannesburg: International Thomson Publishing (Southern Africa) (Pty) Ltd.

Cohen, B. D. 2000. Group psychotherapy as the century turns: Toward a philosophy of care. *Group*. 24 (1) 93–103.

Cohen, M. B. & Mullender, A. 1999. The personal in the political: Exploring the groupwork continuum from individual to social change goals. *Social Work with Groups*. 22 (1): 13–30.

Cohen, M. B. 2002. A tale of transformation: How I became a groupworker. *Social Work with Groups*. Vol. 25 (1/2) 15–22.

Cohn, C. 1993. Wars, wimps, and women: Talking gender and thinking war. In Cooke, M. & Woollacott, A. (Eds.), *Gendering war talk* (pp. 227–244). New Jersey: Princeton University Press.

Coll, C. G., Cook-Nobles, R. & Surrey, J. L. 1997. Building connection through diversity. In Jordan, J. V. (Ed.), *Women's growth in diversity: More writings from the Stone Center* (pp. 176–198). New York: Guilford Press.

Comas-Diaz, L. Cross-cultural mental health treatment. In Comas-Diaz, L. & Griffith, E. E. H. (Eds.). 1988. *Clinical guidelines in cross-cultural mental health*. New York: John Wiley & Sons.

Corey, G. 1990. *Theory and practice of group counselling*. California: Brooks/Cole.

Corey, G. 1995. *Theory and practice of group counselling*. California: Brookes/Cole Publishing Company.

Corey, G. 2000. *Theory and practice of group counselling* (5th ed.). California: Wadsworth Belmont Learning.

Corey, M. & Corey, G. 1997. *Groups: Process and practice* (5th ed.). Pacific Grove, CA: Brooks/Cole.

Corey, M. S. & Corey, G. 2002. *Groups: Process and practice* (6th ed.). Pacific Grove: Brooks/Cole.

Cowger, C. D. & Snively, C. A. Assessing client strengths. In Roberts, A. R. & Greene, G. J. 2002. *Social workers' desk reference*. Oxford & New York: Oxford University Press.

Cox, F. M., Erlich, J. L., Rothman, J. & Tropman, J. E. (Eds.). 1987. *Strategies of community organization: Macro practice*. Itasca, Illinois: F.E. Peacock Publishers.

Curle, A. 1971. *Making peace*. London: Tavistock Publications.

Curle, A. 1991. *Tools for transformation*. London: Hawthorne Press.

Dalal, F. 1998. *Taking the group seriously: Towards a post-Foulkesian group analytic theory*. London: Jessica Kingsley.

Danziger, K. 1997. The varieties of social construction: Essay review. *Theory and Psychology*. 7 (3), 399–416.

Davidson, B. 1998. The internet and the large group [Special section continued]. *Group Analysis*. 31 (4), 457–471.

De Maré, P. 1975. The politics of large groups. In Kreeger, L. *The large group: Dynamics and therapy*. London: Constable.

De Maré, P. 1985. Large group perspectives [9th S. H. Foulkes Annual Lecture]. *Group Analysis*. 18 (2), 79–92.

De Maré, P. 1989. The history of large group phenomena in relation to group analytic psychotherapy: The story of the median group. *Group Analysis*. 13 (3 & 4), 173–197.

De Maré, P. 1998. The development of the median group. *Group Analysis*. 23: 11–27.

De Maré, P. 2000. The median group and the psyche. Chapter 13 in Brown, D. & Zinkin, L. I. (Eds.), *The psyche and the social world*. London: Jessica Kingsley.

De Maré, P., Piper, R. & Thompson, S. 1991a. *Koinonia: From hate, through dialogue, to culture in the large group*. London: Karnac Books.

Dennill, K., King, L. & Swanepoel, T. 1995. *Aspects of primary health care* (2nd ed.). Johannesburg: International Thomson Publishing (Southern Africa).

Department of Health. *Patient's Rights Charter*. Online. Retrieved 28/7/04 from http://www.doh.gov.za/docs/legislation/patientsright/chartere.html

Department of Health. 2002. Regulations relating to the performance of community service by persons registering in terms of the Health Professions Act, 1974: amendment. *Government Gazette*, Regulation Gazette No. 7260 and No. 23047, Vol. 439. Pretoria.

Department of Social Development. 2000. *The state of South Africa's population report 2000: Population, poverty and vulnerability*. Pretoria: Department of Social Development.

Department of Social Development. 2001. *Annual report: 1st April 2000–31st March 2001*. Pretoria: Department of Social Development.

Desjarlais, R., Eisenberg, L., Good, B. & Kleinman, A. 1995. *World mental health. Problems and priorities in low-income countries*. New York: Oxford University Press.

Di Martino, V. 2003. *Relationship between work stress and workplace violence in the health sector*. Geneva: ILO; ICN; WHO; PSI.

Dorrington, R., Bourne, D., Bradshaw, D., Laubscher, R. & Timæus, I. 2001. *The impact of HIV/AIDS on adult mortality in South Africa. MRC Technical Report*. Cape Town: Medical Research Council.

Douglas, T. 1979. *Group process in social work: A theoretical synthesis*. New York: John Wiley and Sons.

Drower, S. 1990. Social work with groups. Chapter 4 in MacKendrick, B. (Ed.). *Introduction to social work in South Africa*. Pretoria: Haum.

Duncan, M., Buchanan, H. & Lorenzo, T. 2004. Politics in occupational therapy education. In Kronenberg, F., Simo-Algado, S. & Pollard, N. (Eds.). *Occupational therapy without borders: Learning from the spirit of survivors*. London Elsevier Publishers.

Dwivedi, K. N. 1993a. Conceptual Frameworks. In Dwivedi, K. N. (Ed.), *Group therapy with children and adolescents – A handbook* (pp. 28–45). London: Kingsley Publishers.

Dwivedi, K. N. 1993b. Introduction. In Dwivedi, K. N. (Ed.), *Group therapy with children and adolescents – A handbook* (pp. 3–13). London: Kingsley Publishers.

Editors Inc. 2002. *SA 2002–3: South Africa at a glance*. Craighall: Editors Inc.

Edwards, M. & Hulme, D. 1996. *Non-governmental organisations – Performance and accountability: Beyond the magic bullet*. London: Earthscan Publications Ltd.

Elias, R. & Turpin, J. (Eds.). 1994. *Rethinking peace*. Boulder and London: Lynne Rienner Publishers.

Erikson, E. H. 1968. *Identity, youth and crisis*. New York: International University Press.

Ettin, M. F. 1997. A view from the other side and call for cultural exchange: Discussion on paper by Eric van Schoor. *Group Analysis*. Vol. 30: 45–48.

Ettin, M. 1999. *Foundations and applications of group psychotherapy, a sphere of influence*. London: Jessica Kingsley Publishers.

Ettin, M. 2000. Fostering a 'group ethos': Truth or dare! *Group*. Vol. 24 (2/3) 229–240.

Evans, J. 1988. Research findings and clinical practice with adolescents. *Group Analysis*. 21, 103–115.

Evans, J. 1998. *Active analytic group therapy for adolescents*. United Kingdom: Jessica Kingsley Publishers Ltd.

Fairbairn, W. R. 1952. *An object-relations theory of personality*. New York: Basic Books.

Favor, C. A. 1994. Feminist ideology and strategies for social change: An analysis of social movements. *Journal of Applied Social Sciences*. 18, 123–134.

Fedele, N. 1994. Relationships in groups: Connection, resonance and paradox. *Work in Progress*. No. 69. Wellesley, MA: Stone Center Working Paper Series.

Fellin, P. 1996. *Mental health and mental illness*. Chicago: Peacock Publishers.

Flores, P. J. 1997. *Group psychotherapy with addicted populations* (2nd ed.). New York: The Haworth Press.

Floyd, K. & Wilkinson, D. 2000. Tuberculosis in the HIV/AIDS era: Interaction, impacts and solutions. In Clarke, E. & Strachan, K. (Eds.), *Everybody's business. The enlightening truth about AIDS* (pp. 150–156). Bellville: Metropolitan Group.

Foulkes, S. H. 1948. *Introduction to group analytic psychotherapy*. London: Maresfield.

Foulkes, S. H. 1964. *Therapeutic group analysis*. London, Allen & Unwin. Reprinted 1984, London: Karnac.

Foulkes, S. H. 1964a. Concerning leadership in group-analytic psychotherapy. Chapter 4 in *Therapeutic group analysis* (pp. 54–65). London: George Allen and Unwin.

Foulkes, S. H. 1964b. Group psychotherapy in the light of psycho-analysis. Chapter 6 in *Therapeutic group analysis* (pp. 87–92). London: George Allen & Unwin.

Foulkes, S. H. 1964c. Group therapy: Survey, orientation, classification. Chapter 3 in *Therapeutic group analysis* (pp. 47–53). London: George Allen & Unwin.

Foulkes, S. H. 1964d. On group-analytic psychotherapy. Chapter 2 in *Therapeutic group analysis* (pp. 38–53). London: George Allen & Unwin.

Foulkes, S. H. 1964e. Outline and development of group analysis. Chapter 5 in *Therapeutic group analysis* (pp. 66–82). London: George Allen & Unwin.

Foulkes, S. H. 1964f. Similarities and differences between psycho-analytic principles and group-analytic principles. Chapter 7 in *Therapeutic group analysis* (pp. 93–100). London: George Allen & Unwin.

Foulkes, S. H. 1968. On interpretation in group analysis. *International Journal of Group Psychotherapy*. 18 (4), 432–444.

Foulkes, S. H. 1973. General dynamic theory. Chapter 8 in Foulkes, S. H. & Anthony, E. J. (Eds.), *Group psychotherapy: The psycho-analytic approach* (3rd ed.). Harmondsworth: Penguin Books. (Original work published 1957.)

Foulkes, S. H. 1975. *Group analytic psychotherapy*. London: Gordon and Breach

Foulkes, S. H. 1982. Psychodynamic processes in the light of psychoanalysis and group analysis. In Scheidlinger, S. (Ed.), *Psychoanalytic group dynamics. Basic readings* (pp. 147–162). New York: International Universities Press.

Foulkes, S. H. 1990. Selected Papers. Edited by Elizabeth Foulkes. London: Karnac.

Foulkes, S. H. & Anthony, E. J. 1957. *Group psychotherapy: The psychoanalytic approach*. London: Pelican Books.

Foulkes, S. H. & Anthony, E. J. 1973. *Group psychotherapy: The psychoanalytic approach* (2nd ed.). Harmondsworth: Penguin Books. (Original work published 1957.)

Freire, P. 1978. *Pedagogy of the oppressed*. New York: Herder and Herder.

Freud, S. 1967/1922. *Group psychology and the analysis of the ego*. New York: Liveright. (Original work published in 1922.)

Friedmann, J. 1992. *Empowerment: The politics of alternative development*. Cambridge, Massachusetts, Oxford: Blackwell Publishers.

Galama, A. & Van Tongeren, P. (Eds.). 2002. *Towards better peacebuilding practice: On lessons learned, evaluation practices and aid and conflict*, Utrecht: European Centre for Conflict Prevention.

Galtung, J. 1996. *Peace by peaceful means: Peace and conflict, development and civilization*. Oslo: International Peace Research Institute; London, Thousand Oaks, New Delhi: Sage Publications.

Garland, J. A., Jones, J. E. & Kolodny, R. L. 1976. A model for stages of development in social work groups. In Bernstein, S. (Ed.). *Explorations in groupwork*. Boston: Charles River Books.

Garvin, C. 1996. *Contemporary group work* (3rd ed.). Boston: Allyn & Bacon.

Geller, M. 1972. Reflections on Selection. In Berkovitz, I. H. (Ed.), *Adolescents grow in groups: Experiences in adolescent group psychotherapy* (pp. 49–62). London: Butterworths.

Gergen, K. J. 1999. *Invitation to social construction*. Thousand Oaks, CA: Sage.

Germain, C. B. & Gitterman, A. 1980. *The life model of social work practice*. New York: Columbia University Press.

Ghirardelli, R. 2001. Silence and the use of objects brought to the session as a resistance in a group with adolescents. *Group Analysis*. 34 (4), 531–537.

Gibson, J., Ivancevich, M. & Donnely, J. 1988. *Organizations – Behavior, structure, process*. Plano: Business Publications.

Gibson, K., Swartz, L. & Sandenbergh, R. 2002. *Counselling and coping*. Cape Town: Oxford University Press.

Gilligan, C. 1982. *In a different voice: Psychological theory and women's development*. Cambridge, MA: Harvard University Press.

Gilligan, C. 1996. The centrality of relationships in human development: A puzzle, some evidence and a theory. In Noam, G. G. & Fischer, K. W. (Eds.), *Development and vulnerability in close relationships* (pp. 237–261). Mahweh, NJ: Erlbaum.

Gilligan, C., Lyons, N. & Hanmer, T. (Eds.). 1990. *Making connections: The relational worlds of adolescent girls at Emma Willard School*. Cambridge, MA: Harvard University Press.

Gilligan, C., Rogers, A. & Tolman, D. L. (Eds.). 1991. *Women, girls and psychotherapy: Reframing resistance*. New York: Haworth Press.

Gingerich, S. Guidelines for social skills training for persons with mental illness. In Roberts, A. R. & Greene, G. J. 2002. *Social workers' desk reference*. Oxford, New York: Oxford University Press.

Goduka, I. N. 1996. Challenges to traditionally white universities: Affirming diversity in curriculum. *South African Journal of Higher Education*. 10 (1): 27–38.

Goldberg, D., Evans, P. & Hartman, D. 2001. How adolescents in groups transform themselves by embodying institutional metaphors. *Clinical Child Psychology and Psychiatry*. 6 (1), 93–107.

Gray, M. & Allegritti, I. 2003. Towards culturally sensitive social work practice: Re-examining cross-cultural social work. *Social Work/ Maatskaplike Werk*. 39 (4) 312–325.

Gray, M. (Ed.). 1998. *Developmental social work in South Africa: Theory and practice*. Cape Town: National Book Printers.

Griffin, R. 1990. *Management*. Boston: Houghton Mifflin.

Grossman, A. & Silverstein, C. 1993. Facilitating support groups for professionals working with people with AIDS. *Social Work*. 38 (2), 144–151.

Gueritault-Chalvin, V., Kalichman, S. C., Demi, A. & Peterson, K. L. 2000. Work-related stress and occupational burnout in AIDS caregivers: Test of a coping model with nurses providing AIDS care. *AIDS Care*. 12 (2), 149–161.

Gutierrez, L. M. 1990. Working with women of

color: An empowerment perspective. *Social Work*. 35 (2):149–153.

Hager, P., Gonczi, A. & Athanasou, J. 1994. *Assessment and Evaluation in Higher education*. Vol. 19, No. 1. 3–16.

Hahn, H. 1994. Dreaming to learn; pathways to rediscovery. *Group Analysis*. 27, 319–328.

Halton, W. 1994. Some unconscious aspects of organisational life: Contributions from psychoanalysis. In Oberholzer, A. & Roberts, V. Z. (Eds.), *The Unconscious at Work* (pp. 12–18). London: Routledge.

Harding, S. 1996. Gendered ways of knowing and the 'epistemological crisis' of the West. In Goldberger, N., Tarule, J., Clinchy, B. & Belenky, M. (Eds.), *Knowledge, difference and power: Essays inspired by Women's ways of knowing* (pp. 431–454). New York: Basic Books.

Hartung Hagen, B. 1983. Managing conflict in all-women's groups. *Social Work with Groups*. 6, 95–104.

Harwood, I. 1998. Advances in group psychotherapy and self psychology: An intersubjective approach. Chapter 3 in Harwood, I. N. H. & Pines, M. (Eds.), *Self Experiences in Group: Intersubjective and self psychological pathways to human understanding*. London: Jessica Kingsley Publications.

Harwood, I. 2003. Distinguishing between the facilitating and the self-serving charismatic group leader. *Group*. 27 (2/3) 121–129.

Harwood, I. N. H. & Pines, M. (Eds.). 1998. *Intersubjective and self psychological pathways to human understanding*. London: Jessica Kingsley Publications.

Heap, K. 1984. *Group theory for social workers: An introduction*. Oxford: Pergamon Press.

Heap, K. 1985. *The practice of social work with groups*. London: George Allen & Unwin.

Hearst, L. 1993. Our historical and cultural cargo and its vicissitude in group analysis [17th S. H. Foulkes Annual Lecture]. *Group Analysis*. 26, 389–405.

Hellriegel, D., Jackson, S. & Slocum, J. 2001. *Management* (South African Edition). Cape Town: Oxford University Press.

Helm, B. 1962. *Social work in a South African city*. Cape Town: University of Cape Town.

Hobbs, M. 1991. Group processes in psychiatry. In Holmes, J. (Ed.), *Textbook of psychotherapy in psychiatric practice* (pp. 57–90). London: Churchill Livingstone.

Hodge, B. & Anthony, W. 1984. *Organization theory*. Boston: Allyn and Bacon, Inc.

Home, A. M. 1991. Mobilizing women's strengths for social change: The group connection. *Social Work with Groups*. 14 (3/4), 153–173.

Hope, A. & Timmel, S. 1995 (rev. ed.). *Training for transformation: A handbook for community workers*, Book 1. Gweru, Zimbabwe: Mambo Press, (86–90).

Hopper, E. 1984. Group analysis: The problem of context. *International Journal of Group Psychotherapy*. 34, 173–199.

Hopper, E. 1997. Traumatic experience in the unconscious life of groups: A fourth basic assumption [21st S. H. Foulkes Annual Lecture]. *Group Analysis*. 30 (4), 439–470.

Hopper, E. 2001. The social unconscious: theoretical considerations. *Group Analysis*. 34 (1) 9–27.

Howe, M. C. & Shwartzberg, S. L. 2001. *A functional approach to groupwork in Occupational therapy*. Philadelphia: Lippincott William and Wilkins.

Human Sciences Research Council (HSRC). 2002. *The Nelson Mandela/HSRC study on HIV/AIDS*. On-line. Retrieved 09/2004 from http://www.hsrcpublishers.co.za/hiv.html

Ijumba, P. 2002. 'Voices' of Primary Health Care facility workers. In Ijumba, P., Ntuli, A. & Barron, P. (Eds.), *South African Health Review 2002* (pp. 181–200). Durban: Health Systems Trust.

Jackson, S., Bijstra, J., Oostra, L. & Bosma, H. 1998. Adolescent's perceptions of communication with parents relative to specific aspects of relationships with parents and personal development. *Journal of Adolescence*. 21, 305–322.

Jacobs, C. 2001. Provincial Administration of the Western Cape. (Suggested) *Protocol and Procedures for care and support for Health Care Workers in its employ*. First Draft.

James, D. C. 1984. Bion's 'containing' and Winnicott's 'holding' in the context of the group matrix. *International Journal of Group Psychotherapy*. 34, 201–213.

James, D. C. 2000. Holding and containing in the group and society. Chapter 5 in Brown, D. & Zinkin, L. (Eds.), *The psyche and the social world*. London: Jessica Kingsley.

James, R. & Gilliland, B. 2001. *Crisis intervention strategies* (4th ed.). Belmont, CA: Brooks/Cole.

Jarvis, T. J., Tebbut, J. & Mattick, R. P. 1995. *Treatment approaches for alcohol and drug dependence*. Chichister: John Wiley and sons.

Jordan, J. V. 1991. The meaning of mutuality. Jordan, J. V., Kaplan, A. G., Miller, J. B., Stiver, I. P. & Surrey, J. L. (Eds.), *Women's growth in connection* (pp. 81–96). New York: Guilford Press.

Jordan, J. V. 1997a. Relational development: Therapeutic implications of empathy and shame. In Jordan, J. V. (Ed.), *Women's growth in diversity: More writings from the Stone Center* (pp. 138–161). New York: Guilford Press.

Jordan, J. V. (Ed.). 1997b. *Women's growth in diversity: More writings from the Stone Center*. New York: Guilford Press.

Jordan, J. V., Kaplan, A. G., Miller, J. B., Stiver, I. P. & Surrey, J. L. (Eds.). 1991. *Women's growth in connection*. New York: The Guilford Press.

Kaldor, M. 2003. The idea of global civil society. *International Affairs*. May, 79 (3), 583–593).

Kane-Berman, J., Henderson, J. & de Souza, C. (Eds.). 2001. *South African survey 2001/2002*. (Statistical Release PO317, 27 November 1996). Johannesburg: South African Institute of Race Relations.

Kaplan, A. G. 1991. The 'self-in-relation': Implications for depression. In Jordan, J. V., Kaplan, A. G., Miller, J. B., Stiver, I. P. & Surrey, J. L. (Eds.), *Women's growth in connection* (pp. 206–222). New York: Guilford Press.

Karterud, S. W. 1998. The group self, empathy, intersubjectivity, and hermeneutics. In Harwood, I. N. H. & Pines, M. (Eds.), *Self experiences in group*. London: Jessica Kingsley.

Keashly, L. & Fisher, R. J. 1990. Toward a contingency approach to conflict resolution: A Cyprus illustration. *International Journal.* 43 (2), (424–453).

Keashly, L. & Fisher, R. J. 1996. A contingency perspective on conflict interventions: Theoretical and practical considerations. In Bercovitch, J. (Ed.), *Resolving international conflicts: The theory and practice of mediation.* Boulder and London: Lynne Rienner Publishers, (235–261).

Kendler, H. 2002. Truth and reconciliation: Worker's fear of conflict in groups. *Social Work with Groups.* Vol. 25 (3) 25–41.

Kennard, D. 1998. *An introduction to therapeutic communities.* Therapeutic Communities 1. London: Jessica Kingsley.

Kennard, D., Roberts, J. & Winter, D. A. 1993. Conclusions. Chap. 13 in *A work book of group-analytic interventions* (pp. 104–115). London: Routledge.

Klein, M. 1946. Notes on some schizoid mechanisms. In Klein, M., Heimann, P., Isaacs, S. & Rivere, J. (Eds.), *Developments in psychoanalysis.* London: The Hogarth Press.

Kohut, H. 1971. *The analysis of the self.* CT: International Universities Press.

Kohut, H. 1977. *The restoration of the self.* CT: International Universities Press.

Kolb, D., Osland, J. & Rubin, M. 1995. *Organizational behavior – An experiential approach.* Englewood Cliffs: Prentice-Hall Inc.

Konopka, G. 1963. *Social groupwork: A helping process.* Englewood-Cliffs, NJ: Prentice-Hall.

Konopka, G. 1972. In Andrews, J. 2001. Groupwork's place in social work: A historical analysis. *Journal of Sociology and Social Welfare.* 18 (4).

Korittko, A. 1991. Family therapy with one-parent families. *Contemporary Family Therapy.* 13, 625–640.

Kurland, R. & Salmon, R. 1999. *Teaching a methods course in social work with groups.* Alexandria, VA: Library of Social Work Education.

Lavikainen, J., Lahtinen, E. & Lehtinen, V. 2000. *Public health approach on mental health in Europe.* National Research and Development Centre for Welfare and Health. STAKES Ministry of Social Affairs and Health.

Lawrence, W. G. 1998. *Social dreaming @ work.* London: Karnac.

Lawrence, W. G. 2000. *Tongued with fire: Groups in experience.* London: Karnac Books.

Le Roy, J. 1994. Group analysis and culture. Chapter 12 in Brown, D. & Zinkin, L. (Eds.), *The psyche and the social world. Developments in group-analytic theory* (pp. 180–201). London: Routledge.

Lederach, J. P. 1995. *Preparing for peace: Conflict transformation across cultures.* Syracuse, New York: Syracuse University Press.

Lederach, J. P. 1997. Building peace: Sustainable reconciliation in divided societies. Washington, DC: United States Institute of Peace Press.

Lederach, J. P. 2001. Civil society and reconciliation. In Crocker, C. A., Hampson, F. O. & Aall, P. (Eds.), Turbulent peace: The challenges of managing international conflict. Washington,

DC: United States Institute of Peace Press, (841–854).

Lee, J. A. B. 1994. *The empowerment approach to social work practice.* New York: Columbia University Press.

Leftwich, A. 1994. Governance, the state and the politics of development. *Development and Change.* 25 (2), (363–386).

Leiderman, M., Birbaum, M. L. & Dazzo, B. 1988. (Eds.). *Roots & new frontiers in social group work.* New York: Haworth Press.

Levin, S. 1991. *Guided meditations, explorations and healings.* The Hollies: Gateway Books.

Lipgar, R. M. & Pines, M. 2003. (Eds.). *Building on Bion: Roots.* London: Jessica Kingsley.

Lipgar, R. M. & Pines, M. 2003. (Eds.). *Building on Bion: Branches.* London: Jessica Kingsley.

Lipman, E. L., Secord, M. & Boyle, M. H. (2001. Moving from the clinic to the community: The alone mothers together program [Letter to the editor]. *Canadian Journal of Psychiatry.* 46, 657.

Lonergan, E. C. 1994. Using theories of group therapy. In Bernard, H. S. & MacKenzie, K. R. (Eds.), *Basics of group therapy.* New York: Guilford Press.

LoveLife. 2000. *The impending catastophe: A resource book on the emerging HIV/AIDS epidemic in South Africa.* Parklands: LoveLife.

Lumsden, G. & Lumsden, D. 1993. *Communicating in groups and teams sharing leadership.* Belmont: Wadsworth Publishing Company.

Lyndon, P. 1995. The median group: An introduction. *Group Analysis.* Vol. 28: 251–260.

Mackintosh, I. 1998. Responding to diversity: toward the development of anti-discriminatory social work practice. Chapter 8 in Gray, M. (Ed.), *Developmental social work in South Africa: Theory and practice.* Cape Town: David Philip.

Madigan, S. 1996. The politics of identity: Considering community discourse in the externalising of internalised problem conversations. *Journal of Systemic Therapies.* Vol. 15, Spring. 47–61.

Maiello, S. 2001. Transgenerational transmission of trauma and violence. *Psycho-analytic Psychotherapy in South Africa.* 9 (2), 13–31.

Maslach, C. & Ozer, E. 1995. Theoretical issues related to burnout in AIDS health workers. In Bennet, L., Miller, D. & Ross, M. (Eds.), *Health workers and AIDS. Research, interventions and current issues in burnout and response.* Harwood Academic Publishers. On-line. Retrieved 29/03/01 from http://www.gbhap.com/aids/05-ch1c2.htm

Mattejat, F. 2001. Treatment planning. In Remschmidt, H. (Ed.), *Psychotherapy with children and adolescents* (pp. 12–39). UK: Cambridge University Press.

Max-Neef, M. 1991. *Human scale development: Conception, application and further reflections.* New York and London: Apex Press.

Maxwell, B. 2000. The Median Group. *Group Analysis.* Vol. 33, 35–47.

McDermot, F. 2002. *Inside groupwork. A guide to reflective practice.* Australia: Allen & Unwin.

McKay, S. & de la Rey, C. 2001. Women's Meanings of Peacebuilding in Post-Apartheid South Africa, Peace and Conflict. *Journal of*

Peace Psychology. 7 (3), (227–242).

McKendrick, B. 1990. The development of social welfare and social work in South Africa. Chapter 1 in McKendrick, B. (Ed.), *Introduction to social work in South Africa.* Pretoria: Haum.

McKendrick, B. 2001. The promise of social work: directions for the future. *Social Work/Maatskaplike Werk.* 37 (2), 105–111.

McLanahan, S. & Sandefur, G. 1994. *Growing up with a single parent: What hurts, what helps.* Cambridge, Harvard University Press.

Meagher, M. 2002. *Partnership or Pretence* (3rd ed.). Strawberry Hills, Australia: Psychiatric Rehabilitation Association.

Mezirow, J. 1991. *Transformative dimensions of adult learning.* San Francisco: Jossey Bass.

Middleman, R. R. & Wood, G. G. 1990. *Skills for direct practice in social work.* New York: Columbia University Press.

Miller, D. 2000. *Work, stress and burnout in HIV/AIDS.* London: Routledge.

Miller, J. B. 1976. *Toward a new psychology for women.* Boston: Beacon Press.

Miller, J. B. 1988. Connections, disconnections and violations. *Work in Progress.* No. 33. Wellesley, MA: Stone Center Working Paper Series.

Miller, J. B. 1991. Women and power. In Jordan, J. V., Kaplan, A. G., Miller, J. B., Stiver, I. P. & Surrey, J. L. (Eds.), *Women's growth in connection* (pp. 197–205). New York: Guilford Press.

Miller, J. B. & Stiver, I. P. 1991. A relational reframing of therapy. *Work in Progress.* No. 52. Wellesley, MA: Stone Center Working Paper Series.

Miller, J. B. & Stiver, I. P. 1994. Movement in therapy: Honoring the 'strategies of disconnection.' *Work in Progress.* No. 65. Wellesley, MA: Stone Center Working Paper Series.

Miller, J. B. & Stiver, I. P. 1995. Relational images and their meanings in psychotherapy. *Work in Progress.* No. 74. Wellesley, MA: Stone Center Working Paper Series.

Miller, W. R. & Rollnick, S. 1991. *Motivational interviewing: Preparing people to change addictive behaviour.* New York: Guilford Press.

Ministry for Welfare and Population Development. 1997. *White Paper for social welfare.* Pretoria: Government Printers.

Mishne, J. M. 1993. *The evolution and application of clinical theory.* New York: The Free Press.

Mohrman, S., Cohen, S. & Mohrman, A. 1995. *Designing team-based organizations.* San Francisco: Jossey-Bass Publishers.

Morgan, A. 2000. *What is narrative therapy? An easy-to-read introduction.* Adelaide: Dulwich Centre Publications.

Moss-Morris, V. 1987. Acquiring a theoretical base for the practice of group therapy in psychiatric units. *The South African Journal of Occupational Therapy.* (November), 16–20.

Mulroy, E. A. 1995. *The new uprooted. Single mothers in urban life.* Westport, CT: Auburn House.

Nagliero, G. 1996. Countertransference in adolescent psychotherapy. *Group Analysis.* 29, 69–79.

Neri, C. 1998. *Group.* International Library of Group Analysis 8. London: Jessica Kingsley.

Neri, C., Pines, M. & Friedman, R. (Eds.). 2002. Dreams in group psychotherapy: Theory and technique. *International Library of Group Analysis.* 18. London: Jessica Kingsley.

Nieto, S. 1992. *Affirming diversity: The socio-political context of multicultural education.* London: Longman Publishing.

Nitsun, M. 1994. The primal scene in group analysis. Chapter 9 in Brown, D. & Zinkin, L. (Eds.), *The psyche and the social world. Developments in group-analytic theory* (pp. 129–145). London: Routledge.

Nitsun, M. 1996. *The anti-group: Destructive forces in the group and their creative potential.* London: Routledge.

Nitsun, M. 1998. The organizational mirror: A group-analytic approach to organizational consultancy, part I – theory [Special section – group analysis and organizations]. *Group Analysis.* 31 (3), 245–267.

Nitsun, M. 2000. The future of the group. *International Journal of Group Psychotherapy.* 50 (4), 455–472.

Nitsun, M. 2000. The shadow of the group in the dawn of the 21st century: The journey from Varnai. *Group.* 24 (2/3) 115–122.

Nitzgen, D. 2001. Training in democracy, democracy in training: notes on group analysis and democracy. *Group Analysis.* 35 (3) 331–347.

Northen, H. 1988. *Social work with groups.* (2nd ed.) New York: Columbia University Press.

Northen, H. & Kurland, R. 2001. *Social work with groups.* New York: Columbia University Press.

Nuttman-Schwartz, O. & Weinberg, H. 2002. Group therapy in Israel. *Group.* 26 (1) 5–15.

O'Brien, C. R. 2003. Community development and conflict resolution: An examination of the potential for complementary strategies in post-settlement contexts, with special reference to Northern Ireland and South Africa. PhD Thesis, Bradford: Department of Peace Studies, University of Bradford.

Olesen, V. L. 2000. Feminism and qualitative research at and into the millennium. In Denzin, N. K. & Lincoln, Y. S. (Eds.), *Handbook of qualitative research* (2nd ed). pp. 215–256). Thousand Oaks, CA: Sage.

Olson, M. & Haynes, J. A. Successful single parents. *Families in Society.* May, 1993. 259–267.

Orley, J. & Sartorius, N. Mental illness in primary health care in developing countries. In Shepherd, M., Wilkenson, G. & Williams, P. 1986. *Mental illness in primary care settings.* London & New York: Tavistock Publications.

Ormont, L. 2000. Where is group therapy going in the 21st century? *Group.* 24 (2/3) 185–192.

Orpen, C. 1981. *Behaviour in work organizations.* Johannesburg: Jonathan Ball Publishers.

Osei-Hwedi, K. 2002. Indigenous practice – some informed guesses: Self-evident and possible. *Social Work/Maatskaplike Werk.* 38 (4) 311–322.

Papell, C. P. & Rothman, B. 1966. Social group-work models: Possession and heritage. *Journal of Education for Social Work.* 2 (2) 66–77.

Papell, C. P. 1997. Thinking about thinking about groupwork: Thirty years later. *Social Work* with Groups. 20 (4) 5–17.

Parran, T. V. 1996. Principles of chemical dependence for the primary care practitioner. Cleveland: Case Western Reserve University School of Medicine.

Parry, J. K. (Ed.). 1997. From prevention to wellness through groupwork. New York: The Haworth Press.

Patel, V. 2003. Where there is no psychiatrist. A mental health care manual. Glasgow. UK: Bell and Bain Ltd.

Pelser, A. J., Ngwena, C. G. & Summerton, J. V. 2004. The HIV/AIDS Epidemic in South Africa: Trends, impacts and policy responses. In Van Rensburg, H. C. J. (Ed.), Health and Health Care in South Africa (pp. 275–314). Pretoria: Van Schaik Publishers.

Perls, F. 1973. The Gestalt approach and eyewitness to therapy. New York: Bantam.

Petersen, I. & Swartz, L. 2002. Primary health care in the era of HIV/AIDS. Some implications for health systems reform. Social Science & Medicine. 55 (6), 1005–1013.

Petersen, I., Parekh, A., Bhagwanjee, A., Gibson, K., Giles, C. & Swartz, L. In Foster, D., Freeman, M. & Pillay, Y. (Eds.). 1997. Mental health policy issues for South Africa. Pinelands: MASA Multimedia Publications.

Pillay, D. 1996. Social movements, development and democracy in post-apartheid South Africa. In Coetzee, J. K. & Graaff, J. (Eds.), Reconstruction, development and people. Johannesburg: International Thomson Publishing, Southern Africa, (Pty) Ltd, (324–352).

Pinar, W. F. & Grumet, M. R. 1976. Toward a poor curriculum. Dubuque, Ia: Kendall/Hunt.

Pines, M. 1975. Overview. In Kreeger, L. (Ed.), The large group: Dynamics and therapy (pp. 291–311). Itasca, Illinois: F. E. Peacock.

Pines, M. 1981. The frame of reference of group psychotherapy. International Journal of Group Psychotherapy. 31, 275–285.

Pines, M. 1983. The contribution of S. H. Foulkes to group therapy. Chapter 16 in Pines, M. The evolution of group analysis. London: Routledge and Kegan.

Pines, M. 1991. The matrix of group analysis: An historical perspective. Group Analysis. 24, 99–109.

Pines, M. 1993. Interpretation: Why, for whom and when. In Kennard et al (Eds.), A workbook of group-analytic interventions. London: Routledge.

Pines, M. 1998. Circular reflections. Selected papers on group analysis and psychonalysis. London: Jessica Kingsley.

Pines, M. 1998a. Change and innovation, decay and renewal in psychotherapy. Chapter 7 in Circular reflections: Selected papers on group analysis and psychoanalysis (pp. 117–129). London: Jessica Kingsley.

Pines, M. 1998b. Psychic development and the group analytic situation. Chapter 3 in Circular reflections: Selected papers on group analysis and psychoanalysis (pp. 59–76). London: Jessica Kingsley.

Pines, M. 2000. Bion and group psychotherapy. London: Jessica Kingsley Publishers Ltd.

Pines, M. 2000. The group-as-a-whole. Chapter 4 in Brown, D. & Zinkin, L. I. (Eds.). The psyche and the social world. London: Jessica Kingsley.

Pines, M. & Hutchinson, S. 1993. Group analysis. Chapter 2 in Alonso, A. & Swiller, H. I. (Eds.), Group therapy in clinical practice (pp. 29–47). Washington DC: American Psychiatric Press.

Postman, N. 1983. The disappearance of childhood. Great Britain: W. H. Allen.

Potgieter, M. C. 1998. The social work process: Development to empower people. South Africa: Prentice-Hall.

Pretorius, J. & Le Roux, J. 1998. Milieu deprivation and its implications for education in the republic of South Africa. Adolescence. 33 (131), 689–698.

Procter, S. & Mueller, F. (Eds.). 2000. Teamworking. Houndmills: Macmillan Press Ltd.

Pullen, G. The therapeutic community and schizophrenia. In Schermer, V. L. & Pines, M. 1999. Group psychotherapy of the psychoses. UK: Jessica Kingsley Publ. Ltd.

Rachman, A. W. M. 1975. Identity group psychotherapy with adolescents. USA: Charles C. Thomas.

Rachman, A. W. M. 1989. Identity group psychotherapy with adolescents: A reformulation. In Cramer-Azima, F. J. & Richmond, L. H. (Eds.), Adolescence and group psychotherapy (pp. 21–41). Guilford, USA: International University Press.

Rachman, A. W. M. 2003. Issues of power, control and status in group interaction: From Ferenczi to Foucault. Group. Vol. 27 (2/3) 89–105.

Rahman, M. D. A. 1993. People's self-development: Perspectives and participatory action research. London: Zed Books.

Rapp, C. A. A strengths approach to case management with clients with severe mental disabilities. In Roberts, A. R. & Greene, G. J. 2002. Social workers' desk reference. Oxford, New York: Oxford University Press.

Raubolt, R. R. 1983. Treating children in residential group psychotherapy. Child Welfare. LXII (2), 147–155.

Rauwald, M. 2002. Introduction to a psychoanalytical therapeutic approach. Lecture presented at the University of Cape Town.

Reid, S. & Kolvin, I. 1993. Group psychotherapy for children and adolescents. Archives of Disease in Childhood. 69. 244–250.

Remschmidt, H. (Ed.). 2001. Psychotherapy with children and adolescents. UK: Cambridge University Press.

Reychler, L. & Paffenholz, T. (Eds.). 2001. Peacebuilding: A field guide. Boulder, London: Lynne Rienner.

Reynolds, P. 1997. Vision: Wellbeing and suffering. In Forster, D., Freeman, M. & Pillay, Y. (Eds.), Mental health policy issues for South Africa (23–31). Pinelands, South Africa: The Medical Association of South Africa Multimedia Publications.

Robbins, H. & Finley, M. 2000. The new why teams don't work – What goes wrong and how to make it right. San Francisco: Berrett-Koehler Publishers, Inc.

Robbins, S. 1991. Organizational behavior – Concepts, controversies, and applications.

Englewood Cliffs: Prentice-Hall Inc.

Roberts, J. (Ed.). 1991. Special categories of patients in groups. Chapter 7 in Roberts, J. & Pines, M. (Eds.), *The practice of group analysis* (pp. 96–127). The International Library of Group Psychotherapy and Group Process. London: Tavistock/Routledge.

Robertson, B., Allwood, C. & Gagiano, C. 2001. *Textbook of psychiatry for Southern Africa.* Cape Town, Oxford University Press.

Rooth, E. 1998. Groupwork as a medium for community development. Chapter 3 in *Developmental social work in South Africa: Theory and practice.* Cape Town: David Philip.

Rosenthal, L. 1971. Some dynamics of resistance and therapeutic management in adolescent group therapy. *Psychoanalytic Review.* 58 (3), 353–366.

Ross, E. 2002. Images of AIDS: Psychsocial issues for affected individuals, families and professional caregivers. *The Social Work Practitioner-Researcher.* 13 (2): 20–32.

Ross, E. & Deverell, A. 2004. *Psychosocial approaches to health, illness and disability. A reader for health care professionals.* Pretoria: Van Schaik Publishers.

Rutan, J. S. & Stone, W. 2001. *Psychodynamic group therapy.* New York: Guilford Press.

Rutan, J. S. Alonso, A. & Groves, J. E. 1988. Understanding defenses in group psychotherapy. *International Journal of Group Psychotherapy.* 38 (4), 459–472.

Saleebey, D. 1992a. Introduction: Power in the people. In Saleebey, D. (Ed.). *The strengths perspective in social work practice.* New York: Longman, 3–17.

Saleebey, D. 1992b. Introduction: Beginnings of a strengths approach to practice. In *The strengths perspective in social work practice.* New York: Longman, 41–44.

Saleeby, D. 1996. The strengths perspective in social work practice: Extensions and cautions. *Social Work.* 41 (3), 296–305. Scheidlinger, S. 1997. Group dynamics and group psychotherapy revisited: Four decades later. *International Journal of Group Psychotherapy.* 47 (2), 141–156.

Santhrock, J. W. 1998. *Child development* (8th ed.). Boston: McGraw Hill.

Schafritz, J. M. & Ott, J. S. 1987. *Classics of organization (2nd ed.).* USA: The Dorsey Press.

Scheidlinger, S. 1982a. *Focus on group psychotherapy; clinical essays.* New York: International Universities Press.

Scheidlinger, S. 1985. Group treatment of adolescents: An overview. *American Journal of Orthopsychiatry.* 55 (1), 102–111.

Schermer, V. L. 2000. Beyond Bion: Basic assumptions states revisited. Chapter 6 in Pines, M. (Ed.), *Bion and Group Psychotherapy.* London: Jessica Kingsley.

Schiller, L. Y. 1995. Stages of development in women's groups: A relational model. In Kurland, R. & Salmon, R. (Eds.), *Group work practice in a troubled society: Problems and opportunities* (pp. 117–138). New York: Haworth Press.

Schiller, L. Y. 1997. Rethinking stages of development in women's groups: Implications for practice. *Social Work with Groups.* 20(3), 3–19.

Schlachet, P. J. 1986. The concept of group space. *International Journal of Group Psychotherapy.* 36, 33–53.

Schlapobersky, J. 2000. The language of the group. In Brown, D. & Zinkin, L. I. (Eds.), *The psyche and the social world.* London: Jessica Kingsley Publishers.

Schlemmer, L. & Smith, J. (2001. Social development. In Kane-Berman, J., Henderson, J. & de Souza, C. (Eds.), *South African survey 2001/2002* (pp. 33–61). Johannesburg: South African Institute of Race Relations.

Schnitzer, P. K. 1998. He needs his father: The clinical discourse and politics of single mothering. In Garcia Coll, C., Surrey, J. & Weingarten, K. (Eds.), *Mothering against the odds* (pp. 151–172). New York: Guilford Press.

Schopler, J. H. & Galinsky, M. J. 1995. Group practice overview. In *Encyclopaedia of Social Work* (19th ed.). Washington, DC: National Association of Social Workers: 1129–1142.

Schubert, W. H. 1986. *Curriculum: Perspective, paradigm, possibility.* New York: Macmillan.

Schwartz, W. 1971. On the use of groups in social work practice. In Schwartz, W. & Zelba, S. (Eds.), *The practice of group work* (pp. 3–24). New York: Columbia University Press.

Seccombe, K., James, D. & Battle Walters, K. 1998. 'They think you ain't much of nothing': The social construction of the welfare mother. *Journal of Marriage and the Family.* 60, 849–865.

Seedhouse, D. 1991. Against medical ethics: A philosopher's view. *Medical Education.* 25: 250–282.

Sharry, J. & Owens, C. 2000. 'The rules of engagement': A case study of a group with 'angry' adolescents. *Clinical Child Psychology and Psychiatry.* 5 (1), 53–62.

Sheinberg, M. & Penn, P. 1991. Gender dilemmas, gender questions, and the gender mantra. *Journal of Marital and Family Therapy.* 17, 33–44.

Shulman, L. 1992. *The skills of helping. Individuals, families, and groups* (3rd ed.). Itasca, Illinois: F.E. Peacock Publishers.

Shulman, L. 1994. Healing the hurts: Single parents. In Gitterman, A. & Shulman, L. (Eds.), *Mutual aid groups, vulnerable populations and the life cycle* (pp. 349–363). New York: Columbia University Press.

Shulman, L. 2002. Learning to talk about taboo subjects: a lifelong professional challenge. *Social Work with Groups.* Vol. 25, No. $\frac{1}{2}$: 39–150.

Shutte, A. 1993. *Philosophy for Africa.* Cape Town: University of Cape Town.

Sidel, R. 1996. *Keeping women and children last.* New York: Penguin.

Silverman, D. 1993. Psychological impact of HIV-related caregiving on health providers: A review and recommendations for the role of psychiatry. *American Journal of Psychiatry.* 150 (5), 705–712.

Skynner, R. 1984. Institutes and how to survive them [8th S. H. Foulkes Annual Lecture]. *Group Analysis.* 17, 91–107.

Skynner, R. 1986. What is effective in group psychotherapy? *Group Analysis.* 19, 5–24.

Slattery, P. 1995. *Curriculum development in the post-modern era*. New York. Garland Press.

Slavson, S. R. 1944. *An introduction to group therapy*. New York: International Universities Press.

Smit, A. 1990. Social work management and administration. In McKendrick, B. (Ed.), *Introduction to social work in South Africa*. Pretoria: HAUM Tertiary.

Smit, A. 1992. Managing for effective welfare service delivery: Issues and concepts. In *Welfare Focus*. 27 (1), 4–8.

Soehner, G., Zastowny, T., Hammond, A. & Taylor, L. 1988. The single-parent family project: A community-based, preventive program for single-parent families. *Journal of Child and Adolescent Psychotherapy*. 5 (1), 35–43.

South African Bill of Rights, 1996. Chapter Two in South African Constitutional Assembly, Act 108 of 1996. Pretoria: South African Constitution.

Spicer, J. 1993. *The Minnesota Model*. Minnesota: Hazelden Foundation.

Spiro, M. 2002. *Processes of transformation in a group psychotherapy intervention for single mothers*. Unpublished Doctoral dissertation. Rhodes University: Grahamstown.

Stein, S. M. 1996. Psychopathy: The legacy of apartheid. *Psycho-analytic Psychotherapy in South Africa*. 4 (2), 41–54.

Steinberg, D. M. 2002. The magic of mutual aid. *Social Work with Groups*. Vol. 25, 1–2: 31–38.

Steinberg, M., Kinghorn., A, Söderlund, N., Schierhout, G. & Conway, S. 2000. HIV/AIDS – facts, figures and future. In *South African Health Review 2000*. Durban: Health Systems Trust.

Steinman, S. 2003. *Workplace violence in the health sector. Country case study: South Africa*. Geneva: WHO, ILO, ICN, PSI.

Stephenson, J. 2000. AIDS in South Africa takes centre stage. *JAMA*. 284 (2). Online. Retrieved http://jama.ama-assn.org/issues/v284n2/ffull/jmn0712-1.html

Stiver, I. P. 1997. What is the role of transference and the unconscious in the relational model? In Jordan, J. V. (Ed.), *Women's growth in diversity: More writings from the Stone Center* (pp. 37–41). New York: Guilford Press.

Stoner, J., Freeman, R. & Gilbert, D. 1995. *Management*. Englewood Cliffs: Prentice-Hall International Inc.

Stroul, B. A. (Ed.). 1987. Community support systems for persons with long-term mental illness: Questions and answers. Maryland: National Institute of Mental Health Community Support Program.

Surrey, J. L. 1985. The 'self-in-relation': A theory of women's development. *Work in Progress*. No. 13. Wellesley, MA: Stone Center Working Paper Series.

Surrey, J. L. 1990. Mother blaming and clinical theory. In Knowles, J. P. & Cole, E. (Eds.), *Motherhood: A feminist perspective*. (pp. 83–88). New York: Haworth Press.

Swanepoel, H. & De Beer, F. 1997. *Introduction to development studies*. Halfway House: International Thompson Publishing.

Swartz, L., Gibson, K. & Gelman, T. 2002. *Reflective practice: Psychodynamic ideas in the community*. Cape Town: Human Science Research Council Publishers.

Swilling, M. 2002. Flames of Hope, South Africa. *Resurgence,* September/October, (No. 214), (p. 23).

Taylor, B. 2001. HIV Stigma and health: Integration of theoretical concepts and the lived experience of individuals. *Journal of Advanced Nursing*. 35 (5), 792–798.

Teffo, L. 1999. Moral renewal and African experience(s). In Makgoba, M. W. (Ed.), *African renaissance*. Sandton: Mafube Publishing Limited.

Terreblanche, S. 2002. *A History of Inequality in South Africa, 1652–2002*. Pietermaritzburg: University of Natal Press and KMM Review Publishing.

The Constitution of South Africa. Act no. 108 of 1996. Pretoria, Government Printer.

Tilbury, D. 1994. *Working with mental illness*. London: The Macmillan Press.

Toseland, R. W. & Rivas, R. F. 1998. *An introduction to group work practice* (3rd ed.). Boston: Allyn & Bacon.

Toseland, R. W. and Rivas, R. F. 2001. *An introduction to group work practice* (4th ed.). Boston: Allyn & Bacon.

Trist, E. 2000. Working with Bion in the 1940's: The group decade. In Pines, M. (Ed.), *Bion and group psychotherapy*. London: Jessica Kingsley.

Truter, B. 2003. 'Now there are no rules': Boundary activity in a psychoanalytically-run group therapeutic intervention for adolescent boys with learning difficulties. Unpublished Masters Thesis, University of Cape Town.

Truth and Reconciliation Commission. 1998. *Truth and Reconciliation Commission of South Africa Report*. Cape Town: Truth and Reconciliation Commission.

Tuckman, B. 1963. Developmental sequence in small groups. *Psychological Bulletin*. Vol. 63 (6), 384–399.

Turner, C. W. 1997. Clinical applications of the Stone Center theoretical approach to minority women. In Jordan, J. (Ed.), *Women's growth in diversity: More writings from the Stone Center*. (pp. 74–90). New York: Guilford Press.

United Nations Development Programme. 2002. *Human Development Report 2002: Deepening democracy in a fragmented world*. New York: Oxford University Press.

Van Dyk, A. 2001. *HIV/AIDS care and counselling* (2nd ed.). Pinelands: Pearson Education South Africa.

Van Rensburg, H. 2004. Primary Health Care in South Africa. In Van Rensburg, H. C. J. (Ed.), *Health and health care in South Africa*. (pp. 412–458). Pretoria: Van Schaik Publishers.

Van Rensburg, H. C. J. & Pelser, A. J. 2004. The transformation of the South African health system. In Van Rensburg, H. C. J. (Ed.), *Health and health care in South Africa*. (pp. 110–166). Pretoria: Van Schaik Publishers.

Van Rensburg, H. C. J. 2004. The health professionals and human resources for health – Status, trends and core issues. In Van Rensburg, H. C. J. (Ed.), *Health and health care in South Africa*. (pp. 315–376). Pretoria: Van Schaik Publishers.

Van Rensburg, H. C. J. (Ed.). 2004. *Health and health care in South Africa*. Pretoria: Van Schaik Publishers.

Vinik, A. & Levin, M. (Eds.). 1991. *Social action in group work*. New York: Haworth Press.

Volkan V. D. 2001. Transgenerational transmissions and chosen traumas: An aspect of large-group identity. *Group Analysis*. 34 (1), 79–97.

Volkan, V. D. 2002. September 11 and societal regression. *Group Analysis*. 35 (4), 456–483.

Wanigaratne, S., Wallace, W., Pullin, J., Keaney, F. & Farmer, R. 1990. *Relapse prevention for addictive behaviours*. Oxford: Blackwell Science.

Watkins, P. 2001. *Mental health nursing: The art of compassionate care*. Oxford: Butterworth-Heinemann.

Watson, R. 2002. Competence: A transformative approach. *World Federation of Occupational Therapists Bulletin*. Vol. 45, 7–11.

Weil, M. 1988. Task group skills: The core of community practice. In Leiderman, M., Birbaum, M. L. & Dazzo, B. (Eds.), *Roots & new frontiers in social group work*. New York: Haworth Press, (131–148).

Weinberg, H. 2001. Group process and group phenomena on the internet. *International Journal of Group Psychotherapy*. 51 (3), 361–378.

Weinberg, H. 2003. The culture of the group and groups from different cultures. *Group Analysis*. 36 (2), 253–268.

Wenger, E. 1998. *Communities of practice: Learning, meaning and identity*. Cambridge: Cambridge University Press.

Westcot, M. E. & Dries, R. 1990. Has family therapy adapted to the single-parent family? *The American Journal of Family Therapy*. 18, 363–372.

Whitaker, D. 2001. *Using groups to help people* (2nd ed.). East Sussex: Brunner-Routledge.

Whitaker, D. & Lieberman, M. A.1964. *Psychotherapy through the group process*. New York: Atherton Press.

White Paper for Social Welfare. 1997. Department of Welfare and Population Development. Pretoria: Government Printer.

White, M. 2002. Workshop notes (Narrative therapy). Online. Retrieved 31/08/2004 from http://www.dulwichcentre.com.au/workshop-notes.htm

Whiteside, A. & Sunter, C. 2000. *AIDS: The challenge for South Africa*. Cape Town: Human & Rousseau.

Wilson, D., Naidoo, S., Bekker, L.-G., Cotton, M. & Maartens, G. (Eds.). 2002. *Handbook of HIV medicine*. Cape Town: Oxford University Press.

Wilson, P. 1991. Psychotherapy with adolescents. Chapter 19 in Holmes, J. (Ed.), *Textbook of psychotherapy in psychiatric practice*, (pp. 443–467). London: Churchill Livingstone.

Winnicott, D. W. 1964. *The child, the family and the outside world*. Harmonsworth: Penguin.

Winnicott, D. 1965. The theory of the parent-infant relationship. In *Maturational processes and the facilitating environment*. London: Hogarth.

World Health Organisation (WHO). 1988. *From Alma-Ata to the year 2000: Reflections at the midpoint*. Geneva: World Health Organisation.

World Health Organisation (WHO). 2004. *TB/HIV. A clinical manual* (2nd ed.). Geneva: World Health Organisation.

World Health Organisation. 1998. Towards a common language for functioning and disablement: The International Classification of Impairments, Activities and Participation. (ICID-H2). Geneva: WHO.

World Health Organisation. 1999. International Classification of Functioning and Disability (ICID-H2). Beta-2 Draft. July. Geneva: WHO.

World Health Organisation. 2002. Department of mental health and substance dependence. *Prevention and promotion in mental health. Mental health: Evidence and research*. Geneva: Department of Mental Health and Substance Dependence.

World Health Organisation. 2002. In Nygren-Kruge, H. 25 Questions and answers on health and human rights. *Health and Human Rights Publication Series*. Issue No. 1. Geneva: WHO.

World Health Organisation. Psychosocial rehabilitation: A consensus statement (WHO/MNH/MND/96.2). Geneva: WHO.

Yalom, I. D. 1983. *Inpatient group psychotherapy*. New York. Basic Books.

Yalom, I. D. 1985. *Theory and practice of group psychotherapy*. New York: Basic Books.

Yalom, I. D. 1995. *The theory and practice of group psychotherapy* (4th ed.). New York: Basic Books.

Index